# HIKING THE ROCKIES
# WITH **KIDS**

# HIKING *the* ROCKIES *with* KIDS

## CELIA MᶜLEAN

Orca Book Publishers

First Edition

**Canadian Cataloguing in Publication Data**
McLean, Celia,
  Hiking the Rockies with Kids

Includes bibliographical references and index.
ISBN 0-920501-72-9

1. Hiking — Rocky Mountains, Canadian (B.C. and Alta.) — Guidebooks.*
2. Family recreation — Rocky Mountains, Canadian (B.C. and Alta.) — Guidebooks.*   3. Rocky Mountains, Canadian (B.C. and Alta.) — Guidebooks.*
I. Title.
GV199.44.C22R634 1992   917.1104'4   C92-091176-5

Cover design by Susan Fergusson
Front cover photo by Roger N.J. Hostin
Inset front cover photo by Christoper Page
Back cover photos by Christopher Page, Eric Langshaw, Celia McClean

**Orca Book Publishers Ltd.**
P.O. Box 5626, Stn. B
Victoria, BC  Canada  V8R 6S4

Printed and bound in Canada

**For Ged and Bronwyn**
**Don't get wet!**

# // Acknowledgements

This book could not have been written without the love and encouragement of my husband Ged and our daughter Bronwyn. I would like to thank Bronwyn for giving me the idea to write the book in the first place, for her buoyant energy in the mountains, her joyous enthusiasm for creation and her patience. Bronwyn has taught me to see all things new again. I wish to thank Ged for being such a good companion and such fun both on the trail and off. His confidence in me and all of his hard work — from proofreading to drawing all of the maps so meticulously — have been a humbling model of self-giving, generosity and love. He is always there when I need him. Thank you both.

This project has received the advice and support of many people. I wish to thank Eric Langshaw, Rosemary Power, Wendy Grant and Dave DeMuy in particular for their invaluable help in confirming information and making suggestions. A special thanks also to the many wardens, naturalists and Parks Canada staff who assisted in gathering information and providing trail details. Thanks also to Lou Mercer, Kate von Kanel and Christopher and Heather Page for their ideas and encouragement. Finally, thanks to Bronwyn, Rachel and Naomi, who hiked so well.

Park maps are based on information from the National Topographic System map sheet numbers MCR 220 and MCR 221, and are printed with the permission of Energy, Mines and Resources Canada.

# // Contents

# // Introduction

Adventure doesn't have to end when children arrive: only changes and compromises are necessary. Families can and do continue to enjoy the wonders of the Canadian Rockies. This hiking guide has been written as an encouragement and as a resource for parents who would like to enjoy the Rockies but who lack the experience and knowledge necessary to feel confident about taking their precious children into an unfamiliar wilderness environment.

The scope of this guide is to provide information, not only on trails easily hiked by families of different ages and abilities, but to provide the necessary contextual knowledge about key concerns expressed by parents. This is why the book discusses issues such as regulations, safety, backcountry health, amusement ideas and alternative activities in such detail. No one guide can cover all topics, but selective information has been included about the geology, history and wildlife of the area, so that parents can share this information with their children and make learning a part of the adventure.

The hikes included within this book do not exhaust the offerings of the Canadian Rockies. There are many more hikes than the sixty-five included here. However, if your family is anything like mine, dull, arduous or hard-to-get-to hikes simply do not have much appeal. The trails included in this book balance the criteria of being scenic and interesting as well as being suitable in length, difficulty and accessibility for family hiking, allowing families to delight in hikes that combine beauty with modest effort. These selected hikes will serve as your family's gateway to one of the world's most spectacular wilderness destinations — the Canadian Rockies. Happy trails.

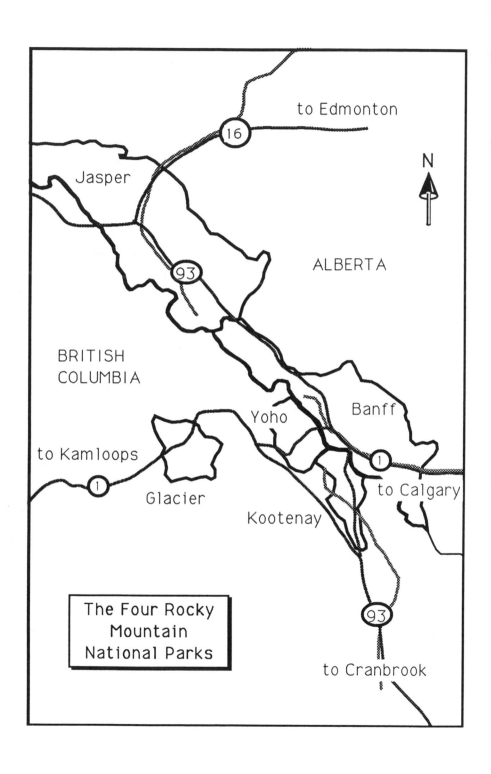

to Edmonton

N

16

Jasper

93

ALBERTA

BRITISH
COLUMBIA

Yoho

Banff

to Kamloops

1

1

Glacier

to Calgary

Kootenay

93

The Four Rocky
Mountain
National Parks

to Cranbrook

# 1 // At A Glance

## Top Twenty Hikes

**Easy:**
- Consolation Lakes
- Fenland Trail
- Paint Pots
- Valley of the Five Lakes
- Emerald Lake
- Johnston Canyon
- Sherbrooke Lake

**Moderate:**
- Angel Glacier
- Eiffel Lake
- Lake Oesa
- Stanley Glacier
- Bald Hills
- Lake Agnes
- Parker's Ridge
- Wilcox Pass

**Difficult:**
- Egypt Lake
- Iceline
- Tonquin Valley
- Floe Lake
- Jonas Pass

# 2 // Ready, Steady, Go

In our normal urban and individualistic societies, we have little opportunity to appreciate and enjoy nature, let alone learn anything from it. Caught up in doing our own thing, our families scatter across town, each member pursuing his or her own interests. A hiking vacation offers families a positive alternative to all of this.

Hiking allows us to enjoy the splendours of nature in its most undisturbed state. Not only can we wonder at the awesome beauty displayed in these powerful yet delicate natural surroundings, we can learn more about our environment and its care. These surroundings can stimulate the senses and the minds of both children and adults alike.

But there is more to hiking than providing an aesthetic or educational experience. Hiking is a shared activity — something that families, no matter how large or small, can do together while also taking individual abilities, personalities and preferences into account. Together, family members cooperate to reach a destination, set up a tent or break camp. As a shared activity, it fosters cooperation among family members who join together in the excitement of planning and preparation and in compromising to allow for individual differences.

The simple companionship on the trail, the long hours spent in the tent during a rain storm, the teamwork needed to ford an unbridged river are all experiences which bond the family together and linger as happy family memories. Some parents might be happy if their kids just wore off their hyperactivity, but hiking and camping also help children learn or strengthen their abilities, explore their physical potential, make decisions and gain greater confidence.

There are scores of reasons why hiking makes a great family vacation or outing. At the top and the bottom of the list, hiking as a family is fun. It is also a challenge.

The most obvious challenge is the physical one. How are we going to lug two toddlers, a baby and all that camping equipment up that steep mountain trail? Can the children walk that far? Can we carry them if they can't make it? There are other challenges, too. Adequate planning and preparation are necessary for a safe and fun trip. The children might need some extra entertaining. But perhaps the biggest challenge of all is a psychological one. Travelling with children is far different than travelling alone or in a group of adults. Family hiking requires families to make major adjustments in their expectations and compromises in their ambitions.

## // Great Expectations

A successful family hike or camping trip must focus on the abilities and needs of your children. Pushing them beyond their endurance or speed in an effort to do a proper "adult" hike will simply create whining, resentful children and frustrated, hassled parents. Competitive sports look for superstars who can outrun and outscore the opposing team and even their own team members. Hiking, on the other hand, caters to the weakest member of the team and accommodates that person's level of ability and interest. If you want to hike with toddlers or babies, you must adjust the distances, level of difficulty and duration accordingly, even if you or other members of the family want to do a more demanding trip.

Another part of this family compromise is a compromise with nature itself. Too often, hikers go out into the wilderness with the intention of conquering it. This attitude of domination expresses itself in individuals who zoom roughshod over the trail trying to set speed records, in hikers who stomp over mosses and wildflowers as they shortcut switchbacks or avoid swampy areas, and in hikers who insist on hiking in mere shorts and T-shirts, without regard to the changeability of the weather. These hikers are more concerned with checking off a hike on their list than with experiencing nature's offerings. They disregard their own fragility and the dignity of their surroundings.

Encourage your family to seek an attitude of cooperation with nature. Absorb its peacefulness; respect its power. Don't race to your destination. Relax and enjoy the sights and smells and sounds. Let your children dawdle over some wildflowers. Take that extra rest stop. Don't worry if other hikers are passing you. Relax. A steady pace will get you there eventually. Hike prepared for the worst conditions and enjoy your good fortune if you carried those annoying, bulky rain jackets for nothing. Stay on the trail. Don't clearcut the flowers. Relax.

Family hiking generally means that you require more supplies than a childless group. More than likely you will end up carrying extra food and clothing — at a minimum — despite your good intentions to make each child carry his or her own stuff. There could also be extra tents, sleeping bags and other equipment adding to your weight. This means that you will be carrying more with you on your hike and carrying it for longer because of the slower pace your kids require. Your own endurance could be pushed to the limit, never mind that of the kids. Take this extra weight into account when you are doing your planning.

Hiking with children is less spontaneous than other types of hiking. Just as you have to make sure kids are always within earshot or eyesight and that they get to school or to bed on time in real life, you have to be prepared to supervise your children and meet their needs at all times when hiking and camping. Forgetting someone's sleeping bag or the food for breakfast may be something adults can put up with, but children have far less patience for these oversights. Check your supplies and check them again for omissions. Your peaceful family will thank you for it.

What can you expect from your children? Each child is different, but most are easier to take hiking than you might think.

**Babies**

Parents tend to worry most about babies, especially if they have only one child. Babies seem so helpless and fragile. Can they really endure the rigours of hiking? In fact, babies are not nearly as fragile as we might like to think. They may get off-schedule, but they will sleep when they need to. Apart from extra care to protect them from the sun and insects, they require little special effort. Be alert to hazards, particularly sticks and small stones that she can put into her mouth, especially if she is crawling and can reach things she shouldn't. Just as at home, use your common sense. The helplessness of babies is an advantage in some ways. Yes, they may need to be carried everywhere and that is tiring for parents, but you have full control over where they are. They don't wander away or have to be dragged reluctantly along a trail when tired.

Expect that your babies (and all other children) will get dirtier on a hike than at home. Try to keep your child clean, but live with stains until you can get to a laundromat. Be prepared to bring along (and pack out) all your necessities, such as diapers and wipes, usually packing extra for emergencies.

### Toddlers

Toddlers are far more work than babies. They will like their freedom to roam and get dirty and will likely push these privileges as far as you will let them. Your main concern with toddlers is their safety, primarily because of their wandering ways. Take special care near rivers, roads, slippery snow patches and steep areas. Belling them like a cat to be able to hear them at all times in case they get lost (or even harnessing them) will help you keep your toddlers safely with you on the trail. More mobile than babies, toddlers must also be kept away from stoves and fires as well as equipment and the first aid kit. Toddlers also require the most amusement of any age group, so you will need to take along extra toys, books, etc. to keep in reserve for the times when the wonders of nature lose your child's attention. (More on this in **Kidding Around**.)

### Juniors

Kids aged five to twelve usually make excellent campers. They are able to walk on their own with less supervision, and they are strong enough to tackle longer hikes. Active and energetic, they will respond well to helping with chores and may even want to assert their own independence by packing their own gear and carrying their own load.

### Teens

Teens are able to hike and take responsibility almost as well as adults, depending on their strength and maturity. They can be included fully in activities such as planning and packing; likely the more involved they are, the better they will like the hiking trip. Some teens want to assert their independence by choosing their own priorities or opting out of a family hike. Taking a friend along on a hike may help overcome this reluctance, but expect that they will want to walk on ahead of you for privacy or take on more dangerous physical challenges such as rock climbing.

## // Endurance

Hiking should be a pleasant outing, not a gruelling ordeal. Expecting too much of your children's stamina can cause disappointment for everybody and a loss of self-confidence in the children if the family is forced to abandon the trip halfway because the kids can't make it. Pushed too far, children will whine and complain incessantly, making you wish you hadn't bothered with the trip. Compromise on distances and the difficulty of terrain for the sake of family happiness. Think of the children as good excuses to walk slowly and to hide your unfitness from the superjocks who whiz by.

Our rule-of-thumb is that we can hike for a maximum of five hours with a five-year-old at about 2 km an hour, making our maximum hike length about 10 km per day. With teenagers, we can cover 3–4 km an hour, depending on the difficulty of the terrain. There are no hard-and-fast rules which dictate that a six-year-old child can hike twice as far and as high as a four-year-old. You know your family best. If your kids are athletic and highly motivated, they may outhike you; if they are bookworms or Nintendo addicts you may have a job ahead of you just to get them out of your tent. If you don't know your family's level of endurance, start on some easy, short trails or day hikes close to your campsite or hotel as a trial run before tackling a major overnight trip or more arduous expedition.

*Hitching a ride at Floe Lake*

Frequent rests and snack stops will improve your family's endurance. A lot of energy is burned up on the trail and this must be restored. If you've planned well and started early, you've got most of the day to do your hike. Take your time.

## // Special Equipment

Babies and toddlers usually need the most assistance on hikes. Small, light babies can be carried against a parent's chest in a Snuggly or in a backpack carrier especially designed for children. In either case, remember that although you may be hot because you are exerting yourself on the trail, your baby is doing nothing but sitting or sleeping. Be sure to keep her warm. Another thing to watch for is maintaining good circulation in your child's legs. Dangling from a Snuggly or carrier for a long time in one position, the legs may have their circulation restricted if the pack's material digs too deeply into the flesh. Check for this problem frequently and move the legs to a new position to relieve the pressure.

Most toddlers like to alternate between walking and being carried. As they grow bigger, this need becomes more and more demanding as the transfer between backpack and the ground becomes more frequent. Eventually, stuffing your child into the backpack and hauling her out again fifteen minutes later just to put her back in again gets to be quite a fussy ordeal. Carrying toddlers in your arms is simpler and can last a little while, but quickly becomes tiring and hard on the back. To limit this, we invented two devices which pulled us through the difficult toddler years.

The "Skookum KiddieSling" is simply a few metres of three-inch webbing fastened in a loop with a snap-in buckle. Slung over one shoulder and under one arm around the parent's body, the KiddieSling is a harness which your child can sit on while being held in your arms. All it does is help you bear the weight of your child. The other advantage is that it is quick and easy to get in and out of, avoiding the hassles of backpacks when your children constantly change their minds about where they want to be.

Our second invention, the "Land Canoe," is a rickshaw-like trailer

*Taking it easy in the Land Canoe*

which let us carry a toddler and most of our gear far into the back country on overnight camping trips. We made the Land Canoe by attaching a standard bicycle wheel to two arms of ash, which had been arched and pre-stressed with cables for extra strength. To the arms, we laced a bucket made of plastic ground-sheet material to carry our daughter and most of the gear. Bronwyn sat in a little seat, complete with cushion and seat belts, that had been cut from a dishtub; we could safely carry two toddlers. The Land Canoe was harnessed to a hip belt and a daypack so that the weight was pulled by hips and shoulders; we used our hands primarily for balancing. Hikers stared at us wherever we went with this contraption, but it let us do long trails with a minimum of effort and allowed Bronwyn to relax like a queen or get out and walk whenever she wanted without wasting much time and effort transferring her back and forth. Although we have outgrown it, the Land Canoe is still in use by other families and has been helpful in allowing disabled children to participate in hiking adventures.

The Land Canoe worked well on most mountain terrain, except trails that were exceptionally rooty, which required a second person to lift its back end up over obstacles. It easily managed steep grades and switchbacks. We discovered that it needed a brake for downhill journeys because its weight on the downhill would force the bearer forward, a motion resisted by the knees. The other thing we learned was to pack our heaviest equipment as low down and as close to the wheel as possible so that the wheel would bear the majority of the weight.

Feel free to imitate our design.

## // Sharing the Load

The biggest problem with family hiking, especially backpacking, is the sheer weight and volume of everything you have to carry. Backpacks can be stuffed only to overflowing and parents can bear only limited amounts of weight, especially when carrying the weight longer while walking at the slower pace children require. This problem is especially daunting when your children are unable to carry much weight themselves and may, in fact, also have to be carried.

This is a problem that is not going to go away, but it can be reduced. The trick is to take with you the minimum amount of gear, clothing and food that you can safely and comfortably get away with. This requires a lot of forethought and planning on your part. The following are lists of essential items required for three types of hikes: the nature hike, the day trip and the overnight backpacking trip. These lists are additive, so the backpacking list includes the items listed under the nature hike and day trip. Adjust the quantity of listed items to meet the needs of every person going on the hike.

**Nature Hike:**

*For each person:*
- ✓ daypack
- ✓ jacket
- ✓ sunglasses
- ✓ snack food
- ✓ whistle for each child
- ✓ bear bell

*For the family:*
- ✓ first-aid kit
- ✓ sharp pocket knife
- ✓ insect repellant
- ✓ 5 metres of rope or webbing
- ✓ toilet paper and trowel
- ✓ garbage bags
- ✓ matches or lighter
- ✓ map or knowledge of the trail
- ✓ flashlight

**Day Trip — all of the above plus:**

*For each person:*
- ✓ lunch
- ✓ 1/2 litre of water per person
- ✓ extra socks
- ✓ wool or pile hats and mitts
- ✓ extra food for snacks and emergencies
- ✓ extra sweaters/jackets
- ✓ rain gear

**Backpacking Trip — all of the above plus:**

*For each person:*
- ✓ backpack
- ✓ sleeping bag
- ✓ insulating pad for sleeping and sitting on
- ✓ eating utensils, plates and cups
- ✓ change of clothing (2 changes per child per day)

*For the family:*
- ✓ tent (possibly two if children are old enough to sleep in their own tent)
- ✓ cook set
- ✓ stove (possibly two for a large family)
- ✓ fuel
- ✓ food for meals (see **Eating Right**)
- ✓ drinks (tea, hot chocolate, juice crystals etc.)
- ✓ water purifier or tablets
- ✓ flavourings (salt, pepper, sugar, bouillon cubes, favourite spices)
- ✓ dish soap, scrubber
- ✓ toilet kit: brush, comb, toothbrushes and paste, soap
- ✓ water bottle or container reserved for untreated water (label this one)
- ✓ water bottles or containers for treated water
- ✓ towel
- ✓ kleenex
- ✓ toys, games and amusements (see **Kidding Around**)

**Special Needs:**
- ✓ diapers
- ✓ wipes
- ✓ bibs
- ✓ harnesses for wandering toddlers

**Optional:**
- ✓ candle lamp
- ✓ binoculars
- ✓ guide books
- ✓ camera

✓ notebooks                ✓ tripods
✓ rubber rafts or canoes (we've seen it done!)
✓ the kitchen sink

Somehow, you have to get all of this stuff into your backpack or daypack. Many things you should try to do without: ie. razors, pillows, shampoo, portable radio, etc. Cut out as much as you can, and then cut down again. When you think you've cut out everything you don't need, pack up your pack and walk around the block with it to check its weight. You'll likely find that you will want to remove some more items. Here are some tricks we've learned for reducing the weight and bulk.

- Take the extra time to pack well, compacting items to their smallest bulk.
- Fold clothing, then roll it into tube shapes for easy packing with minimum wrinkles.
- Fold bulky items like sweaters and jackets meticulously.
- Compartmentalize items by separating them into different bags: ie. one bag for each person's clothing, one bag for food, one bag for first-aid and toilet kits, etc. This makes unpacking far easier and more organized.
- Pack heavy items near the top of the pack and close to your back. This allows you to counterbalance the weight most easily, meaning you need to lean forward less to compensate for the weight dragging on your back.
- Try to get everything except the insulating pads inside your pack. Tying items such as cups and pots onto the outside is sloppy and will gradually become irritating, as they bounce at every step.
- Use film cans as containers for: toothpaste, spices, dish soap, matches, etc. These are tight, waterproof containers which will hold enough supplies for most hikes while reducing the weight and bulk of supplies significantly.
- Use travel-size toiletries.
- Share items such as towels.
- Improvise pillows out of clothing or bagged boots (which are surprisingly comfortable).
- Take time to make precise estimates of your food needs.
- Separate out quantities of food that you will eat rather than packing store-size bags in and lugging the remainder out.
- Use nesting (stackable) pots, plates and cups.
- Fill empty cavities of the cook set with food and spices to save space.
- Fill unstackable, empty cups with food and smaller items to save space.
- Carry as much food as possible in dried form ie: choose dry spaghetti and powdered sauce over canned, ready-made spaghetti, flat noodles over hollow or curled ones, etc.
- Save the bags from boxes of wine. They make great, compressible water carriers and can be used a long time before they wear out.
- Pack necessities such as snacks, sunscreen and your camera near the top of the pack for easy access.

## // Equipment

Hiking and backpacking are inexpensive activities — once you get past the hurdle of accumulating the necessary equipment. Family camping, especially, can get to be an expensive proposition when you have to buy adequate sleeping bags, tents and footwear for everyone. Ouch!

If you are fortunate enough to have friends, family or even total strangers who can lend you some equipment, by all means take advantage of them. If you do have to buy, you will have to balance your needs with what you can afford, obviously. As a general rule-of-thumb, buy the best equipment you can afford. It will last longer, be more comfortable and likely see more use. This rule is especially true if you plan to spend a lot of time in the wilderness over several years; however, if you will rarely hike or camp, don't be lured into spending more than your level of activity warrants.

Unless you plan to buy everything at once, buy your equipment in order of priority. Proper walking shoes, rain gear and warm weather clothing should be first on your list. Daypacks next. If you expect to camp a lot in roadside campgrounds, buy sleeping bags and tents next. Last of all, buy backcountry equipment such as backpacks, single burner stoves, water pumps, etc. Until your family has gained experience and decided it actually likes hiking, there is no point spending money on equipment that might never get used.

Most outdoor stores sell a wide selection of carefully designed, excellent equipment. The better stores will have staff who are willing to spend extensive amounts of time helping you select the equipment that will meet your needs best. Take the time necessary to do this research. It is beyond the scope of this guide to discuss specific hiking/camping products on the market today, as this information changes so quickly from year to year. Ultimately, what you select depends very much on your own preferences, needs and finances. However, here are some suggestions which may help you make your buying/borrowing decisions.

**Warm Weather Gear**

Staying warm in the mountains is similar to staying warm in the winter. Hikers don't have to bundle up in ski suits, but must remember that although the weather may be fine, the environmental conditions here are more severe than at home and the weather is highly changeable. Despite this, hikers generally wear everyday, comfortable clothing and require little special equipment. It is essential to keep the head and torso warm. Fully 25% of body heat can be lost through the head, so be sure everyone wears hats on cold days. The torso, with its vital organs, must also be well insulated. Mitts, warm socks and even scarves can add to your comfort. Think winter-in-the-summer, and you are sure to take along enough warm weather gear.

An important aspect of staying warm is staying dry. This requires a good rain jacket and rain pants. Thoroughly waterproof shell jackets, anoraks and ponchos will keep hikers dry, especially if used in combination with a lightweight pair of rain pants to prevent rain from dripping off the jacket onto legs. Jackets should have hoods to keep water off the head and to help keep the head warm. A rain jacket can often double as a windbreaker, which is essential in the windy Rockies, particularly if the family is hiking at high altitudes, near passes or close to glaciers.

Wool and pile (sometimes called fleece) clothing are best suited to keeping hikers warm. Cottons, polyesters and nylons don't retain heat well and are useless to hikers if they get wet. Even if wet, wool and pile will keep you warm. Wool will stretch if it is wrung out, so hikers will be wet but warm; pile can be wrung out, making hikers more comfortable and the clothing lighter without the weight of the water trapped in wool. Wear either, unless you have dry clothing with you. Wool is the traditional and natural material, but pile is lighter, warmer and dries more quickly. Wool hats, socks, sweaters, gloves and even pants are extremely useful items to have along in case of cooler weather. Jackets, pants and gloves are the most commonly available pile items. Pile clothing has the advantage of being fashionable and popular with kids, especially children who find wool itchy. Whether choosing wool or pile, remember that neither material resists wind very well and jackets must be layered with a wind-proof jacket overtop. Single-jacket pile/wind combinations are popular and economical compromises, but often don't provide adequate protection from rain.

Layering clothing permits hikers to adapt to their conditions. When exerting yourselves up slopes, you can peel off several layers to put them back on again when you reach a windy ridge. Avoid heavy clothing; several lighter layers allow greater adaptability to hiking conditions. The layering also traps air between the layers, providing extra insulation. Deluxe silk undershirts do a terrific job of keeping adult bodies warm, but are rarely available in children's sizes. Sportswear marketing is big business, but hiking clothing for children can be kept simple because their needs are different from those of adults. For example, breathable rain jackets, such as those made of Gore-tex material, are preferred by adults who sweat a lot. Children don't sweat nearly as much, so the need for this specialty clothing is not as great. Standard rain gear suitable for school is just as suitable in the Rockies.

### Footwear

Twenty years ago, no one went along the mountain trails without enormous, heavy hiking boots. Times have changed. Heavy boots have, by and large, been replaced by lightweight hiking shoes which are often the same shoes people wear everyday around town. Tennis shoes, canvas-topped shoes and any lightweight sneaker are inadequate for all but the easiest day hikes, mostly because their soles are not durable enough on rocky terrain; however, hiking footwear does not need to go to the other extreme of the calf-high, blister-creating prisons that old-style hiking boots often were.

Hiking shoes require a good fit to avoid blisters, a stiff sole to provide comfort and agility when hiking over rocks and roots, and a lugged sole to provide good traction. They should be rugged and durable, as waterproof as possible and should be somewhat breathable to minimize sweaty feet.

Hikers with weak ankles should get shoes that rise up above the ankle to give it extra support and stiffness.

When purchasing hiking shoes, be sure to spend a lot of time in a pair walking around and, especially, walking up and down ramps to check to see whether the foot slips forward or backwards in the shoe when on a slant. If the foot does move, try a different size or style of shoe. Many hikers have lost their toenails and suffered great discomfort when descending mountains because their toes have crashed into the tips of their shoes for hours on end. Kids, especially, don't need this discomfort.

Hiking shoes for children are a problem. Hiking boots for children are usually unavailable until a child is about six and has reached Size 1. They are almost as expensive as shoes for adults. Children will outgrow them before they wear them out, and the potential for handing them down to younger siblings is limited because of the close fit the shoes need to avoid causing blisters. Hiking shoes are built to be stiff so that they give sole and ankle support over rough terrain, but this construction means the shoe tends to fight feet. Any tight or rubbing parts of the shoe are quite likely to cause blisters. Also, finding wool (for warmth when wet) hiking socks that fit children is next to impossible.

Knowing this entire litany of problems, we went out and bought hiking shoes for Bronwyn as soon as her feet were big enough. They sit in the closet and she always insists on wearing her rain boots instead. The rain boots offer no sole support and have very little traction or other features that are advisable in hiking shoes, but they seem to get our daughter everywhere she needs to go in the Rockies without the painful blisters she kept getting from the hiking shoes. We've learned the expensive way that the combination of a good pair of sturdy running shoes and boots for the wet spots will likely be sufficient for most children.

### Daypacks

Daypacks are small, lightweight versions of backpacks and are used primarily for short hikes to carry food, extra clothing and other supplies, such as film. The best daypacks are waterproof, have at least two compartments and hug the body closely. Having more than one compartment allows hikers to arrange supplies so that they are accessible. Snack food kept in an outer compartment is easier to reach than food dumped into the sack-like main compartment. Well-padded, adjustable shoulder pads make the weight of the pack more comfortable; a hip belt unites the pack to your body and keeps the pack from swaying as you walk.

Choose a pack size that fits your needs, and always beware of cheap versions. Get a larger pack if only one person is carrying all the supplies, smaller packs if each person takes their own food and clothing. Children are best off with packs made for children; adult packs are too long for kids and will bang against their bottoms as they hike. A daypack for each of your children will make them feel like real hikers, not just tag-alongs, and will allow them to carry some of their own stuff. Carrying their own packs makes children feel grown-up and responsible and raises their sense of adventure and self-esteem. No other piece of equipment is quite so important to increasing a child's interest in hiking. The added advantage is that when kids carry more, parents carry less.

### Backpacks

There are two types of backpacks: internal and external frame packs. Internal frame packs hide the suspension system within the pack, while external frame packs hang from a frame and are separate from it. Internal frame packs are the most versatile because the frame can be fitted to your back and will hug it tightly, allowing it to be carried more easily. They are a favourite for mountaineers and skiers, who need the pack to hug the body tightly over rough terrain and through heavily wooded forests. External frame packs don't look as tidy, but are cooler to hike in because the pack is held a small distance from the back. They also have a larger capacity than the internal frame packs, likely making them the preferred option for families.

Wide, padded and adjustable shoulder and hip belts are a necessity to customize the fit and comfort of these packs. We prefer packs with several compartments over sack-like packs because the compartmentalized packs allow for better organization. Everything seems to sift to the bottom in single compartment packs, meaning a lot of frustration and digging when you want to find something and a lot of repacking when you've found it. Good planners will be able to use single compartment packs well because of the attention they give to where things get put. Buying the biggest pack is not always the best option because you will be tempted to fill it with more than you need. And then you have to carry all that weight around.

### Tents

Tents come in all shapes and sizes. Your key considerations here are weight, compactness, living space and waterproofing. The lighter the tent, of course, the easier it is to carry. Avoid "hardware store special" tents. These are usually heavy and cumbersome, and they likely won't last very long. If possible, get a tent with low-weight aluminum poles. We prefer dome tents over triangular tents just because domes tend to give more headroom and a feeling of greater space, especially on days when we are closed in by rain or bad weather. We also prefer tents that have two doors, providing better ventilation and making it easier to get in and out in a hurry (such as midnight trips to the outhouse). Many tents now come with special vestibules which provide extra room just outside the tent. These vestibules are ideal for expanding your space and storing equipment or wet rain gear.

Whatever tent you buy, get one that is self-supporting. Tents that require pegs to build the structure often cannot be put up in the mountains because the pegs can't be driven into the stone or gravel surface. We peg our tent only to keep it tied down in the wind. If we can't drive our pegs in, we often weigh down our tent with our equipment or rocks.

Be sure that any lightweight tent you buy is also fully waterproof. Take the time to seal the seams from moisture with seam-sealer. Get a tent with a fly for added protection from rain and snow. Try to get a fly that comes as close to the ground as possible. Flies that cover only the top half of the tent will drip directly onto the tent when it rains. The gap between the fly and the tent also provides a small degree of insulation to keep your living space warmer in cold weather; the farther down the fly goes, the better this insulation will be. This may be hard to believe, but try taking the fly off on a cold evening and you will quickly feel the difference in temperature. Also, purchase a tent with as few seams as possible on the ground, to minimize water seepage from the ground through the seams.

Finally, most tents come loosely stuffed with their flies and poles in a single, large bag. They don't have to stay this way. Experiment with ways of rolling your tent up into a compact tube, then find or sew a waterproof bag just big enough for the tent to fit in. Do the same for your fly. By doing this you will reduce the bulk of your tent significantly and make getting it into your backpack a lot easier. Use the larger bag for loose storage between hiking trips. Remember to dry your tent thoroughly before storing it to prevent mildew and rotting.

### Sleeping Bags

We prefer down sleeping bags, even for children — as long as they have passed the diaper and bedwetting stages. Down bags are luxuriously comfortable because of their warmth and their tendency to shape to the body. They are washable, highly compressible and packable and can last virtually forever when cared for properly. Down is a particularly good sleeping bag material for families to use because it is so light and compressible. With so many people to pack for, bulk and weight considerations are very important. However, on the downside, down bags are very expensive and are useless when wet. Because they must be fluffy to be warm, they often are not so warm underneath you because they are being compressed.

Synthetic bags made of various types of materials such as Holofil and Polarguard have the major advantages of continuing to provide warmth even when wet, even though they are not as comfortable as down and are about twice as large when compressed into a stuff sack. Comfort will be a major issue with your children; bulk is a major packing issue to consider. Synthetic bags also have a fairly limited life and are usually expected to last for only a few years of regular weekend use. In the short term, they are cheaper than down, but will ultimately be more expensive if they must be replaced after only a few years' heavy use.

Apart from the cost considerations, choose your sleeping bags according to your needs and expectations. If you have a good, rainproof tent, require compactness and intend to do a lot of camping, choose down. If you do a lot of wet weather or canoe camping, or if packable size and long life are not issues for you, choose synthetic bags. Whatever you choose, don't go for the summer-camp specials often found in department stores. It is always a temptation to get these cheap bags for your kids, but ask yourself: Would you want to sleep in one? If it's not good enough for you, it's not good enough for your kids.

Remember to choose a sleeping bag according to its warmth rating. Choose a rating appropriate to your expectations of where and in what conditions the bags will be used. Summertime hikers in warm climates have no need for sleeping bags rated to −25°C and there is no need to pay for more than you need. Typically, a three-season bag rated to −5°C is more than sufficient. One option to consider is making a long-term investment in an adult-sized, summer-weight down bag for your children. Until the kids grow into them, the bags can be folded over top of them like a sock, giving the kids extra warmth and allowing the bag to be used for five to fifteen years or more.

### Insulating Pads

Some people tough it out without insulating pads, considering them luxuries. For family camping, however, some comforts really help to keep morale up. Insulating pads are not only more comfortable to sleep on than bare ground, they also provide insulation, to keep body heat from dispersing into the ground and the cooler ground temperature from invading your bodies. They are also useful for sitting on during picnics and for covering the dewy seats of picnic tables at breakfast. On a rainy day, they will keep you up off the wet ground should you have to camp in a wet area.

Pads known commercially as Therm-a-Rest pads are the deluxe insulating pads. Acclaimed by most hikers as the most comfortable pads, these are self-inflating foam-filled air mattresses. The downside is that they are expensive and easily damaged. However, repair kits and protective carrying bags are available.

Closed cell foam pads are a much cheaper option and have the advantage of still being usable if torn. They are abrasion- and ultraviolet-resistant. Because of their durability, these pads can be positioned under rather than inside the tent, retaining their insulating value and adding the advantage of letting them protect the tent floor from punctures as well as preventing the need for a groundsheet.

### Cooking Equipment

Lightness and compactness are the criteria for cooking sets. A nesting set of lightweight steel cooking pots that can double as plates is a necessity for backcountry cooking. If you have to have a two-ton cast-iron frying pan, by all means take it along, but you will think twice about it when you feel its weight on your back. Aluminum cooking pots are also available, but are losing favour among hikers, despite their light weight, because of the health concerns associated with ingesting this soft metal. Cooking is a camping activity that has been much romanticized. Many hikers feel that the ideal method is to cook everything over an open fire. Forget it. Not only can backcountry fires be hard to start and maintain, they are dangerous and illegal in most areas because of the risk of forest fire and the ugly scars they leave on the land. Not only this, smoke will sting your eyes, invade your clothing and blacken your pots. Think twice before you choose this option.

Quite a number of stoves are on the market, each with its own advantages. Before buying, make sure your intended fuel is available where you will be hiking; only alcohol fuel is allowed on airplanes. White gas is available at many hardware stores and gas stations, while alcohol can be found at pharmacies. Butane fuel cartridges are readily available at hardware stores and are convenient, but they work best when full and, therefore, under high pressure. As they empty, they become less efficient because they lose pressure. We have used alcohol stoves, noted for their safety, but favour hotter and fuel-efficient white gas stoves.

Another factor when considering stoves is their stability. Tipping over a pot of hot stew while it is on the burner can not only ruin your supper, but cause a fire or ruin your stove as well. Try to get a stove with good supporting legs and arms large enough to keep a pot stable. Windscreens made of heavy foil will keep your stove going and keep the heat focused on your pot instead of warming up the great outdoors.

### Water Purifiers

Water purifiers are not absolutely necessary, but they are a convenient security. The risk of contracting giardiasis from contaminated water in the Rockies is steadily increasing with the growing popularity of backcountry hiking. (See **Good Health** for more details on the causes and symptoms of giardiasis.) Water can be purified by boiling it, although experts disagree on whether two, three, five or twenty minutes is a long enough boiling period. If boiling water, play it safe and boil it as long as possible. The disadvantage to this is the time and fuel that the method consumes.

Chemicals such as iodine and chlorine do not kill the *Giardia lamblia* parasite.

Water purifiers are a more expensive option than boiling, but provide an extra measure of security. Filters work without chemicals by forcing water through a core, usually made of ceramic. *Giardia lamblia*, cysts, sediments, bacteria, in fact, anything larger than a couple of microns, will be trapped on the filter. Filters must catch everything greater than two microns to prevent the *Giardia lamblia* parasite from passing through. There are filters available that filter particles down to .1 microns. Filters do not filter out particles of minerals or chemicals that have bonded to the water molecule, such as iron or sea water. Water with iron or salt in it will retain its colour or salinity even though it has successfully gone through the filter. Filters usually come equipped with cleaners to allow repeated use for many years. Most filters come with a measuring device which indicates when the ceramic core needs to be replaced. Replacement parts are available. Carrying a filter everywhere your family goes guarantees the availability of clean water while weighing no more than a one-litre bottle of water.

When drinking backcountry water, be sure to keep your containers separate. Never pour clean water into a container that has been contaminated with unpurified water or you will defeat the purpose of the filtration exercise.

Children will enjoy participating in filtering the water, but will likely quickly tire from the minor exertion needed to pump enough water for the family.

## // Base Camp

One of the most practical concerns for families is figuring out where they will stay. Hotels, motels, chalets and campgrounds are all options available to families throughout the parks. Your choice will depend on the type of experience you are after and your budget. If your family chooses the hotel/motel method of accommodation, expect to book early and pay relatively high prices during the peak summer months. Families that can manage to visit during the fall or spring shoulder seasons will find the prices lower and the area less congested with other tourists. For fine backcountry experiences, it is possible to reserve space in huts operated by the Alpine Club of Canada. By staying in these huts, your family can enjoy a dry night under a roof in the wilderness without having to pack a tent. Foam pads, stoves and cutlery are provided, but families must take in their own bedding, food and stove fuel. Huts must be shared with other guests and the staff, so these are appropriate options only if your family doesn't mind close quarters and if the children are well-behaved and respectful of others and their property. To use the huts, non-members pay $10–15 per adult and $5 per child. Annual membership is $45 per person and reduces the adult price by $5 per night. See **Resources** for further information.

Camping is the most common and least expensive option. Apart from the many free campsites in the backcountry throughout the parks, there are thirty-three roadside campgrounds for tents and trailers, plus five group camping campgrounds. For family camping, there are fourteen campgrounds in Banff, ten in Jasper, five in Yoho and four in Kootenay Park. These campgrounds vary in the numbers of sites from sixteen (Cirrus Mountain) to 781 (Whistlers) and also vary greatly in the facilities offered. Only eight campgrounds have showers (Tunnel Mountain trailer court and Villages I and II, Johnston Canyon in Banff; Whistlers and Wapiti in Jasper; Kicking Horse in Yoho; Redstreak in Kootenay). Others have hot and cold running water, electrical hook-ups and flush toilets. Still others have only cold water. Be prepared to end up in campsites that have only water pumps and outhouses. If your family style requires full facilities, arrive at these campgrounds before noon to guarantee yourself a site because they fill up early during the peak season.

Campground living can be an adventure in itself. Collecting and splitting firewood available at no charge in bins, building a campfire, picnicking, fetching water and meeting other campers are all activities children enjoy thoroughly. Unlike commercial campgrounds, the facilities in park campgrounds are intended to allow families to stay close to nature: there are no video arcades and movies to entertain children. Most campgrounds are very basic, but a few of the larger ones have small playgrounds for children. Come prepared with games and activities to keep the little ones amused. During the summer, park naturalists offer evening programs on the wildlife, park history and the environment especially for families. Many of these programs start late in the evening so that it is dark enough for slide shows. They are a good excuse for bending the bedtime rules.

Whether you opt for a hotel or campground, staying in one spot for several days before moving on is a good idea. Children will want to have a "home" in this unfamiliar environment. Also, packing and moving around takes a lot of time and planning that can be avoided. Staying put for a while may mean driving extra distances, but makes for a more relaxed and comfortable vacation.

# 3 // Kidding Around

A family's nervous system can suffer shock while hiking. There you are, walking along the trail with kids in tow, with none of the usual activities to entertain them: no TV, no video games, no baseball diamonds, no school. Kilometre after kilometre of slow-moving scenery, no matter how beautiful, can strain the attention span of even the most fascinated child. What makes it even harder is that you all have to stay together *all the time* on the hike without a break from each other, especially when younger children require constant care and supervision. You have to find lots to do — and you have to pack most of it with you.

Keeping children amused on the trail or in the campground is a challenging task, one that often forces parents to opt for less demanding vacations. The difficulty lies mostly in figuring out what will entertain your children without breaking your back with its weight and bulk. You need to find objects and pastimes suited to your children's ages and interests. These have to be light. They also have to be small enough to be crammed into pockets and the spare corners of your daypack or backpack. Durability is helpful and environmentally preferred, but not absolutely essential.

It does get easier. As children grow older, they need fewer things and activities for amusement, and they hopefully will be able to enjoy the peacefulness and absorb the natural beauty around them. They will also begin to choose their own amusements and carry them in their own backpacks, relieving you of most of this concern.

The following suggestions are listed roughly according to age group, but many objects listed for younger children will be enjoyed by the older ones, too.

## // Up to Two Years Old:

✓ favourite doll, even if large; it can be strapped to the outside of a pack
✓ small stuffed animal      ✓ cloth books
✓ plastic farm animals      ✓ small ball
✓ plastic rings or blocks to fit together      ✓ rattles
✓ deflated beach ball      ✓ pail and shovel
✓ spoons

## // Two to Five Years Old:

✓ balloons      ✓ frisbee (one that doesn't go too far)
✓ paper airplanes      ✓ crayons and colouring books
✓ Silly Putty      ✓ one favourite toy
✓ kite      ✓ magnifying glass
✓ kaleidoscope      ✓ bug-collecting kit
✓ paperback books to read to them (3-4 for an overnight trip)
✓ finger puppet      ✓ magazines (ie. *Chickadee*)
✓ yo-yo

*Friends make hiking more fun*

## // Six to Twelve Years Old:

- ✓ paperback novels to read themselves or to have read to them
- ✓ crosswords
- ✓ small musical instruments like harmonicas, kazoos, mouth harps, recorders
- ✓ scissors and paper
- ✓ activity books with puzzles, mazes, games etc.
- ✓ friends (these don't usually fit in a backpack)
- ✓ fishing rod and line (fishing permits are required)
- ✓ Walkie Talkies
- ✓ skipping rope

## // Teens:

- ✓ car-travel games such as chess, checkers or backgammon
- ✓ small tape-player
- ✓ books on anything
- ✓ hobbies and crafts: knitting, origami etc.

## // Activities

Once you have reached your destination, or if you are camping, there is still lots to do. The added advantage here is that most of these ideas can be packed in your head, ready when necessary. You are limited only by your imagination. Keep things simple and try to include everyone.

Setting up the camp, preparing meals, keeping the area tidy, collecting wood, hauling or pumping water . . . all of these chores can be done as fun games that include children and make them feel like important contributors to the camping experience. Don't worry if the kids don't do things properly, as long as they are not endangering themselves or the equipment. They are learning independence and responsibility, even if you have to correct their efforts later. Don't rush these events, either, unless darkness is setting in. Rushing will only leave time on your hands and kids to be amused.

If you are blessed with more than one child — your own or your children's friends who have been borrowed for the occasion — they will likely be able to keep themselves busy for several hours playing imagination games and exploring. Often companionship is the best amusement. Parents, children and friends can while away the time telling stories, talking about family issues, planning for the future and generally getting to know each other better. Hiking vacations provide a beautiful setting for building and deepening relationships.

Kids everywhere love to learn new things, especially if the information is presented to them in an interesting way. Enjoying the backcountry together, your whole family can learn a lot about the wonders of nature, painlessly and through firsthand experience. A lot of this learning can be done quite simply by asking the kids questions to get them to think about what they are seeing.

Try some of the following activities, adapting them to your children's ages and interests.

- Each child can keep a notebook or sketchbook identifying natural objects. Older children can draw them and take notes on the characteristics and locations of these objects.
- Identify the many flowers and plants you see. Are they in the sun, in the swamp? Are they just budding or already in bloom? What grows near them? Are there berries?
- Watch for animals. Can you find where they live? What do they eat? What is the difference between a pika and a marmot, a deer and an elk?
- Kids have a great interest in paw prints and feces left behind by animals. Books identifying these are available and following these signs is a fun way to identify and "track" animals along the trail.
- Identify the trees. What does a larch tree feel like? How are red pine needles different from those of an Engelmann spruce? What kind of birds live in each type of tree? Why are the aspen trunks black to uniform height?
- Watch the sky and predict the weather.
- Watch for birds. Can you imitate their songs? What do they eat?
- Collect non-living objects such as fallen pine cones, twigs and branches for crafts and projects.

When naturalism wears thin, there are countless other activities to keep children busy:

- make up names for the mountains and rivers; compare them to the real names
- spelling bees
- math contests
- guessing games like "I Spy" and "20 Questions."
- counting games: who is the first to see 100 Glacier Lilies?
- story-telling: each person contributes a sentence, or, tell three stories each and the others guess which one is made up and which ones are true.
- talk to your kids; get to know them
- stargazing; a chart will help with identification
- marshmallow roasting, over stove or fire
- collect objects for crafts
- paint rocks
- start a sing-along
- make masks out of pie plates
- go to bed early
- bug out and be tourists for awhile. Go shopping, watch a movie, plan the next hike or get more supplies.

## // Morale Boosting

Let's face it. Hiking can be tough work. Children often need a lot of encouragement to make it up a set of switchbacks or to complete a hike in good humour. Setting reasonable expectations in the first place and then graduating to longer or more arduous hikes will do a lot towards helping a child happily accomplish a hike and look forward to the next one. You can do a lot on the trail to boost your children's morale. Watch for opportunities constantly and try the following:

- Praise each successfully forded river, each switchback ascent, each notable accomplishment.

*Fun on an improvised swing*

- Be patient when the children dawdle or stop to look at something. Enjoy the moment with them.
- Walk with and beside your children whenever possible.
- Be available to assist or carry the children over difficult spots, such as narrow bridges or muddy paths.
- Take frequent rest and snack stops.
- Refrain from spooking everyone with bear stories etc.
- Take along surprises like chocolate bars, a favourite book, new toys.
- Provide minor destinations which the children can use as benchmarks of their progress towards the final goal.
- Talk about what they will see at the final destination or about what they can do when they get there.
- Take your children's friends along. Kids seem to hike much better when they have a pal. Often they are hard to keep up with.
- Take a break from hiking every few days and do something entirely different.
- Hike with other families. Children can occupy each other and families can share responsibilities, food, knowledge and activities together.
- Let the children take turns "pathfinding" or leading the family up the trail. Imaginative children can dramatize this into an adventure reenacting the expeditions of explorers, adventurers and even pirates.
- At junctions, let the children make the decision (within reason) about which way to go. Let them be the map-readers occasionally.
- Let the children decide when and where to take a lunch break.
- If you must abandon the hike because the children can't make it, accept your fate gracefully and avoid blaming anyone.

# 4 // Walking Softly

The imposing grandeur of the Rocky Mountains is justly famous as one of the great untamed wilderness areas of the world. Appearing to be robust, this mountain ecosystem is really a fragile, delicate environment which must be enjoyed with great care and respect. Each year, millions of tourists arrive in these mountain parks to wonder at their beauty. The pressures of these seasonal population increases take a heavy toll on the wildlife, plant life and terrain which combine to create the distinctive beauty of this area. These parks have been preserved to protect the mountain environment forever while we enjoy them. Please, please, remember to experience the Rockies with care, so that your children's children can revel in the wonders of this amazing place.

## // Park Regulations

Most backcountry campgrounds are run on a quota system to minimize overcrowding and overuse. Because of this system, free permits are required for backcountry camping. These permits are mandatory and must be obtained if your family plans to stay overnight in the backcountry. They are available from information centres and warden offices. These permits do not have to be returned.

- Permits are not required for day hikes.
- Camp only in designated campsites.
- Some trails or areas are temporarily restricted for safety reasons (ie. bears). It is illegal to enter these areas.
- Fires are permitted only in fireboxes. Fires are illegal in many campgrounds. You are sure of a warm meal if you take your own stove.
- Chopping wood from living trees is forbidden.
- Plants and natural objects such as rocks and fossils may not be picked, removed or destroyed.
- Animals must not be disturbed, touched or fed.
- No hunting — ever.
- A fishing permit is required for any fishing. Available from park information, administration, campground and warden offices, as well as some tackle shops, the annual permit costs $10 and the seven-day permit costs $5. Information on lakes and rivers where fishing is permitted in the parks can be found in the pamphlet "Fishing Regulations", published by Environment Canada Parks Service.
- Food must be properly stored by hanging it in a bag from a tree or bear pole, or, if you are camping in a car-accessible campground, the food should be stored in bear-proof caches or the car. Coolers will do little do deter animals from raiding your supplies.
- Pets must be on leashes at all times. It is actually best to leave your pets, especially dogs, at home. They can easily get lost or injured and often annoy the wildlife, particularly bears. (We've heard of several pets being preyed upon by owls. One family took their rare, pregnant

*Boardwalks and bridges minimize trail damage*

cat camping with them because they thought she would be safer than at a sitter's. The cat and unborn kittens (valued at $300 each) made one lucky owl a sumptuous meal.)

- All garbage must be disposed of in bear-proof receptacles. Any garbage created in a backcountry site must be packed out for proper disposal. This includes organic waste. Orange and banana peels, for example, can take two years to rot.
- Stiff fines and/or eviction from the parks can result if you ignore these regulations.

## // Trail Conditions

The trails in the Rocky Mountains are among the best and best-maintained in the world. Most of the trails in the Rockies are wide, gently sloped and clearly marked. Major rivers are usually bridged, as are many of the known boggy areas. (This is in marked contrast to most trails in the United States, which are narrow and usually unbridged to limit access.) Trail crews put in long, hard hours each year to build new bridges, clear out blowdown areas and improve boggy areas. The wardens hike or ride the trails regularly to check their condition. Information on trail conditions, such as snow, boggy patches and washed-out bridges, can be found at the information centres.

Trail conditions vary from year to year because of varying damage done by winter storms, avalanches, high water levels, time and vandals. Sometimes the trail you want to do hasn't yet been cleaned up by trail crews. You may find yourself climbing over trees pushed down by avalanches, fording icy rivers or slogging through swampy or snowy patches still remaining from the winter. Most snowy or wet areas will be at the higher elevations or in areas shaded from the drying sun. Late snow can be a problem even in July and can be found in small amounts on some trails year round.

Finding boggy patches, avalanche debris or unbridged rivers can be a problem, especially if you have to get your children through or over them. Not only can you get wet and/or dirty, especially from the ankles down, but avoiding these impasses often takes you off the trail, and your traffic begins the erosion process, which can take years to repair. A step over a log may be small for parents, but it can be a monumental leap for a small child. A few of these can be an adventure; too many will leave children exhausted and complaining. Children are also easily scratched and bumped when passing through these areas or when leaving the trail. When you encounter difficult trail conditions — and you will — try to follow these tips:

- Never shortcut up or down switchbacks.
- Wear waterproof footwear, which will allow you to go through muddy areas rather than going off the trail (even a bit) to get around them.
- Clear light deadfall from the path as you go rather than leaving it for everyone else to step over.
- Be cautious climbing over or under trees brought down by avalanches. Test the trees' stability before climbing on or under them.
- Give horses and their riders the right of way. Keep to the side of the trail and don't move until they have passed.
- Walk single file on narrow trails.
- Give way to oncoming hikers, especially those going downhill. Take a break.
- Do not bushwhack. You risk injury and getting lost, as well as trampling the plants.
- Ford unbridged rivers facing upstream. It is easier to balance this way.
- On snow-covered slopes, dig your feet into the snow to get a secure footing and to avoid sliding. Consider "roping up" with webbing to tie children to a securely footed adult to keep them from slipping down the slope.

## // Backcountry Camping

Once you get to your backcountry destination, it's time to pick your site and make camp. This is a great opportunity for your children to be explorers. They can look over the camping sites, find the outhouse, seek out the best tree or bear pole for hanging food and locate the best spot for getting water. If you happen to be camping with another family, this is a good opportunity for mutual learning and teaching as you help each other set up.

Be sure to establish boundaries for the children. Wading in rivers, scrambling up scree slopes and wandering from the campground alone should be strictly forbidden children of all ages. Vigilance is needed to keep everyone safely together. Children should also be reminded to respect other campers in the area and to avoid unnecessary noise or walking too close to occupied campsites.

Most backcountry campgrounds are very basic. Don't expect tables, washing up areas and split firewood. Bear poles have been set up at most backcountry campgrounds and should be shared with other campers. The outhouses usually have some toilet paper in them, but take your own just in case.

There is much you can do to make your camping experience as comfortable as possible. Involve the children in picking your site. Suggest that they look for a flat site reasonably close to water, the outhouses and any available fireboxes. In most cases the designated sites are obvious: they are the flattest, most worn looking areas. If possible, try to avoid sites that are already wet and that would allow water to seep through your tent floor. Also, if it is raining or

*Huddled in camp*

looks like it might rain, avoid sites that are lower than the surrounding ground. We ignored this dictum once and found our tent floating in a puddle after a severe rainstorm because all the water had run into our dip and stayed there.

If you can't avoid rolling or slanted sites, pitch your tent and organize yourselves so that you sleep with your head at the highest level; otherwise you may dream that you are falling all night long. Especially on stony or wet ground, try putting your insulating pads beneath your tent rather than inside it. This will protect the tent floor and keep you drier while still providing just as much insulation.

At night, we bring almost everything except food and toiletries inside the tent. Doing this can make your tent crowded, but backpacks and their contents make good pillows and footrests. You can also use them to cover parts of the tent not protected by your insulating pads. Bringing your gear inside protects everything from the weather and guarantees you have everything you need when you need it. We make an exception for footwear, which is usually dirty and often wet. Shoes are left outside because keeping the tent clean and dry is a high priority. Often, we will just shove boots or shoes under the floor of the tent near the door. We will bring them inside if it is pouring rain or if there are leather-loving porcupines in the area. If you want to bring your boots inside, turn a stuff-sack inside out and put a pair of boots in it. By interlocking the boots around their L-shapes, you can make a surprisingly comfortable pillow.

Cook at least 100 metres from your tent. Dispose of cooking and dishwashing liquids, as well as toothpaste and washing-up waters, at the same distance. If animals do come into the campground, you want them to stay far away from you. Hang all food in a tree as far as possible from the trunk for the night. Avoid leaving food out unattended while you go exploring. Clark's nutcrackers, crows and chipmunks will have a feast, thanking you for carrying all that weight up the trail just for them.

Pack out all of your garbage — extra food, diapers, cans, everything. This includes organic garbage such as fruit peels, rice and coffee grounds. Yes, it will rot, eventually, if the animals don't eat it and harm their digestive systems first, but the wilderness is not a compost bin for human waste. When in doubt, pack it out. You are responsible for the cleanliness of your site and for leaving it as you found it for the next group of hikers who visit the area. It is lighter and takes less space on the way out, anyway. A good habit is to leave the area cleaner than you found it. Your young environmentalists can be put to work for a good cause.

If there is an outhouse, use it. The convenience of bushes or just beyond the tent flap when your children have the call of nature in the middle of the night simply aren't environmentally sound options in the wilderness — or anywhere. Human waste around the campsite can create animal-attracting odours and is inconsiderate of future campers on your site. Feces deposited close to surface water will eventually seep their germs and possible parasites, such as the *Giardia lamblia*, into the water, contaminating it. If you are on the trail or there happens to be no outhouse, burn all paper used and bury feces with a trowel. When you do use the outhouse, use a minimum of toilet paper because it is the rotting paper, more than the wastes, that contributes to the outhouse's characteristic smell.

Do not use the outhouses as garbage cans. This is an offensive practice committed by lazy, inconsiderate slobs. Leftover food, cans, disposable diapers etc. will all attract animals to the outhouse, possibly making it a dangerous place to go.

Parents with children in diapers need not despair — too much. The contents can be dumped in the outhouse, but the remaining diaper must be bagged and packed out. Paper won't degrade and cloth, of course, can be used again. If you are forced to wash a cloth diaper, do so 100 metres away from any surface water, using water you have carried to the washing site. Don't worry too much about stains and set the diapers on a rock or bush to dry and bleach in the sun.

## // Wildlife

The wildlife in the parks is wonderful to watch — at a distance. You may disappoint your children, but resist their temptations to feed the birds and animals. The wildness of these animals should be respected for the sake of their dignity and health and for your own safety. These animals are not pets, nor are the Rockies an enormous petting zoo. Feeding the birds and animals makes them dependent upon human food and will encourage them to become campground nuisances. Many animals have died because they have consumed too much human food. Our foods tend to be highly processed, full of sugar and fatty. While usually not so healthy for us, either, these foods can deal a rapid death blow to many animals. Also, all animals can accidentally or purposefully nip or wound people who venture too close to pet or feed them. For more on this topic, see **Playing it Safe**.

# 5 // A Sense Of Place

## // Geology

### Making Mountains

The Canadian Rockies straddle the Alberta/British Columbia border in Western Canada and extend 1,450 kilometres north from the international boundary to the Liard River just south of the Yukon border. Although there are several mountain ranges between the Pacific Coast and the expansive prairies, the name "Rockies" does not apply to all of these ranges. Just 150 kilometres wide, the Rockies are the most easterly range of mountains and are fronted by the interior plains on the east and the Rocky Mountain Trench in the west.

The Rockies began 1.5 billion years ago under the sea. Slowly, seabed sediments accumulated and were compressed into sandstone, limestone and shale. The Canadian Rockies rose up out of the sea about 120-75 million years ago — making them older than the American Rockies, the Himalayas and the Alps. Unlike many other mountain formations, such as those in the Pacific Rim, the Rockies were formed almost entirely through the movement of continental plates and without much volcanic activity. The sedimentary rocks accumulated in layers until they began to be thrust upwards as the western continental shelf pushed northeast about 120 million years ago. This thrusting activity lasted approximately 75 million years. During this time, the flat sedimentary rocks slid, folded and broke as they ascended toward the clouds as much as 4,000 metres above sea level.

Of course, as soon as these new mountains emerged, erosion began to wear them down again. Recent glaciation in the last two million years has been carving mountain valleys and making the peaks more prominent. In places, a depth of more than ten kilometres of rock has been removed by the wind and the glaciers. Silently, this dramatic process is still going on in these middle-aged mountains.

Because of their geological history, the Rockies are composed almost entirely of sedimentary rock. There is little igneous or metamorphic rock in the Rockies. There are oil, gas and coal in these mountains, but no precious metals such as gold and silver.

## // Mountain Ranges

The central region of the Canadian Rockies covers the four national parks discussed in this guidebook. (For the sake of brevity and interest, the geology of the northern and southern regions will be ignored.) This central region can be roughly divided into four broad areas: the foothills, the front ranges, the main ranges and the western ranges. The main and western ranges are the oldest, and the ranges get younger as you move east toward the prairies.

### Foothills

The foothills are a transitional area linking the flat prairies to the jagged peaks of the mountains. Gradually becoming more tilted and broken as they run in parallel southeast/northwest lines approaching the west, the shale and sand-

*Overthrust
Mt. Rundle in the
Front Ranges*

stone foothills subdue the grassy prairie expanses with rolling hills and increasingly dense forests.

### Front Ranges
The front ranges are highly folded limestone mountains which tend to tilt or overthrust downward toward the southwest. Postcard-perfect Mt. Rundle is a prime example of this tilt. Gradually worn by glaciers on its southwestern side until entire downward-tilting layers tumbled to the valley below, Mt. Rundle's upward-tilting northeastern side could not be eroded so quickly and remains taller than the southwestern side. The front ranges repeat themselves in a sequence of four parallel lines of limestone peaks alternating with more easily eroded shale valleys.

### Main Ranges
West of the front ranges are the main ranges, subdivided into eastern and western main ranges. The eastern main ranges, including the Continental Divide, which sends water to either the Pacific or Atlantic Ocean depending on which side of the divide the water falls, are about 500 metres taller than the front ranges, and the rock tends to lie flat rather than folding over itself as it does in the front ranges. These mountains are known as castellated mountains and, naturally, Castle Mountain is a good example of this range because of its blocky construction and horizontal folds. The rock in this range tends to be dominated by pinkish quartzite, pale dolomite and darker limestone, and so these mountains are more colourful than the front ranges. In this range, the western slopes are steeper than the eastern ones, primarily because of thicker buildups of ice and the faster flow of rivers to the closer Pacific Ocean on the western side than to the Atlantic on the eastern slope.

The western main range begins at Field in Yoho Park. West of Field, the

*The Mt. Louis dogtooth in the Front Ranges*

rock is primarily soft shale instead of the harder quartzite. This means the mountains here are more rounded and eroded. Much of this shale is slightly metamorphosed by heat and pressure to become greenish slate.

### Western Ranges

A tiny area between Golden and Radium Hot Springs is known as the western ranges. This area is made of folded shale, as are the southwestern sloping main ranges, but the western ranges have been bent backwards by pressure from the Purcell Mountains and slope to the northeast.

## // Mountain Types

At first, all mountains look the same: big and pointed. But gradually, experience and observation allow mountain-watchers to distinguish between mountain types. Here are the five main types of mountains in the Rockies:

### Castellated

These are the big mountains of the parks. Found in the eastern main ranges, these mountains were built in flat layers of limestone, quartzite and dolomite sandwiching layers of shale. Famous examples are Castle Mountain, Mt. Temple and Mt. Edith Cavell.

### Dogtooth

Dogtooth mountains point straight to the sky because they were thrust vertically upwards during mountain building. They are found mostly in the front ranges and western main ranges. Mt. Louis near the 1A junction close to Banff townsite is a good example.

### Horn

Horn mountains are mountains that have been eroded on several sides by cirque glaciers, giving them a classic pyramid-like appearance. Good examples are Mt. Assiniboine in Mt. Assiniboine Provincial Park, Cirque Mountain, Howse Peak and Mt. Fryatt. Horn mountains are usually found in the eastern main ranges.

### Overthrust

Overthrust mountains are tilted heavily in one direction, with layers beneath the tilt being eroded away to form steep cliffs. These are found most often in the front ranges. Mt. Rundle near Banff townsite is the classic example of an overthrust formation.

### Sawtooth

Long ridges eroded by winds to produce a distinctive many-pointed edge are known as sawtooth mountains. Found mostly in the front ranges, these mountains seem similar to overthrust mountains, but owe their shape more to erosion than to mountain-building compression. The Queen Elizabeth and Colin Ranges in Jasper are good examples.

## // Mountain Regions

The four Rocky Mountain parks discussed in this book fall in the central region of the Rocky Mountains. Within this region, the mountains have three ecological zones: the montane forest, the subalpine and the alpine zones.

### Montane Zone

The montane forests include the valleys and wetlands, the foothills and the lower slopes of the mountains. The eastern slopes are drier and less densely covered with trees than the wetter western slopes. The eastern slopes grow primarily aspen, white spruce and lodgepole pine, as well as shrubs such as kinnikinnik, shrubby cinquefoil and juniper. The western slopes are wetter and include additional trees such as larch. South of Jasper, both the southern and western slopes will also be populated with Douglas fir. Asters, bluebells, pasque flowers, hollyhocks, fireweed, Indian paintbrush etc. can all be found in the montane forest. Of all mountain zones, the montane zone is most abundantly filled with animal and plant life. It is also the most heavily affected by humans.

The montane zone is where most hikes begin. The trails at this level are usually cool and forest enclosed. Hikers should watch out for roots, slippery mud, and deadfall.

### Subalpine Zone

The subalpine zone accumulates the heaviest snowfall and is generally damp and cool. Extending from the montane forest to the treeline at the beginning of the alpine zone, the subalpine zone begins with a mix of white and Engelmann spruce; higher up, the slopes are typically covered with lodgepole pine and aspen. At the highest levels, subalpine fir, whitebark pine and larch trees dominate the forest. Growth is often stunted here because of the cool air, higher snowfall and longer winter. The mid-mountain forests are thinner than the montane forests and can include open meadows. Flowers in this zone include trilliums, Indian paintbrush, columbines, shooting stars, fireweed, lilies, monkshood etc. The subalpine zone is the largest of the three mountain zones.

Hikers here will find that the forest is thinner than in the montane zone, making the views better. The trails will alternate between sunny, open mead-

*A subalpine meadow in the Tonquin Valley*

ows rife with wildflowers and cool forests. Hikers should be careful of the steeper slopes and loose rocks on the trail.

### Alpine Zone

The alpine zone includes all land above the treeline: glaciers, scree slopes and meadows. The true alpine areas are easy to recognize because of their lack of trees, but exactly where this zone begins and where the subalpine zone ends is a debatable question. On southern and western slopes and in warmer climates, the treeline that separates the alpine and subalpine zones will be at higher elevations than on eastern or cooler slopes, and so the location of the alpine zone will vary, even on individual mountains. On average, the treeline ends at about 2,200 metres. Generally, as you approach the alpine zone, the trees will grow shorter and more sparsely, often in small groups rather than spread out across a slope. In the final stages, known as the krummholz zone (German for "crooked wood"), the trees will be twisted and low, growing only in sheltered areas. When you leave the trees completely behind, you are definitely in the alpine zone. This zone is noted for its wildflowers: glacier lilies, pussytoes, stonecrops, globeflowers, anemones, white dryas, grass of parnassus, saxifrage, fleabane, buttercups, heathers etc. Most of these flowers have cup-shaped petals to get the greatest benefit from the sunlight.

The alpine zone is the favourite zone of almost all hikers, young and old alike. The views are unimpeded by forest and can often be spectacular. Scree and snow slopes should be crossed carefully. Particular care must be taken to avoid stepping on the beautiful but fragile plants which grow here.

## // Glaciers

Glaciers are beds of ice and snow that lie on mountainsides at high

*The Leanchoil Hoodos stand guard*

elevations or on shady slopes. Glaciers form when more snow accumulates than melts. The snow gradually compresses into ice over time and under the weight of more snow layers. The glaciers seen in the Rockies today are merely the scattered remains from the last ice age, known as the Wisconsin Glaciation, which began about 75,000 years ago and ended about 11,000 years ago.

Glaciers are the most erosive force in the mountains: they are the mountain shapers. Glaciers are seldom in a state of equilibrium; they are usually advancing or receding. They recede when more ice is melting than is being formed; they advance under the opposite conditions. As glaciers move, they grind away at mountains, rocks and anything else in their paths, leaving behind a mess of rock and mud known as glacial till. Hills or mounds of till are known as moraines. Glaciers have changed these mountains from being round and smooth to jagged. They have carved cirques, tarns and river valleys.

Most of the remaining glaciers are receding: less than a hundred years ago, the Columbia Icefield extended over the area where the Icefields Parkway now runs; the Crowfoot Glacier has lost one toe and the famous Angel Glacier is shrinking.

## // Hoodoos

Hoodoos are ghostly pillars of glacial till capped by harder lime deposits which protect the softer columns below from erosion by rain and, to some extent, wind. The unprotected till around the hoodoos has been worn away, leaving the pillars exposed. Some hoodoos are up to 20 metres high; they are pale brown in colour and imbedded with small stones. Many of the protective caps have finally worn away, although it is known that many of the caps have been kicked off by early settlers in the area and destructive tourists. Beheaded hoodoos will erode far more quickly than those few remaining with their caps.

Hoodoos can be found throughout the mountains. The most visited are those easily seen from the Hoodoo trail on Tunnel Mountain in Banff, near Castle Mountain, and on Highway 93 by Dutch Creek, just south of the Fairmont Hot Springs. The best examples of hoodoos, however, are the Leanchoil Hoodoos, which can be reached by a steep hike at the western end of Yoho Park.

## // History

Just as the geological history of the Rocky Mountains has been shaped by the push and shove between continental plates, glaciers and the wind, so, too, the human history of these mountains has been one of conflict and erosion.

### Early History

The Native peoples of Western Canada were the first people to settle in the Rocky Mountains. Likely arriving in a southern migration from Alaska about 60-20,000 years ago, these people are thought to have dwelled on the eastern, sheltered slopes of the Rockies, at least during the summer months. Animal remains, spear points and knives found at Vermilion Lake near Banff provide the first datable record of human activity, placing human settlement at the end of the last glacial period, 10,000 years ago. We know little of this early Indian culture because our knowledge depends on scant archaeological evidence. We do know that these people were migratory hunters and gatherers.

### Before the Europeans

Prior to European exploration of the area at the end of the eighteenth century, the east and west slopes of the Rockies south of the Saskatchewan River were inhabited most successfully by the Kootenays; between Jasper and Prince George lived the Sarcee; the Beaver tribes lived north of Jasper toward the Peace River; and the Dene lived north of the Athabasca River. As Europeans explored and settled eastern Canada, Stoney tribes (Assiniboine) headed west in the early 1700s, fleeing the white invasion and its ravaging diseases, such as smallpox. In their turn, the Stoneys pushed the Kootenays further west and fought bloody wars with the Blackfoot, Blood and Peigan tribes who remained on the prairies. The Sarcee Indians were pushed south by the more northerly Cree at this time, increasing the inter-tribal competition for territory and food. The acquisition of horses and, later, of guns, intensified the tribal rivalries and the bloodiness of their wars. During this period, smallpox claimed the lives of sixty percent of these tribes. Gradually, the Stoneys became the dominant tribe in the central Rockies, using the Bow Valley as a central corridor for travel and trade between the tribes.

### The Fur Trade

The fur trade that had enticed Europeans to eastern Canada had moved west by the 1780s. Members of the North West Company were initially responsible for the early non-Native explorations of the Rockies. Many places now bear the names of these early adventurers. Alexander MacKenzie, a partner in this company, completed the first overland trip across western Canada in 1793 by taking a northern route along the Peace River and over the mountains until he found the Fraser River, which he followed to the Pacific Ocean. Trading posts were established at the edge of the prairies between this time and 1805, but exploration was limited to minor forays into the front ranges. David Thompson, an employee of the North West Company, explored around the Kananaskis area and up the Bow River in 1800, but was forced out by Blackfoot Indians. Simon Fraser explored the Rocky Mountain Trench in 1805 and followed the river which now bears his name to the Pacific in 1808.

The North West Company merged with the Hudson's Bay Company in 1821 and the fur trade intensified, bringing with it naturalists and botanists like Thomas Drummond and David Douglas, who identified, classified and sketched the flora and fauna of this wild, savage land. There were even a few missionaries, most notably Robert Rundle, a Methodist minister who led a small congregation of Stoneys near Banff in the 1840s and who is now remembered by his namesake, Mt. Rundle, likely the most famous and most photographed mountain in the Rockies.

Yet when the Hudson's Bay Company decided to begin shipping furs via the coast rather than by land around 1850, explorations of the area all but ceased, and there was little non-Native presence in the Rockies. The most notable exploration prior to the 1880s was John Palliser's 1858 expedition which explored the Rockies for the purpose of finding areas suitable for settlement. Palliser's deputy, Dr. James Hector, did most of the exploration of the region, crossing and recrossing the mountains and valleys and discovering the Kicking Horse, Bow and Vermilion Passes so critical for transportation through the mountains today.

### The Railway

When British Columbia became a province of Canada in 1871, one of its conditions for membership in the new country was that it be linked to the rest of the country by a trans-continental railroad. The northern Yellowhead Pass was originally chosen as the route across the mountains until the dry prairies to the south were discovered to be fertile and suitable for farming. Also, political motivations dictated that a more southerly route be found to prevent competition from American railways. In 1881, the Canadian Pacific Railroad, under Sir Sanford Fleming, decided to take a southern route through this rich farming area to attract settlers who would pay for CPR operations. It didn't matter that the CPR didn't know of any route through the mountains. They would find one. Major A.B. Rogers was selected to survey a route and was responsible for selecting the Kicking Horse Pass as the way over the Great Divide.

By 1883, the CPR had reached "Siding 29," now known as Banff. Careless workers and hazardous blasting caused wildfires to blaze through the forests of the Bow Valley, creating environmental damage and visual eyesores which would last for decades. By 1884, the railway had crossed over the Kicking Horse Pass and began making its terrifying and steep descent toward Craigellachie to join the railway ascending from the Pacific. The last spike was driven in 1885 and the transcontinental railway was complete.

### Hot Springs

The CPR, however, needed money to finance its operations, and to get money, it needed people. Fleming saw the mountains as a haven for wealthy tourists — just as the Swiss Alps were — but it wasn't until three CPR workers discovered hot springs on Sulphur Mountain above Banff that tourism's treasure chest was opened. The springs had been known and sacred to the Native tribes for centuries, but were first found by Peter Younge and Benjamin Pease in 1875. They stuck around for a short time, hoping to stake a claim, but soon gave up and the springs were forgotten. They were rediscovered by Bill and Tom McCardell and Frank McCabe. These three formed a fragile partnership and tried to stake a claim to the springs by squatting in the area. Several disagreements and bad deals later, these early entrepreneurs were paid off and relinquished their claim to the federal government. The federal government decided to protect the area because it recognized the value the springs would have as a spa and sought to eliminate the wildfire of commercial speculation that surrounded them.

### Canada's National Parks

The fortunate intervention of the federal government saw the 1885 creation of the world's third national park: Rocky Mountains Park. Only 26 square kilometres of land were reserved, but it was a beginning. Unlike Yellowstone Park in the United States, which had been set aside fourteen years earlier but desecrated by entrepreneurs, tourists and thieves — the reckless and the lawless — Canadian federal government regulations preceded commercial development and gave Canada's first national park a chance to remain a wilderness environment rather than being rampantly exploited for profit.

More land was added to the park system: Yoho in 1886; the Lake Louise area in 1892; Jasper in 1907; and Kootenay in 1920. The boundaries of these parks changed several times as land was added and taken away. The most serious withdrawal of land occurred in 1911, when Rocky Mountains Park was reduced from 17,500 to 4,700 square kilometres and Jasper from 13,000 to 2,600 square kilometres to allow mining and logging in the reserved area. Gradually, this reduction was reversed and the four national parks now cover more than 20,000 square kilometres. In 1930, the National Parks Act established these boundaries and renamed Rocky Mountains Park Banff National Park and dubbed the initial group of four parks the Canadian National Parks.

Even though the emphasis of government policy slanted the development of the national parks towards making them wilderness areas — not profit centres — government policy was sorely lacking in many areas. The wilderness was treated carelessly, and wildfires started by careless construction and tourists continued to spread through the valleys. The majestic beauty of Rocky Mountain Park was left scarred and ugly. Trophy and sport hunting was permitted until 1890 and even long after this date, animals were classed as either good or bad. The bad animals, primarily predators such as coyotes, were shot by bounty hunters until the mid 1930s. Park officials did not realize that this slaughter affected the food chain and allowed elk, made extinct in the area but reintroduced in 1917, to thrive so well that the populations of deer and bighorn sheep were threatened. Although the land was set aside as a wilderness preserve, this was done more to promote tourism and the financial health of the CPR than for the benefit of the environment. Early developments focused on improving transportation and building luxury hotels for wealthy tourists. The land and wildlife went largely unprotected until a small warden service with police powers was established in 1909 to prevent poaching and to fight fires. There was much to learn.

### Modern Times

As the number of visitors to the parks grew each year, the area was gradually developed. A second national railway made its way through the northern Yellowhead Pass in 1913. The first car arrived at the park gates in 1904, but was immediately banned, supposedly to protect the wildlife but also to maintain the transportation monopoly held between the CPR and the Brewster family's outfitting company. Cars were not allowed into the parks until 1915. Roads were gradually built. The Icefields Parkway was a Depression-era make-work project finished in 1940 as a single-lane dirt track. The Trans-Canada Highway did not cut through the parks until 1962. Now this highway has been twinned through much of the park area, adding more cars and controversy over the effects of the highway on the wildlife. Much of Banff Park has been fenced along the highway to decrease encounters between animals and cars, conflicts animals invariably lose.

The four national parks are now visited by several million people each year. Famous the world over for their serene beauty and remote wildness, there is an increasing need to protect the Rockies from the very people who come to enjoy them. The pressures of development and increasing tourism, like erosion, can all too easily destroy this unique wilderness that we have come to see.

## // Animals

### Black Bear

Black bears can be either cinnamon-coloured or black and can weigh as much as 250 kilograms They range throughout all zones of the mountains, but prefer the lower valleys and wooded areas. Less aggressive than the grizzly and more inclined to a vegetarian diet, the black bears eat young plants and bark in the spring and berries, dandelions and fruit in the summer and fall. These bears have grown accustomed to humans and haunt campgrounds in search of easy food.

Black bears mate during early summer, but the embryo is not implanted in the uterine wall of the womb until October or November. The cubs, small as puppies, are born in January or February. The mother may or may not wake up from her hibernation and the blind cubs nurse and sleep unattended until she wakes up in April. The cubs are weaned at about six months, but stay with their mother until the following spring, when they are ready to mate.

These bears do not truly hibernate, but sleep lightly with little drop in body temperature or heart rate. During this dormant period, they use up about 5,000 calories a day — almost as much as during the rest of the year — and yet they do not eat or drink during this time. They can do this partly because they gorge themselves on 20,000 calories a day in the summer and fall and store up the excess energy as fat.

Primarily nocturnal, black bears can be found near most Banff campgrounds, along the Icefields Parkway, most campgrounds in Yoho and in the McLeod Meadows area of Kootenay.

### Grizzly Bear

The grizzly bear can be easily distinguished from its more common cousin because the grizzly has a longer, flatter face and a pronounced hump over its shoulders. Unlike the single-toned black bear, the grizzly has fur that is shaggier and multicoloured, ranging from black to silver; his ears are smaller than the black bear's ears and his claws are plainly visible, whereas the black bear's claws are seldom seen. The grizzly is also usually larger, weighing between 200 and 350 kilograms. If hikers are unsure what type of bear they have seen, it was a black

*Grizzly Bear*

bear. A grizzly is too impressive to leave any doubt about what it is.

Like the black bear, the grizzly can occasionally be found in any area of the mountains, but it prefers avalanche slopes and open meadows. It is usually found at low altitudes in the spring and in the alpine zones in the summer. These bears are omnivorous and will eat everything from cow parsnip, horsetails and whitebark pine seeds to ground squirrels, fish and elk. Grizzlies have been known to eat as many as 200,000 buffalo berries in one day!

Grizzlies mate and hibernate in the same manner as black bears, although the cubs stay with the mother an extra year or two and are not ready to mate until five or six years old. They have a reputation for fierceness and for attacking humans, their only predator. They will defend their cubs to the death, but will almost never attack people unless they feel threatened.

Grizzlies are rarely seen, but can be found in the Skoki region and the Cascade Fire Road area of Banff, throughout Yoho, particularly in the Lake O'Hara and Amiskwi Valley areas, north of the Columbia Icefield, and in the Wolverine and Goodsir Pass areas of Kootenay.

### Moose

These huge, solitary animals are even larger than grizzly bears and weigh up to 450 kilograms. They are distinguished by ungainly long legs, which allow them to wade into swamps or pass through heavy snow, thick antlers, a rounded nose and a shaggy flap of skin, known as a bell, under the chin. They are a dreary beigy-brown in colour.

While other ungulates are in the valley bottoms during the winter, the moose stays higher up on the slopes, browsing on willow, dogwood and aspen twigs. In the summer they wade through swamps in search of water plants.

The antlers of the bull moose begin to grow in April and the rut begins in early fall. Unlike elk, which rut enthusiastically, moose usually just make a show of defiance and give in to the dominant bull. The cows give birth to a single calf (sometimes twins) in May or June. The calves are completely dependent upon their mothers for protection for the first year. This makes the cows very protective and very dangerous to intruding hikers, especially when the calves are is very young.

Moose are best seen at dawn or dusk along slide paths, burns or near swampy areas. Look for them near the Columbia Icefield, Vermilion Lakes in Banff, the Natural Bridge in Yoho, McLeod Meadows in Kootenay and the Banff/Kootenay boundary.

### Elk (Wapiti)

These commonly seen animals had to be reintroduced to the national parks during World War I, but have become well established. The elk is easily recognized by the oval whitish patch on its rump and tail, its long, dark brown neck, head and legs and its lighter brown body. In winter, the elk wears a shaggy mane on its neck and it looks somewhat like an antlered llama.

These grazing animals live in herds, although the males usually leave the females and younger elk in the valley bottoms while they head for the hills in the summer. These nocturnal feeders can eat almost anything from lichens to grass to planted gardens. When food is scarce in the winter, they eat aspen bark. Rutting season begins in August and lasts until November. During this time, the dominant stags defend harems of as many as 30 females (hinds) by fighting off competitors with their massive antlers. These racks are worn only by the males, who lose them each February or March and grow new ones beginning in April. Each year, the stag grows a bigger rack. The hinds usually bear one fawn in May or June. These fawns are often born on islands and must swim to shore hours after birth. They are weaned in September, but don't breed until their third fall.

*Rutting male elk; left elk has a radio collar for park research*

Elk are commonly found throughout the parks and are often the victims of car accidents because they gather near the highways. Whistlers campground in Jasper, between Banff and Lake Louise, McLeod Meadows in Kootenay and along the highway west of Field are prime viewing locations. Your chances of seeing elk are best at dawn and dusk. The elk is the animal on the Canadian quarter.

### Mule Deer

These small deer were once the only deer in the Canadian Rockies. Often mistaken for the white-tailed deer, the mule deer can be distinguished by its narrow, white tail with a prominent black tip (white-tailed deer show the white tail only when raised like a flag), very long ears and larger eyes. The rack is smaller than that of buck elks.

The mule deer browses on grasses and flowers in the spring and summer,

*Mule Deer*

leaves in the fall and the twigs of aspens, junipers and evergreens in the winter. The does and their young usually stay in the valley bottoms year-round, but the solitary bucks ascend to the alpine zones during the summer.

Like other ungulates, the mule deer begins its rut in the early fall. Unlike elk and moose, however, the mule deer bucks spar with each other more out of clique rivalry than for rights to the does. The bucks don't gather harems as elk do. The does usually deliver a single fawn in June after their first pregnancy. After this, they usually deliver twins. The fawns are hidden in brush for a month until they are able to walk well. Mule deer, like other ungulates, are best viewed in the early morning or evening. They are commonly seen in the Palisade area east of Jasper, near the west gate of Yoho and on the Bow Valley Parkway west of the town of Banff.

## Mountain or Bighorn Sheep

The bighorn sheep, famous for their curled horns and brutal rutting, once roamed in huge herds, but have become extinct in many places because of hunters and poachers. Even now, their craving for salt brings them down to lick the highways, which are salted in winter, and the bighorns are being slaughtered by collisions with cars. The fencing along the Banff highway has been put up as an attempt to keep these animals, as well as other ungulates, off the highway.

*Bighorn ram (foreground) and ewe*

Both the male and female grow horns, which, unlike antlers, grow from birth and are not shed annually. The ram's horns curl backwards, sometimes drawing a full circle, while the female's horns are rough, grey-brown spikes. Females are often confused with mountain goats, but the goats have shiny black and straighter horns than the sheep. The goats are also pure white, while the sheep of both sexes are mostly brown with white edging on the rump, legs and muzzle. The ewes weigh about 75 kilograms while the rams weigh 125 kilograms and are much larger. The sheep shed their winter coats in June and have a ragged, mangey appearance.

Bighorns eat grasses, flowers and leaves, seeking out open or windblown areas as they travel together in flocks of about a dozen. The rams head above treeline in the summer while the ewes and young stay lower down.

During the spectacular fall rutting season in November and December, the rams will charge each other from a distance of about 15 metres and crash into each other again and again, sometimes for almost a full day, until one gives up. Usually a single dominant ram will impregnate the ewes. Single lambs are born in late May and hidden from predators for a week. They are weaned at six months and mature in two to three years.

Bighorn sheep can be spotted in Sinclair Canyon near Radium, near Mt. Norquay and Lake Minnewanka in Banff, north of the Columbia Icefield, and at the Miette Hot Springs and at the junction of Maligne Road and Highway 16 in Jasper.

## Mountain Goat

These agile, elusive climbers frequent the crags and cliffs of the alpine zone. Easily recognized by their shaggy white (sometimes yellowish) coat, square face and spiky black horns, mountain goats are not goats at all, but antelopes. Both the billies and the nannies have horns, and the two sexes are difficult to tell apart. The female's horns curve sharply at the tips, while the billy's horns begin their curve earlier. Females are more

*Mountain goat ewe and kid*

easily seen because they stay in the valley bottoms longer with their young than the independent males, who head to the peaks sooner.

Usually roaming the rocks and ridges in small flocks of half a dozen, mountain goats survive mostly on grass. When food is scarce in the winter, they will eat twigs and fir needles. During the November rut, the billies roll in the dust, thrash at plants and fence with their horns against their competitors. The victorious billy often gathers a harem around him. The nannies give birth in late May to single or twin kids, who stay with their mothers for more than two years.

Mountain goats are shy, but can be seen at mineral licks 38 kilometres south of Jasper and at Nigel Creek, both sites on the Icefields Parkway, and at Disaster Point, about 30 kilometres east of Jasper on Highway 16. They can also be seen near Mt. Wardle at a mineral lick in Kootenay, near the Leanchoil Hoodoos and on the cliffs above Yoho's Kicking Horse campground.

### Beaver

Weighing up to 20 kilograms the beaver is the largest rodent in the Rockies. It is distinguished by its large incisors used for gnawing trees, a thick brown fur coveted by the historic fur traders and modern coat-makers, and a hairless tail used for dam construction and for whacking the water to sound an alarm.

These nocturnal rodents live in the marshes and lakes of the mountains, particularly near their favourite foods, the bark of aspens, willows and birches. They will also eat leaves, twigs and some seeds. Beavers are well known for their tree-felling and dam-building activities. Dams are built with mud and sticks to create a pond, used for safe travel to their food supplies. While the pond grows to its full size, the beavers live in bank burrows; when the pond reaches its limit, the beavers will build a stick-and-mud lodge, usually on an island or a protected area of the shore. The lodge can be up to three metres high and six metres wide. Access is gained by underwater tunnels which lead to a dry chamber for the beaver family.

Beavers do not hibernate. They breed in mid-winter and give birth to about four kits in later spring. The young live with the family about a year, until they are kicked out when the next litter is born. The younger beavers can be recognized by a white spot on their noses.

There are beaver lodges throughout the parks in wetland areas, particularly on the Vermilion Lakes near Banff, the Cottonwood Slough near Jasper townsite, in the Leanchoil Marsh and on the east end of Wapta Lake in Yoho, and along the Athabasca and Miette Rivers. The Fenland Trail near Banff offers spectacular examples of half-chewn trees.

### Porcupine

This large nocturnal rodent is second only to the beaver in size, weighing up to eight kilograms. It is easily recognized by its protective blanket of 30,000 quills. These modified hairs are hollow, barbed spines which are sharp enough to penetrate skin and clothing. Contrary to popular belief, porkies do not throw their quills at predators; usually, they protect their heads and bellies by turning their backs against their predators and fluffing up their quills. The tail lashes back and forth, sometimes causing a few loose quills to detach. Because the quills are barbed, they work their way into an animal's skin and often need to be removed by pushing them right through the wound. (Keep dogs at home in porcupine territory.) A would-be predator with a mouthful of quills will likely starve to death. Only the wolf, wolverine, lynx and fisher can successfully turn a porcupine over to attack its unprotected belly.

Porcupines prefer to eat leaves, but will strip trees of their bark when leaves are unavailable. They do not actually eat the bark, but are after the sweet cambium layer that lies beneath it. Porkies have an insatiable appetite for salt and wood resins. They will gnaw on anything made of plywood — signs, outhouses, huts. They also love rubber and are known to eat entire boots or the brake lines of cars.

Porcupines find natural shelters in piles of boulders or deadfall. They breed in the late fall and the females deliver a single baby in May or June. The open-eyed baby is born with fur and (soft) quills. Most rodents deliver large litters of blind and naked babies. The baby porky is weaned in a few weeks but hangs around its mother for a full year.

Porcupine sightings are almost guaranteed on the Takkakaw Falls road, the Tumbling Glacier campground in Kootenay and the trail to the Lake Agnes Teahouse above Lake Louise. They are rarely seen in Jasper. Dusk is the best time to see porcupines; usually they will be climbing trees or shuffling through the underbrush.

### Hoary Marmot

This member of the squirrel family is often confused with the half-sized Columbian ground squirrel. The marmot looks more like a groundhog, to which it is related, and grows to about 75 centimetres and almost six kilograms. Black paws, a "hoary" coat of coarse brown, white-tipped fur and a dark patch on the forehead which continues in lines over the ears to the neck distinguish this bold, ambling creature. Known as "Whistlers" or "Whistle-pigs," marmots communicate with each other by a long, loud whistle.

Marmots prefer to live among larger rocks of the alpine zone where they dig grass-lined burrows which protect them from all predators except grizzlies. Marmots will eat grasses, leaves and flowers between April and September. The rest of the time, they hibernate in their burrows. A litter of four or five babies is born in July.

Marmots are quite unafraid of humans and can often be seen sunning themselves on rocky landscapes. Bow Summit, on the Icefields Parkway, Lake O'Hara, Moraine Lake, near Stanley Glacier in Kootenay and at Cairn Pass in Jasper are all popular places to find marmots.

### Pika (Rock Rabbit)

This guinea-pig look-alike is actually related to rabbits and hares. Pronounced Pii-ka, this endearing little creature is recognized by its small, round shape, grey body, round ears and lack of tail. You will likely hear it before you see it, for it sits motionless on the scree slopes and warns its colony of danger with a sharp little cry: "Eeeek!"

Pikas live in the alpine zone close to the treeline, among small loose rocks known as scree. Here they eat grass, lichens, young leaves and flowers. Near the end of the summer, they will harvest grasses, leave them to dry in the sun and then store them in runs or under boulders. A lot of food must be stored this way for pikas do not hibernate and are active all year round. Pikas will eat their own dung, selecting special green pellets of partly digested food.

Pikas live in colonies, but each animal has a territory about 50 metres by 50 metres in size. The female has a litter of three to five babies in May and often a second litter in July. The young are born furry and are weaned in less than two weeks. They are fully grown in a few months and live three or four years.

Pikas can be found in most high country in the mountains, particularly around the Opabin Plateau in Yoho, near Moraine Lake, the Floe Lake area in Kootenay and in the Nigel Pass area of Jasper.

## // Birds

### Bald Eagle

The bald eagle is the largest eagle and second largest bird in the rockies (next to the tundra swan, which is rarely seen). It has a wingspan of 203 centimetres and is 82 centimetres long. Distinguished by its white head and tail and its brown body plumage, the bald eagle feeds primarily on fish. It also eats carrion, ducks and water animals, such as muskrats. Its squeaky voice mocks its dignified reputation.

Bald eagles migrate to the United States and the west coast for the winter unless they can find open water in the mountains. Breeding in mid-spring, they usually nest in the same coniferous tree each year and hatch a pair of white eggs. The older nestling usually kills the younger one. Bald eagles have been recorded as living forty-eight years in captivity.

*Bald eagle*

Look for bald eagles in most wetland areas, such as the Vermilion Lakes, the Cottonwood Slough near Jasper townsite and the Ottertail River flats in western Yoho.

### Golden Eagle

The golden eagle soars high above alpine meadows and mountain tops. Brown over its entire body, this eagle gets its name from the sheen of its neck when viewed at close range. Slightly smaller than the bald eagle, this rare bird has a wingspan of 200 centimetres and is about 80 centimetres long. Like the bald eagle, the golden eagle has a weak, chirruping voice that doesn't match its size.

Golden eagles eat alpine animals such as marmots, hares, pikas and sometimes the carrion flesh of mountain goats and sheep, although these last two animals are not known

*Golden eagle*

to be killed by golden eagles. Golden eagles mate for life and build huge nests of sticks (three metres across by one metre deep) on alpine cliffs. They lay two blotchy white eggs which hatch in about forty-five days, a few days apart. The older nestling usually kills the younger one. Golden eagles can fly at speeds of up to 200 kilometres per hour, but usually soar at 50 kilometres per hour. They live up to forty years.

Look for golden eagles in high alpine areas and meadows. Wilcox Pass, the valley above Moraine Lake, the Opal Hills and the southern part of the Kootenay River valley are all places where this rare bird may be seen.

*Black-billed magpies*

### Black-billed Magpie

This common bird is related to ravens and crows, but is easily identified because of the contrast of its black and white coloration. Most of the bird is black, except for the white underbelly and wing sections. Noisy garbage-eaters with a rasping hack, magpies also eat eggs, nestlings and carrion.

Black-billed magpies usually live and fly in small flocks. The birds pair off and mate for life. They breed in mid-spring and nest on low-lying bushes near water in domed nests made of sticks, lined with mud. Between five and twelve eggs are laid and hatched. Magpies remain in the mountains year-round near garbage dumps, picnic sites and townsites.

### Clark's Nutcracker

These campground visitors are known for their incessant and harsh cawing as they petulantly demand goodies from campers. This bird has uniformly grey feathers with black and white wings. It is often confused with the gray jay, also known as the whiskey jack, which is smaller and has a dark area at the back of its head. The Clark's nutcracker has a longer, blacker beak than the gray jay. As its name implies, Clark's nutcracker uses its beak to dig into cones and crack seeds. It will also eat bugs, often pecking into rotten wood for ants and beetles. This bird hides its food in a hoard for winter on branches or in the ground and can remember where to find it.

The indistinguishable male and female birds mate for life, building bulking nests on coniferous trees in April. They lay two or three greenish eggs with brown spots. These eggs hatch in just over two weeks. The young leave their nests in three weeks and hound their parents for food.

Watch for these birds between April and November, particularly at campgrounds and picnic sites and in the southern and central subalpine woods.

*Steller's jay*

### Steller's Jay

This bird is the official provincial bird of British Columbia. As the only crested jay commonly seen in the Canadian Rockies, it is easily identified by its dark, crested head and upper back and blackish-blue feathers on the rest of its body. (The blue jay is rarely seen in the Rockies and has a lighter blue colouring, a white chest and face and white bars on its wings.) This shy bird eats mostly pine seeds, bugs and berries and is rarely a campground nuisance. Its call sounds like a hacking cough.

The Steller's jay remains in the parks year-round, but is seen most often at low elevations in the winter. Its nest is made of mud-lined sticks in the spring, when four bluish-green eggs are laid. They hatch in about sixteen days and the nestlings follow their parents around for several weeks after learning to fly.

Look for these birds on western slopes; south of the Crowsnest Pass, they will also be found on eastern slopes. Emerald Lake Lodge, Sulphur Mountain, Saskatchewan River Crossing and Radium Hot Springs are all likely places to find this bird.

### Rufous Hummingbird

This little helicopter is the more common of the two hummingbirds found in the Rockies. Less than 10 centimetres long, hummingbirds are identified by their very small size, long, thin beak, the hum of their wings and their ability to hover and fly backwards. The male of this species is reddish in colour all over with an especially brilliant patch of red on his throat. The female has a green back and a white underbelly.

Able to reach speeds of 80 kilometres per hour, rufous hummingbirds require enormous amounts of food to keep their little bodies going. They eat constantly. Mostly, they eat sugar by sipping nectar from flowers; they also eat small bugs. They always carry extra food in their crops to survive the night. In extreme situations, such as cold weather, they can become dormant for a few days. The rufous hummingbird migrates to Mexico for the winter, but returns each spring to hatch out a pair of tiny white eggs in nest in coniferous shrubs.

Look for this tiny bird wherever there are flowers, especially on bright meadows. They particularly favour red flowers, such as columbines and Indian paintbrush.

## // Flowers And Shrubs

### Alpine Forget-Me-Nots

This delicate sky-blue flower with a sunny yellow centre blooms in clusters in alpine and subalpine meadows in July. While blooming, the flower has a highly fragrant smell. Curiously, the flowers become brighter blue at higher altitudes. The stalks vary from 10 to 50 centimetres tall.

### Bull-Thistle

Common in marshes, montane meadows, roadsides and disrupted areas, these thistles have attractive purple heads which bloom in July and August. Don't go too close, though, the leaves are thorny and sharp. This thistle can be up to one metre high and its nectar is a favourite food of butterflies.

### Calypso Orchid

This beautiful true orchid, also known as a Venus Slipper, grows in moist montane forests and is recognizable by its slipper-shaped violet lip hanging beneath a crown of radiating purple spikes. Black-tipped yellow stamens extend over the flower's lip. This orchid has only one basal leaf. The flower usually grows in patches in moist montane forests. It blooms May to July.

### Columbine

Columbines are easily identified by their bushy, heavily lobed and dark green basal leaves and by the rather complicated blossoms which droop from straight stems. Columbines can be yellow, red or blue. The yellow and red columbines often hybridize. They usually flower in montane woodlands and subalpine meadows in July, but can be found as late as August at higher elevations.

*Dwarf Dogwood*

### Dwarf Dogwood

Dwarf dogwood pleases at any time of the year. The strongly lined leaves grow in fours or sixes and cover large areas of woodland with their vibrant green colour. Bold white flowers bloom in June and July. In August, the blossom is replaced by a cluster of bright red berries, sometimes called bunchberries. The berries are edible but quite bland. Dogwoods can be found in most moist and shady montane forests throughout the Rockies. It is the flower of the dogwood tree, not the flower of the Dwarf dogwood, that is the provincial flower of British Columbia.

### Elephant-head

The tiny pink blossoms on this flower look like little elephants in profile. The blossoms are borne on a 25-centimetre spike with thin, sawtoothed leaves. They grow in wet montane and subalpine meadows, but especially favour areas with highly alkaline soils, such as those near mineral springs. They bloom from late June to August.

### Fireweed

This showy, pink flower is common in open meadows, roadsides and burns from mid-July to early fall. It is known to move into areas shortly after they have been disrupted by fires, hence the name. Another theory suggests that the plant derives its name from the bright orange and red colours taken on by the narrow leaves in the fall. Fireweed blooms are large, about 2 centimetres across; the lower blossoms bloom first. The stems are unbranched and can grow between 30 centimetres and 2 metres tall. It is eaten by many grazing animals and is a favourite of the grizzly bear. Look for this flower on roadsides, near the Stanley Glacier burn and on sunny meadows.

### Glacier Lily (Avalanche Lily, Dogtooth Violet)

This unmistakable flower is the only yellow lily in the Rockies. Appearing as early as April as the snow recedes at low elevations, this brilliant yellow flower rising from two broad basal leaves will briefly dominate the highest alpine meadows, turning them into a sea of yellow. By August, most of these lilies have disappeared. The nodding flowers are distinctive not only for their colour but for the sharp backwards curl of the petals. Look for these flowers almost anywhere, but especially on high meadows in early July and in rich, moist soil near streams.

### Horsetail

This unusual-looking plant is easily identified by its segmented, green stem, which stands about 30 centimetres tall. The horsetail grows two kinds of shoots: unbranched shoots topped with fertile seed cones and infertile shoots with delicate branches radiating from the segment joints. It is most common in wet areas but can survive in drier areas. Look for horsetail primarily in marshy areas such as the Fenland trail, in wet woods, on roadsides and meadows.

### Indian Paintbrush

This flower does, indeed, look like a well-used and bristly paintbrush. Although there are more than 200 species of this densely spiked flower, making it the best-known flower in the mountains, it is usually recognized as being in two types: red and yellow. The colour can range from green to purple and is actually carried on the bracts, not the petals. Flowering from June to late August from a single stem, these plants grow parasitically off the roots of other plants. Look for these flowers in sunny meadows at any elevation below 9,000 feet.

### Kinnikinnik (Bearberry)

Spelled forwards or backwards, this attractive ground-covering shrub can be recognized at all times of the year. In May and early June, the Kinnikinnik bears bell-like white flowers with pink tips. By late summer, the round berries have become bright red. These will stay on the bush over winter unless they are eaten by bears, birds and rodents. The evergreen leaves are thick and glossy, growing from woody stems. They are eaten by deer and mountain sheep during the fall and winter. The leaves were used by Native peoples to smoke mixed with tobacco; Russians still use the plant as a source of tannin. The berries are mealy but edible and were used by the Natives to mix with saskatoon berries and animal fat to make pemmican, a dietary staple. Look for Kinnikinnik in dry areas, sandy soil and south-facing slopes below timberline.

### Labrador Tea

This short shrub has flat, leathery evergreen leaves that look like they belong to an azalea and is, in fact, a relation. The leaves are up to 6 centimetres long and are notable for their glossy tops and rusty undersides. Small white flowers bloom in soft tufts in June and July. The shrub grows in shady montane and subalpine forests. Natives made tea from dried leaves and sometimes used the leaves for tobacco.

### Moss Campion

A cushion plant that can take twenty-five years to mature, Moss Campion grows only in the alpine zone. The tiny leaves grow close to the ground and compress together in a round, flat dome which can be up to one metre wide. Relatively large pink flowers

*Moss Campion*

bloom from the time the snow melts even into late August. Moss Campion is not actually moss. Moss does not grow flowers.

### Shrubby Cinquefoil (Yellow Rose)

This common, showy bush grows almost everywhere in the mountains and is easily recognized by its bright yellow blossoms which bloom from June through early October. The

*Shrubby Cinquefoil*

blossoms are five-petalled (hence the French name) and grow on many woody, shredded branches, which bear heavily indented, needle-like leaves. The round bush grows to about 1.5 metres high. This plant keeps its leaves in the winter. Although not a preferred food, animals will graze on it. The cinquefoil serves as an indicator plant. If it has been heavily eaten, it means that too many range animals are competing for a scarce food supply. Look for this bush throughout the parks.

### Skunk Cabbage

This large leafy plant is recognized by the yellow hood which shelters a small yellow spike of flowers and by the skunk-like smell given off by the broad green leaves when they are crushed. Blooming in early spring, April and May, skunk cabbage grows on the western slopes of the Rockies in marshes and wetlands. Skunk cabbage roots were made into flour as part of the Natives' staple diet.

### White Pasque Flowers

Also known as anemones or prairie crocus, these thick-stocked white flowers are among the first alpine flowers to poke through the snow in the early spring. When the flower goes to seed, it becomes a waving head of silky hair that looks like it belongs in a book by Dr. Seuss. The leaves are short and furry. The fuzzy stem can be up to 30 centimetres high. This flower tends to grow in large colonies.

*Wild Rose*

### Wild Rose

Several species of wild rose commonly grow in the Rockies. All bear pinkish five-petalled flowers and grow serrated oval leaves in groups of seven or nine. Not all of the species have thorns. Roses prefer to grow in fire succession forests and in sunny areas.

## // Trees

### Engelmann Spruce

Engelmann spruce is often confused with white spruce; in fact, these two species interbreed. Growing to 30 metres, these trees have brown, easily shredded bark and bear long cones near their tops. The needles are square, short and prickly, compared with flat fir needles and long, round pine needles. Engelmanns can be distinguished from the similar white spruce by noting that the Engelmann is able to grow at higher elevations and is common in the subalpine "krummholz zone," where trees are scrubby and twisted. The Engelmann's needles are more curved and prickly than those of the white spruce, and its cones are thinner and more flexible.

### Larch

Three species of larch grow in the Canadian Rockies: Lyall's larch, the Western larch and the tamarack or American larch. All are distinctive because they are coniferous trees, but not evergreens. In early October, their soft, delicate needles turn a stunning shade of gold and then drop off. During the winter the trees appear to be dead until new needles grow in May. Lyall's larch grows in the subalpine zones just below timberline. It is short (5-10 metres) and scraggly. The Western larch grows up to 30 metres at low elevations and is straight and uniform in shape. The tamarack is the same size as Lyall's larch, but prefers to grow in bogs at low elevations.

### Lodgepole Pine
This straight, thin tree is the most common tree in the Canadian Rockies and derives its name from its usefulness in making wigwams. Found below 6,000 feet in dry areas, this tree will reach a height of 25 metres but requires full sunlight to grow. It can be easily identified because it is the only pine in the Canadian Rockies with paired needles. Pollen from this tree is blown throughout the mountains in June and July and can often be seen piling up like scum on quiet lakes and marshes. The seed cones are hard and oval, usually taking years to release and germinate seeds unless a forest fire causes the cones to open quickly and creates the carbon-rich soil conditions necessary for the growth of seedlings. Most lodgepoles live 100 years and are succeeded by shade-tolerant spruce, which grow under the pines.

### Trembling Aspen
This member of the willow family is the most common deciduous tree in the Rockies. Usually growing in groves of genetically identical clones at low elevations, this tree with smooth, white bark and serrated, waxy leaves that flutter in the wind can grow to 40 metres in sheltered areas. Aspens will often have black scars on their bark. This is caused by damage done by animals. Mule deer will rub the trees with their antlers to leave their scent; deer, elk and small mammals will eat the bark during hard winters and bears will scratch the trees as far as they can reach to stake out territory. The aspen can be distinguished from the similar white birch because the aspen's bark does not peel easily and the aspen's leaves are larger and more finely and bluntly toothed.

*Trembling Aspen*

# 6 // Banff

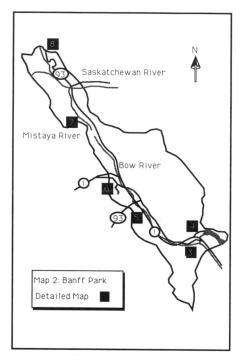

Map 2: Banff Park
Detailed Map ■

Canada's first national park is also its most famous. With an area of 6,641 square kilometres, Banff National Park is second to Jasper National Park in size, but is the most visited, drawing more than three million visitors each year. It is also the most highly developed of the four adjacent national parks, with more trails, attractions and facilities than the others.

Founded in 1885 as a 26-square-kilometre federal reserve to protect the valuable hot springs now known as the Cave and Basin, Banff grew sporadically as land patches were added and taken away until it reached its present size in 1930. The Canadian Pacific Railroad, run by shrewd business-men, promoted tourism to sweeten its financial operations, which were drained in building the trans-continental railroad. The CPR promoted the Rockies heavily and built several Swiss-style chalets and teahouses which can still be visited today at scenic destinations, as well as the Banff Springs Hotel and the Chateau Lake Louise.

Tourists flocked to the area, lured by the hot springs and the spectacular scenery. To capitalize on the tourist industry, entrepreneurs quickly built bathhouses and a sanatorium at the hot springs, as well as many hotels, restaurants and stores nearby. Outfitters, mountain guides and bounty hunt-ers explored the area, built backcountry lodges and carved their niche in the tourist market. Mountain climbers scaled the slopes; photographers popular-ized the natural beauty.

By the late 1930s Banff had become a popular winter destination be-cause of its now-famous ski slopes. Although the other parks are open in the winter, none attract the same volume of tourists or operate with the same intensity. The 1984 Winter Olympics in Calgary began another spurt of devel-opment of malls and condominiums which is still continuing.

As a result of this history, Banff has far more easily accessible trails than the other parks and Banff townsite has the largest population and offers the greatest number of activities and attractions of the four parks.

# Cave And Basin Loops

**Level:** Easy    Wheelchair Accessible
**One Way:** Discovery .4 km; Marsh .5 km
**Time:** 30 minutes each
**Elevation Gain:** 5 metres (15 feet) for Discovery; nil for Marsh
**Maximum Elevation:** 1,375 metres (4,515 feet)
**Trailhead:** Entrance to Cave and Basin facilities at end of Cave and Basin Road, Banff townsite.
**Map:** 3 (pg 57)

Visitors to the Cave and Basin facilities often neglect to enjoy the two short boardwalk trails nearby: the Discovery Trail and the Marsh Loop Trail. Both are wheelchair accessible.

The Discovery Trail takes strollers backwards in time from the renovated swimming facilities/exhibition to the hot springs which served as a catalyst for the creation of Canada's national parks. The trail begins at the stairs on the left side of the Cave and Basin entrance. Climb these stairs (a wheelchair lift inside the building and a ramp at the back of the building are also available) and watch the swimmers cavorting in the lukewarm pool. The boardwalk leads to a reconstruction of the pool used in the very early days of the parks. Doubling back up the ramp and then turning right above shortcutting stairs, the boardwalk comes upon the opening in the ground where the three railway workers discovered the hot springs and staked their claim. Wheelchair accessibility ends here. Beyond this, stairs lead to a loop which runs past mineral ponds and a small spring where children will delight in watching the warm water bubble up through the sand and algae.

The Marsh Trail is a slightly longer boardwalk loop trail, which is also accessible to wheelchairs. Going counter-clockwise, the trail leads past sulphur-smelling wetlands where the warm water encourages the growth of orchids, asters and sunflowers. These flowers usually grow in warmer climates at lower elevations. A horse trail cuts through the middle of the loop, but your path out onto the marshes is plainly evident straight ahead. At the edge of the marshes, watch for the killdeers and robins that winter here in the ice-free waters. At the northern (left) edge of the marsh-front section of the loop, stairs lead down to a bird blind on the right and a fish observation area on the left. Behind the blinds, watch for kinglets, red-winged blackbirds, snipes and ducks. From the fish observation area, watch for four types of fish, including the Banff Longnose Dace, a very rare fish found nowhere else in the world. Return to the main loop and continue through a forest to the parking lot.

# Fenland Trail

**Level:** Easy    Wheelchair Accessible
**Loop:** 2.1 km
**Time:** 45 minutes
**Elevation Gain:** None
**Maximum Elevation:** 1,370 metres (4,500 feet)
**Trailhead:** Parking lot on W side of Mt. Norquay Rd. after crossing N of the CPR tracks leaving the town of Banff
**Map:** 3 (pg 57)

This wheelchair-accessible wetland hike is popular with outdoor enthusiasts of all kinds, especially joggers and cyclists. However, the trail is wide and tranquil, allowing many uninterrupted opportunities to view the natural succession from marsh to forest, and presents excellent possibilities for animal and bird watching. The shallow marsh and the neighbouring Vermilion Lakes will gradually become drier through the natural infilling of silts and water plants. Slowly, the marsh will become a meadow and, finally, a mature forest. The succession process can be observed in all of its stages in the Fenland/Vermilion area.

After leaving the parking lot, the trail immediately crosses a bridge and presents hikers with a junction. The self-guiding trail goes counterclockwise, but either direction can be chosen. Ponds, channels and marshes dominate in some sections; horsetails and wintergreen populate wet, shady areas; shrubs and willows are growing in the more open areas. The last stage of the succession is also underway where many mature white spruce stretch towards the sky.

Beaver can often be seen swimming in the early evening. Even if you don't see them, the evidence of their activities is everywhere: halfway around the trail, hikers can spot beaver dams and the channels these industrious creatures have cut through the long grasses. Near the end of the trail are several large trees half-gnawed by overly ambitious beavers — a sight that never fails to delight children of all ages. The work of the beavers has expanded the wetland areas, making it an ideal area for water-loving creatures such as moose and muskrats. Bushes and willows that look mangled or scarred have been browsed by local deer and moose. Kids will enjoy the bridges and floating sticks and make-shift rafts in the river.

The Vermilion Lakes, which can be seen from the western edge of the trail, provide one of the best habitats for birds in the Rockies. About 200 species of bird have been sighted here. Many of these birds are migratory, like the osprey and bald eagle, but some, like the barred owl and the ruffed grouse, make their home here year round. Take your binoculars on this hike.

*Lunch on the Fenland Trail*

*Mt. Norquay beyond the Marsh Loop*

# Marsh Loop

**Level:** Easy     Wheelchair accessible, but not paved on most of it.
**Loop:** 2.7 km
**Time:** 1 hour
**Elevation Gain:** Negligible
**Maximum Elevation:** 1,370 metres (4,500 feet)
**Trailhead:** Cave and Basin parking lot at end of Cave and Basin Road.
**Map** 3 (pg 57)

This loop trail can be done in either direction. The most obvious access is straight past the Cave and Basin down the paved section towards Sundance Canyon. About .5 km down the road, the Marsh Loop trail begins at a right fork heading towards the marsh and the Bow River. This option is easier for families requiring wheelchair access because it is mildly downhill to the junction. The counter-clockwise option gets hikers into the marsh sooner and begins to the right of the Cave and Basin Road as it draws alongside the parking lot.

From the junction, the flat, sandy trail angles northward toward the Bow River and offers fine views of Mts Cory (2,789 m), Edith (2,254 m) and Norquay (2,523 m). Within a kilometre, the trail curves right to the east and heads between the placid, turquoise Bow River on the left and the grassy marshes on the right. The marsh is often windy, so take jackets even on warm days. The nectar of bull thistles and other flowers are favourite foods for the many butterflies that flit through the marsh. Many birds can also be seen at this northwestern end of the trail: red-winged blackbirds and many varieties of teals, kinglets, snipes and ducks all make their home here. Further along, as the trail leaves the Bow and heads for the parking lot, look for beaver dams. The trail enters a small lodgepole pine forest and proceeds directly to the parking lot's edge. At this end of the trail, the forest floor is covered with horsetail.

Expect to share this trail with horses, joggers and mountain bikers. If hiking counter-clockwise beginning at the parking lot, head straight away from the lot, following horse trail #2. The left-right trail runs between the Cave and Basin and the Recreation Grounds.

# Middle Hot Springs

**Level:** Easy
**One Way:** 1.6 km
**Time:** 45 minutes
**Elevation Gain:** 100 metres (325 feet)
**Maximum Elevation:** 1,470 metres (4,825 feet)
**Trailhead:** Far end of Park Administration building gardens by the washrooms. The park building is at the S end of Banff Avenue across the bridge.
**Map:** 3 (pg 57)

Wander through the grounds of the Park Administration building, particularly the lovely Cascade Rock Garden, then head for the Middle Hot Springs. The trailhead is between the far end of the gardens and the washroom facilities. At the beginning of the trail, note the contrast between the wild garden on the right with its untended wildflowers and the highly cultivated garden on the left. Many seeds from the cultivated garden have blown over to the natural forest and domestic flowers have established themselves in this setting.

The cinder path leading westward up the flank of Sulphur Mountain is straightforward but often cut through by animal trails and other trails abandoned in this heavily used area. Continue up the trail through a sparse, grassy forest of lodgepole pine until it ends at a wide gravel road about 1.4 km from the trailhead. If the wind is right, you may be able to smell the faint odour of sulphur from here. Turn right at the road and follow it until reaching the springs.

There are two caves at the springs; the water emerges mostly from the left-hand cave. The water there and in the small pool at its mouth is warmer than in the other cave. With care not to damage the area, small children can enjoy the novelty of taking a quick dip in the warm, sulphurous water au naturel or with a bathing suit. The algae in the stream emerging from the basin is white and greasy-looking because of the mineral content of the water. The flat, cleared meadows here make a pleasant spot for a secluded picnic.

Hikers can cheat on distance by driving 1.7 km up Mountain Avenue towards the Upper Hot Springs. Where the road curves, there is an access road on the right. Park here and walk less than .5 km to the springs. This is a quicker route, but it is not nearly so pleasant as the longer trail.

# Tunnel Mountain/Hoodoos

> **Level:** Easy
> **One Way:** 4.8 km
> **Time:** 90 minutes
> **Elevation Gain:** 92 metres (300 feet)
> **Maximum Elevation:** 1,462 metres (4,800 feet)
> **Trailhead:** Follow Buffalo St. in Banff townsite along the Bow River.
> Trail begins at a small parking lot above Bow Falls, at the
> base of Tunnel Mountain Drive.
> **Map:** 3 (pg 57)

Yes, this too is a hike you can cheat on and get most of the way by car. But then you would miss seeing climbers on the limestone cliffs of Tunnel Mountain, the peaceful Bow, ancient Douglas fir trees and the breezy wildflower meadows.

Leaving cars behind, the trail descends immediately by stair into the forest, which blocks views of Bow Falls. To see the falls, head right and down rocky ledges to the river's edge. Otherwise head left along a wide, undulating trail through the grassy forest. More stairs descend steeply into the valley bottom and the trail remains flat as it wanders through flower-filled meadows and past huge Douglas fir with charred, fire-resistant bark. Many of the forests in the Bow Valley were destroyed by wildfires caused by careless blasting and workers more than a century ago. The Douglas fir were able to repel the flames and survive. Lodgepole pines, which need fire to release their seeds, have taken over many parts of the forest that burned. This is a good place to look up and watch the climbers making their crab-like moves along the rockface of Tunnel Mountain.

Many trails cut across and diverge from the main trail. Any one of these trails can provide interesting options; you are sure to find your way back to the main trail if you follow the general direction of the river flow. The sandy beach at the river's edge beneath the cliffs makes a pleasant picnicking or fishing spot.

Leaving the beach, the trail ascends and descends a ridge and then passes through more meadows. About 2.8 km along the trail, a junction offers hikers the choice of climbing .5 km up the left fork to the back of several resort hotels and out to Tunnel Mountain Road, or of continuing further along the valley bottom by taking the right-hand fork and then climbing more gradually towards Tunnel Mountain Road (about .7 km). Either option allows hikers to continue east by paralleling the road through grassy, wildflower meadows to the hoodoos.

The hoodoos are gnome-like pillars of glacial sediment which have managed to withstand erosion from wind and rain better than the softer sediments around them. Usually protected by a caprock, the hoodoos remain while the softer sediments are gradually worn away. Most of the caprocks have been knocked off by thrill seekers and the hoodoos are gradually wearing down. Please keep children from climbing on or otherwise damaging what remains. A boardwalk from the parking lot takes you as close as you can get to the hoodoos.

You can return to your car by the trail or by either Tunnel Mountain Road or Tunnel Mountain Drive. The Drive is higher up the mountain and gains elevation but is a more straightforward option; the Road climbs less but is longer and requires that hikers turn left at Moose Avenue and follow St. Julien Road through the Banff Centre before turning right upon meeting Tunnel Mountain Drive. The walk through the Banff Centre is a pleasant diversion.

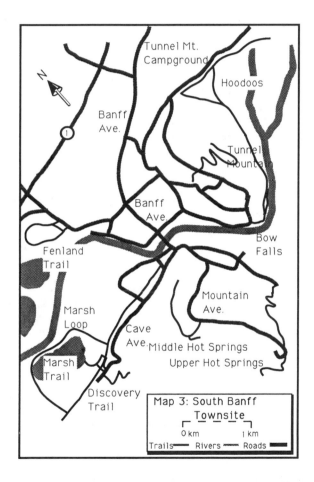

Map 3: South Banff Townsite

# Tunnel Mountain

**Level:** Moderate
**One Way:** 2.3 km
**Time:** 1 hour
**Elevation Gain:** 280 metres (910 feet)
**Maximum Elevation:** 1,670 metres (5,428 feet)
**Trailhead:** Large parking lot on St. Julien St. in Banff townsite, near Banff Centre.
**Map:** 3 (pg 57)

This well-marked and well-maintained switchback trail heads to the summit of Tunnel Mountain and provides the best view of Banff townsite and the Bow Valley in the area. Beginning at the parking lot, climb the steep, broad path west towards Tunnel Mountain, ascending some stairs to Tunnel Mountain Road at .3 km. Cross the road (which has another parking lot for shortcutters) and begin the well-graded gravel switchbacks, which climb back and forth for 2 km to the summit of the mountain. Although the mountain is forested with Douglas fir and lodgepole pine, hikers are rewarded with periodic, ever-improving views of the Bow Valley area.

The trail branches at the top because of different routes taken by many hikers over many years; finding the summit, however, is easy. Just head to the highest point. The summit is flat and cleared where a fire lookout tower once stood. Here hikers have a commanding view of Mt. Norquay (2,523 m), Mt. Edith (2,554 m) and Mt. Cory (2,789 m) to the north on the right, of Sulphur Mountain (2,271 m) on the left to the south and the Bow Valley extending to the west. There is no water on the trail, so take along your own. Also, expect to share the trail with mountain bikers, many other hikers and even joggers.

The trail's close proximity to Banff makes it a popular destination. It gives children a real feeling of accomplishment to "bag a peak."

*Banff Springs Hotel from Tunnel Mountain*

# Aylmer Lookout

**Level:** Moderate backpack
**One Way:** 11.8 km
**Time:** 5 hours
**Elevation Gain:** 560 metres (1,900 feet)
**Maximum Elevation:** 2,050 metres (6,900 feet)
**Trailhead:** Lake Minnewanka parking lot 9 km N of Banff townsite on Lake Minnewanka Rd.
**Map:** 4 (pg 60)

Lake Minnewanka (Devil's Lake) once provided the Native peoples with a route into the mountains. The lake was originally about 5 km wide and 14 km long when Sir George Simpson, governor of the Hudson's Bay Company, passed by on his east-west trip around the world in 1841. A 1912 water storage dam and a 1941 dam for a power plant lengthened the lake by 8 km and raised the water level by 25 m. The raised water level provided power for Banff, but also submerged all evidence of the Native trails and campgrounds, a forest and the remains of a tourist village, known as Minnewanka Landing, which operated at the turn of the century.

The major part of the hike is actually quite easy and flat, but the Aylmer Lookout trail is rated moderate because of the final, stiff 500-m ascent to the fire lookout, which offers scenic views of immense Lake Minnewanka below and tall Mt. Aylmer (3,162 m) running along a ridge above the lookout. Many adult hikers do the return trip in a day, but for families, the steepness of the final 3 km makes it preferable to combine an easy overnight camping trip with a moderate day hike up to the lookout the following day.

The trail to the aspen-enclosed, shoreline campground gains little elevation. Passing through the parking lot and picnic area towards the Stewart Canyon bridge, 1.6 km from the trailhead, the trail is relatively easy. Keep an eye out for herds of mountain sheep along the entire trail but particularly near the bridge, one of their favourite hangouts in the Rockies. After crossing the canyon, the trail remains wide and veers left and moderately upwards. (There is a narrow trail which heads immediately right after the bridge and hugs the cliffs of the shoreline until descending to a wide sandy point on the shore. If beach access is all you are after, go for it; otherwise you will find this a time-consuming dead end.)

The trail bends and climbs over a hump and then emerges above the lakeshore. It continues with gentle ups and downs until it crosses a small river, the first encountered on this hot trail. The campground/lookout junction lies just beyond the river at about 7.8 km. Take the right fork to reach the campground almost immediately and find yourself a quiet spot in one of the loveliest leafy campgrounds in all of the Rockies. Skipping stones into the lake from the shore or playing hide-and-seek among the aspens can close an idyllic day here. This is a great area to play and watch the alpenglow on the mountains. Leave your gear at the campsite to lighten the load up to the lookout.

The ascent to Aylmer Lookout the next day is a classic "grunt." Gaining about 500 m in less than 3 km, this trail is hot and arduous. Take the ascent slowly and easily and be sure to carry lots of water for each person as the trail is almost waterless. At the 10.1 km junction, take the right fork for the lookout, 1.7 km further along. The lookout sits on one of Mt. Aylmer's ridges and affords magnificent views of most of Lake Minnewanka, Mt. Inglismaldie (2,964 m) and the slightly taller Mt. Girouard (2,995 m) across the lake to the south and Mt. Rundle (2,949 m) across the Bow Valley to the southwest. The straight trail will take energetic hikers 250 m higher to the park boundary and Aylmer Pass at 2,285 m and 13.5 km from the trailhead.

Mountain sheep are plentiful at the lookout. The sheep are not shy, but do not approach or feed them: they are unpredictable. Also, check your bodies for ticks, which ride and feed on the sheep. After descending from the lookout, you can pick up your camping equipment and hike out the remaining distance or enjoy another quiet evening by the lapping waters.

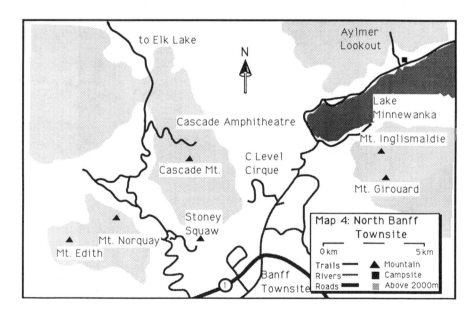

# Cascade Amphitheatre

> **Level:** Moderate
> **One Way:** 6.6 km
> **Time:** 4 hours
> **Elevation Gain:** 610 metres (2,000 feet)
> **Maximum Elevation:** 2,195 metres (7,200 feet)
> **Trailhead:** Far end of first Mt. Norquay parking lot (#3) off Mt. Norquay Rd. N of Banff townsite.
> **Map:** 4 (pg 60)

No one yet has put on a Greek tragedy at Cascade Amphitheatre, but the bowl-like shape carved into the mountain rock by a receding glacier certainly recalls the imposing ancient theatres where Oedipus Rex and Antigone were once performed.

Popular as a day hike, the Cascade Amphitheatre trail begins at the easily accessible Mt. Norquay ski area and also shares its route with the Mystic Lake and Elk Lake trails. Your family is unlikely to be alone on this hike. Still, other hikers drop off at the junctions and the amphitheatre has enough room for everybody.

The early trail at the ski area can be rather confusing because of the busyness of buildings, lifts and crossing trails, but by following a service road northwest and ignoring a horse trail that cuts across it, you will come to a more evident track and enter the forest within 1 km. After descending into the Forty Mile Creek valley and crossing the bridge at 3.1 km, the trail begins its climb up the dry and usually waterless western slope of Cascade Mountain. Twinflowers, arnica, harebells, calypso orchids and columbines grace the heavily forested slopes. Head right at the 4.3 km junction. The straight path heads to Elk Lake, 9.2 km further along. The climb continues steadily until reaching the lip of the amphitheatre, where the trail drops down and allows families to wander through the wide alpine meadow. As the trail ascends, it offers increasingly good views of the Elk Valley to the north and, to the west behind your direction, the five north to south peaks of Mts. Brewster (2,859 m), Louis (2,682 m), slightly hidden Cory (2,789 m), Edith (2,554 m) and Norquay (2,523 m).

The amphitheatre itself is a wonderful place to nap, picnic, roam or simply take in the wide assortment of wildflowers: shrubby cinquefoil, buttercups, mountain avens, paintbrush etc. Wide open, almost treeless and sheltered by the semi-circle of the limestone cliffs of Cascade Mountain (2,998 m), the amphitheatre makes a great place to fly a kite.

# C Level Cirque

**Level:** Moderate
**One Way:** 4 km
**Time:** 2 hours
**Elevation Gain:** 455 metres (1,500 feet)
**Maximum Elevation:** 1,920 metres (6,300 feet)
**Trailhead:** Upper Bankhead parking lot off Lake Minnewanka Road, 3.5 km from the Trans-Canada Highway, at far, forested end of parking lot.
**Map:** 4 (pg 60)

Plunging into a lodgepole pine forest immediately, this trail is forest-enclosed for its entire length, offering only fleeting glimpses of the Lake Minnewanka area and the mountains south to Canmore. The two main points of interest on this moderate trail are mining vents from the old Bankhead coal mining operations and the steep horn of Cascade Mountain at the trail's end. The destination's mundane name refers to the highest of three mining levels operated by the Bankhead coal mine: the C Level.

The trail is stony and steep for the first kilometre, but even this section is reasonably moderate. There is no water on the trail until reaching the cirque, so take along enough for everybody. At 1.1 km, the cement shell of a mining building is passed, followed by a cement foundation and a half-dozen fenced vents and shafts. The path runs along a black seam of coal here. By wandering to the edge of the slope by the small slag pile, hikers can get one of the few good views of Lake Minnewanka and the Two Jack Lake area. The trail climbs more moderately through the forest and makes a long curve to the southwest. Few wildflowers grow here, although strawberries may be found. Just before reaching the cirque, the forest opens to provide views of the Bow Valley. Then the trail descends to the rocky cirque area. The cirque is an impressive amphitheatre steeply carved by a glacier into the east slope of Cascade Mountain. An enormous scree slope falls down into the cirque bottom. Once, this cirque contained a tarn, but, lacking a glacier to feed it, the tarn has dried up and left behind a flat meadow being overtaken by alpine willows and shrubs. In early summer this area is abundant with glacier lilies. There is a small pond below the cirque, but hikers should purify the water before drinking it.

# Stoney Squaw

| | |
|---|---|
| **Level:** | Easy/Moderate |
| **One Way:** | 2.3 km |
| **Time:** | 1 hour |
| **Elevation Gain:** | 118 metres (385 feet) |
| **Maximum Elevation:** | 1,184 metres (6,123 feet) |
| **Trailhead:** | First parking lot at Mt. Norquay Ski Area, #3, at end of Mt. Norquay Road, 6 km from the Trans-Canada Highway. Trail begins at entrance to parking lot. |
| **Map:** | 4 (pg 60) |

The trail to the top of Stoney Squaw Mountain between Mts. Norquay (2,523 m) and Cascade (2,988 m) provides several good viewpoints of the Banff townsite, the Bow, Spray and Sundance valleys. The trail itself is narrow and somewhat dark as it winds up the mountainside through a dense forest of lodgepole pine and Engelmann spruce and the path is a bit rooty. The trail is alternately easy and moderate and the forest is cool but waterless. It is a fine place to look for mushrooms. (Do not pick any; park regulations forbid picking or destroying plants, and some mushrooms are poisonous.) Arnicas and twinflowers also bloom here. Gradually the trees become younger and thinner and, at about 2 km, the trees disperse to permit views of Banff townsite. The trail then leaves the edge of the slope and heads north, down into a gulley, and then makes the final steep ascent to the summit, which offers a close view of Cascade Mountain. Near the summit, a bent tree offers children an unusual chair to sit in.

Most hikers return by the same route, but it is possible to continue northward and drop down from the summit ridge to find a trail through the heavily forested northern slope of the mountain. This trail meets a ski run, which should be followed until it meets an access road. Follow this road left back to the parking lot.

# Boom Lake

**Level:** Easy
**One Way:** 5.1 km
**Time:** 2 hours
**Elevation Gain:** 185 metres (600 feet)
**Maximum Elevation:** 1,895 metres (6,210 feet)
**Trailhead:** Highway 93 at the Boom Creek Picnic area 7.1 km from the Eisenhower Junction heading towards Radium.
**Map:** 18 (pg 136)

The shady, wide trail that leads to lovely Boom Lake is often patched with slowly melting snow and intersected by many little bogs and streams, especially in the early season, so good waterproof boots are a necessity on this easy hike until mid-summer.

Unlike many of the higher alpine lakes situated in scree and meadows, Boom Lake's stunning views of rock walls and glaciers are also graced with a heavy forest which comes right down to the water's edge. The trees, in fact, provide the name for the lake because many fallen trees lie across the lake's outflow in a natural log boom.

The moderately graded trail rises from the bridge crossing Boom Creek at the trailhead and makes its way on a very wide, cleared trail through a middle-aged forest of lodgepole pine, alpine fir and spruce. Dogwood and strawberries line the trail. At 2.3 km the trail reaches a junction. The right branch goes to Taylor Lake. Keep straight and continue the easy climb until reaching the narrow footpath that leads to the lake over a rockslide at 5 km.

For most of the hike, the heavy forest prevents good views of the surrounding area. However, the view at the lake is worth the minimal effort required to get there. The north face of Boom Mountain towers in a 600–metre rock wall above the southern shore of the lake in an impressive reach to the sky. At the far end of the lake, the broad glacial expanses of Mt. Quadra (3,173 m) on the left and the smaller Bident Mountain (3,084 m) on the right can often reward hikers with a safe view of a spring avalanche. The lake provides a rocky perch for a picnic and opportunities for a bit of rock scrambling by the shore.

*Mt. Quadra (left) and Mt. Bident from Boom Lake*

# Citadel Pass

**Level:** Easy day hike or backpack
**One Way:** 9.3 km
**Time:** 4 hours
**Elevation Gain:** 165 metres (550 feet)
**Maximum Elevation:** 2,360 metres (7,750 feet)
**Trailhead:** Interpretive centre at upper terminus of Sunshine Meadows gondola. Lower terminus is at the Bourgeau Parking Lot 9 km along the Sunshine Village road, 9 km W of Banff on the Trans-Canada Highway.
**Map:** 5 (pg 68)

*NOTE: This hike is only possible for families if the gondola is operating. Summertime operations have been sporadic. A 6.5-km access road leads from the parking lot to the trailhead, but most families will not want to add this to the hiking distance. Kids will love the gondola ride.*

Getting above the treeline is a favourite adventure for children and adults alike. Although long, this marvellous hike is easily done, partly because the spectacular views encourage great enthusiasm among hikers. This hike is best done in late summer, to allow the snow to melt and the trails to dry. Do not leave the trails: the meadows are fragile and can be easily destroyed by careless hikers.

Begin the hike along a wide gravel road for .2 km and then take the left branch immediately after passing the avalanche control cabin to head towards the summit of the Great Divide. The summit, 1.3 km from the trailhead, forms the Alberta/British Columbia border 100 vertical metres above the junction. The trail makes its moderate way through a scattered subalpine forest. As forest gives way to alpine meadows, expect to see wide expanses of sun-loving alpine flowers: moss campion, alpine forget-me-nots, pussytoes, pasque flowers, Indian paintbrush, and scores more. The view from the divide is stunning. Back to the northwest, there are views of the Bow Valley and the front ranges. To the south lies the famous horn of Mt. Assiniboine (3,618 m) and to the northwest lie the Simpson Pass and the Monarch Ramparts.

Just below the summit, at 1.3 km, there is a junction. The trail straight ahead goes to photogenic Rock Isle Lake, another worthwhile destination. A .5-km (one way) side trip will take hikers to a viewpoint over the lake. From there, the trail continues around the lake another .7 km to its outlet and can continue as a 3-km loop around Grizzly and Larix lakes before returning to Rock Isle Lake.

Back at the junction, head left for Citadel Pass along a fairly level trail into Mt. Assiniboine Provincial Park. At 5.2 km, the trail climbs a small ridge below what is known as Quartz Hill. The trail then drops down to Howard Douglas Lake at 5.8 km. There is a campground at this lake for hikers wishing to make an extended stay. Dropping gear here would make the remaining distance less demanding for children.

Passing through this basin, the trail climbs again until reaching Citadel Pass between Fatigue Mountain (2,959 m) on the left and Citadel Peak (2,608 m) on the right to the southwest. Beneath the pass, the trail descends quickly towards routes leading to popular and dramatic Mt. Assiniboine.

*Rockbound Lake and meadows near Citadel Pass*

*Haiduk Lake with Mt. Ball in background on left*

# Egypt Lake

> **Level:**   Difficult backpack
> **One Way:**   12.4 km
> **Time:**   6 hours
> **Elevation Gain:**   655 metres (2,150 feet)
> **Elevation Loss:**   335 metres (1,100 feet)
> **Maximum Elevation:**   2,330 metres ( 7,650 feet)
> **Trailhead:**   Bourgeau Parking Lot 9 km along the Sunshine Village
>    road, 9 km W of Banff on the Trans-Canada Highway.
> **Map:**   5  (pg 68)

Egypt Lake is one of the most popular overnight hikes in the Rockies because it provides a base for exploring a number of turquoise subalpine lakes with mysterious names associated with ancient Egypt. As a family backpacking trip, it rewards children with great views and lots of opportunity for exploring. The hike should be reserved for reasonably strong children because it requires the gradual 650-metre ascent of Healy Pass and then descends half that elevation towards Egypt Lake, meaning the elevation loss has to be recovered on the hike out. Snow is often on the trail into late July; fun to slide on, it also can cause wet feet, so be prepared.

There are several routes into Egypt Lake, but the Healy Pass trail is the shortest. Beginning at the western end of the parking lot at the base of Sunshine Village, a famous area for skiing, head along a wide ski-out trail before heading right into the forest along a narrower trail at .8 km. This trail will slowly climb up Healy Creek through the forest and cross by bridge over Healy Creek at 3.1 km. After passing the remains of an old cabin at 5.2 km and a campground at 5.5 km, the trail will rise more quickly and reach another campsite and junction at the 7.7 km mark.

At this junction, the trail to the left heads up to spectacular Simpson Pass, another possible route to Egypt Lake, but one that is often snow-covered and soggy late into the season. Keep climbing straight for Healy Pass and climb through the meadows dotted with delicate alpine larch to the 2,330 m pass. From the pass, it is possible to see Mt. Assiniboine (3,618 m) to the southeast. Also to the south but quite immediately in view is the Monarch (2,904 m). The ridge of this icy mountain extends down to Healy Pass and is known as the Monarch Ramparts. To the north lies the Massive Range with Mt. Brett (2,984 m) on the left and slightly shorter Mt. Bourgeau (2,931 m) on the right. Below, the deep turquoise jewel of Egypt Lake can be seen. From this high point, the trail descends quickly back into the forest to Egypt Lake at 12.2 km. Take the left trail for the shelter cabin and campsite. By making this campsite your base, the family can easily while away another day or two in the area by making daytrips to the other exotically named lakes in the area.

From the campground, the trail turns left and switchbacks up into the Whistling Valley, reaching Whistling Pass in 3.3 km. Both of these areas are named for the whistling hoary marmots that live here. The trail takes families first to Scarab Lake at the edge of the treeline by descending for .6 km from the junction 1.9 km from the Egypt Lake campsite. Mummy Lake is reached by crossing the Scarab Lake outlet above the 100-metre waterfall, which falls down to Egypt Lake, and making progress up a short scree slope. The Whistling Valley can be reached by returning to Scarab Lake and then taking the main trail another 1.5 km upwards to a pass between the Pharaoh Peaks and Haiduk Peak. Haiduk Lake is found by descending the pass for 2.2 more km on a rocky trail.

Pharaoh Lake and Black Rock Lakes lie 2.4 km north of Egypt Lake. Take the trail from Egypt Lake down Pharaoh Creek for .5 km and then ascend a steep fork on the west to switchback for .8 km up to Pharaoh Lake. Beyond this lake, head north again for 1.1 km along a somewhat tangled trail to Black Rock Lake.

The entire Egypt Lake area is very heavily used during the peak season in the summer and is often one of the first overnight trips attempted by novice hikers. Expect a lot of company and ensure your children respect the space and privacy of others.

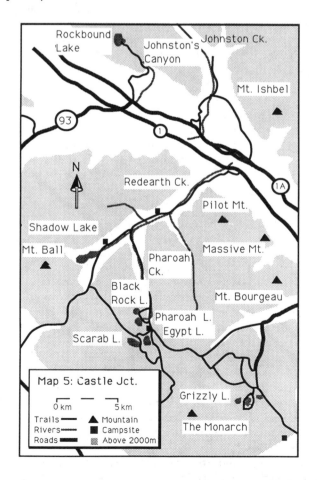

# Johnston Canyon and Ink Pots

> **Level:** Easy
> **One Way:** 5.8 km to Ink Pots
> **Time:** two-and-a-half hours
> **Elevation Gain:** 215 metres (700 feet)
> **Maximum Elevation:** 1,645 metres (5,400 feet)
> **Trailhead:** Parking lot next to the Johnston Canyon Lodge on the Bow Valley Parkway (Highway 1A), 18 km W of the 1A junction.
> **Map:** 5 (pg 68)

Johnston Canyon is one of the most popular trails in all of the national parks. Hikers won't find solitude here in this tight and cosy canyon, but they will be intrigued by the rushing waters which have carved a beautiful and impressive canyon into the dolomite cliffs. Unlike the other canyon trails in the parks, this hike runs inside the mouth of the canyon rather than along its lip, giving a more intimate view of the erosive forces of water.

The first 1.1 km of this hike has been paved to make it accessible to high numbers of hikers and to prevent further erosion in the area. Catwalks hang along the cliff edges and steel railings also prevent accidental dips in the swift river. Self-guiding pamphlets and the occasional interpretive sign are available to explain the geological significance of the erosion that slowly but continually deepens and changes the canyon.

Upon reaching the lower falls at 1.1 km, hikers can view its 10-metre plunge into an oval pothole from the bridge. Entering the natural tunnel left behind thousands of years ago by the river for a wet, close-up view above the falls is an irresistible attraction. The river once coursed through this tunnel, but changed its direction as it wore away softer rock to the side.

Reach the more majestic 30-metre upper falls by heading left just before the lower falls bridge. Most hikers stop, satisfied with the lower falls, but hikers can leave most of the crowd behind by ascending the stairs up and out of the canyon, past several small waterfalls and through a stand of Douglas fir and lodgepole pine before reaching the upper falls at 2.7 km. At 3.2 km, the trail joins an access road, which runs about 2 km through a forest of white spruce and lodgepole pine toward the Ink Pots. Fireweed, arnica, roses and Indian paintbrush are common along this section. As the trail narrows, it leaves the forest and descends to the subalpine meadows of the Johnston Valley, where the Ink Pots are found at 5.8 km.

The Ink Pots are a cluster of six karst springs which bubble up water at a constant temperature of 4°C. Karst springs are found in limestone formations and are marked by crystallized solution, such as quartzite, around their edges. They are sometimes, but not always, associated with the presence of caves. The Ink Pots mark a pleasant place for a picnic. Before turning around, the grassy meadows beneath Castle Mountain (2,729 m) and Mt. Ishbel (2,850 m) can be explored and searched for wildflowers. The meadow is a wonderful wide open area for playing tag or frisbee and even for flying kites.

# Shadow Lake

**Level:** Moderate/backpack
**One Way:** 14.3 km
**Time:** 5 hours
**Elevation Gain:** 460 metres (1,500 feet)
**High Point:** 1,860 metres (6,100 feet)
**Trailhead:** Redearth Creek parking lot on Trans-Canada Highway,
12.2 km W of Banff townsite overpass.
**Map:** 5 (pg 68)

Large and photogenic, Shadow Lake is a popular family destination, because of the great views of rough and chunky Mt. Ball (3,307 m), and a base for hikes to Egypt Lake, the Whistling Valley and Gibbon and Ball Passes.

The trail itself is rather dull. The destination provides most of the scenic rewards. A short trail from the parking lot meets the Redearth Fire Road within .3 km and follows it for another 10.5 km. While the hike through a pine and fir forest is not exactly awe-inspiring, neither is it terribly steep or difficult. Several creek crossings add interest. The ascent is gradual and reasonably easy for children. At 7.2 km, the road crosses Redearth Creek by bridge. There is a campground here.

At the 10.8 km mark, there is a fork in the road. Keep straight for Shadow Lake, or, if this hike is being used to get directly to Egypt Lake, turn left and head up the low-lying trail of Pharaoh Creek. Continuing toward Shadow Lake, the trail opens up a bit and occasional views of Mt. Ball lie ahead. A campsite in the midst of a meadow lies further ahead. Here you can drop your packs and hike another 1 km up to the lake. A right-branching trail at kilometre 13.4 takes hikers to Gibbon Pass, but keep straight to get to the lake.

From the lake, it is possible to hike a trail that skirts the south shore for a kilometre and then heads up toward Haiduk Lake, over Whistling Pass and down to Egypt Lake. If you extend your trip to include Egypt Lake by this route, keep left when you reach the junction that leads to Ball Pass.

# Consolation Lakes

**Level:** Easy
**One Way:** 3 km to lower lake
**Time:** 1 hour
**Elevation Gain:** 90 metres (210 feet)
**Maximum Elevation:** 1,950 metres (6,400 feet)
**Trailhead:** End of Moraine Lake Rd, 12.4 km from its junction with
the 1A highway up to Lake Louise.
**Map:** 6 (pg 76)

Few family hikes are more rewarding for the minimal effort needed to get to the lower of the two Consolation Lakes. At the very least, this hike is a good excuse to drive to Moraine Lake, which lies icy blue beneath the stunning Ten Peaks rising 1,000 m into a 15-km-long ridge of rock and ice above it. This is the scene on the back of the Canadian $20 bill. It's worth far more in real life.

After absorbing Moraine Lake's incandescent beauty, head toward the rockpile and cross the railed bridge at the lake's outlet. Hikers wanting a better view of Moraine Lake can take the short .4-km hike up the Rockpile trail and then return the same way to continue on the Consolation Lakes trail. The trail over the rockpile boulders is well worn and obvious, but still involves some careful footing to keep a steady balance. This rugged section was not left behind by a receding glacier, but was created by an avalanche of rock which fell from the Tower of Babel, or which floated on top of a glacier and was deposited here.

The trail skirts the rounded slopes of the Tower of Babel and climbs almost unnoticeably through a mature forest beside Babel Creek. At 1.6 km, it meets a junction. Go straight for the Consolation Lakes, left for Taylor Lake. Soon the forest trail levels out and gives way to an open meadow full of summer flowers, especially Indian paintbrush and roses. Before reaching the lake, hikers will hear the whistles of the marmots warning each other of approaching danger. This lake is one of the prime marmot habitats in the Rockies. Hearing them is guaranteed on any trip here and you will quite likely be lucky enough to see several as they sun themselves on rocks and forage for grasses and flowers, such as shrubby cinquefoil.

Upon reaching the shores of the lake, hikers can pick their way along the immense boulders that have fallen from the Tower of Babel until finding the perfect picnic site. Children can spend hours here climbing over the rocks and exploring. Upper Consolation Lake can be reached by fording the lower lake's outlet on fallen logs and then following the wet, rocky eastern shore of the lake for about 1 km.

Named in contrast to Desolation Valley on the other side of Moraine Lake by Ross Peacock in 1899, Consolation Lakes remain somewhat severe because of the quantity of rock and scree that has fallen from the mountain slopes. The view is nevertheless impressive as Mt. Bident (3,084 m) and Mt. Quadra (3,173 m) rise majestically above the lake. To the north lies magnificent, snowy Mt. Temple (3,544 m), the highest peak in the Lake Louise area.

# Eiffel Lake

**Level:** Moderate
**One Way:** 5.6 km
**Time:** 2 hours
**Elevation Gain:** 350 metres (2,360 feet)
**Maximum Elevation:** 2,255 m (7,128 feet)
**Trailhead:** Moraine Lake, past the lodge. Moraine Lake is at the end of Moraine Lake Rd, 12.4 km from its junction with the 1A highway up to Lake Louise.
**Map:** 6 (pg 76)

This is a spectacular hike. Beginning on the western shore of Moraine Lake, the trail climbs over and beside rivers for the first 1.1 km. At this point, a series of eleven switchbacks begin to climb up through the alpine fir and spruce forest littered with arnica and Indian paintbrush and offering great views through the trees of the indescribably blue lake below and the jagged Wenkchemna Peaks (still popularly known as the Ten Peaks, the English translation of Wenkchemna) across the valley. Once the trail begins the switchbacks, there is no water available. The switchbacks are moderate, but tired children will be encouraged to know that once the switchbacks are finished at 2.4 km, there is no noteworthy elevation gain for the remainder of the hike. At the end of the switchbacks, the trail meets a signed junction. Head straight for Eiffel Lake; the right trail climbs 3.4 km to Sentinel Pass.

From the junction, the Eiffel Lake trail stretches westward toward Wenkchemna Pass. Almost entirely above the treeline, the remainder of the hike provides awe-inspiring, unobstructed views of all ten of the Ten Peaks. The narrow and somewhat rocky trail passes through meadow after meadow of fireweed, pasque flowers, sunflowers and even columbines. Watch for porcupines among the low shrubs. Up the valley, towards the lake, hikers will understand why discoverer Walter Wilcox named this area Desolation Valley: massive rockslides and glacial debris make the valley floor hostile to almost all vegetation. Eiffel Lake, found in a small depression left by a rockslide falling from Neptuak Mountain (the final peak), is reached at 5.6 km, but is 200 m below the trail. The lake gains its name from the impressive peak hovering above it to the north, itself named Eiffel Peak (3,085 m) because of its resemblance to the famous tower. Watch for golden eagles and marmots in this area.

Just 3 km beyond the lake, Wenkchemna Pass seductively beckons. One of the highest accessible passes in the Rockies at 2,605 m, this pass looks closer than it is. Most children especially enjoy hiking above the treeline and may insist on continuing beyond the initial destination. Do so only with older or especially agile children. The trail is safe, but narrow over several scree slopes. Although marked by cairns, the trail is easily lost over the final ascent through a large rockfall and hikers may have to do some bouldering to get to the top. The pass — one of the highest accessible by trail — is very windy, desolate and cold but permits a view down into a steep valley belonging on the north to Yoho Park and to Kootenay Park in the south. The steep valley below is the upper end of Kootenay's Prospectors' Valley, an area often forbidden to hikers because of grizzly bears.

*Eiffel Lake looking toward Wenkchemna Pass*

*Lake Agnes Teahouse*

# Lake Agnes

**Level:** Moderate
**One Way:** 3.4 km
**Time:** 2 hours
**Elevation Gain:** 367 metres (1,200 feet)
**Maximum Elevation:** 2,100 metres (6,778 feet)
**Trailhead:** W of the Lake Louise Chateau. Park in the Lake Louise
parking lot and walk in front of the chateau to the trailhead.
**Map:** 6 (pg 76)

This glossy lake was named for Lady Agnes MacDonald, the wife of Sir John A. MacDonald, but perhaps more famous for riding on the cowcatcher of a train from Lake Louise over the terrifying Kicking Horse Pass. It also offers a step into park history at a quaint teahouse left over from the days of early Swiss-style tourism, as well as wonderful views from above Lake Louise and access to curious-looking mountain knolls known as the Beehives. The short but steep trail begins easily along a paved path on the far (northwestern) shore of Lake Louise and then immediately branches off to the right to ascend up switchbacks through a mature, thick forest of alpine fir and Engelmann spruce. The first good views of Lake Louise are visible only once you have gained about 200 m of elevation at 1.6 km. At 2.3 km, the trail passes through a gate and joins a horse trail just before coming across pretty Mirror Lake at 2.6 km beneath the Big Beehive. From this lake hikers can see the teahouse and the waterfall at the outlet of Lake Agnes above. From Mirror Lake, there are two options. The main route heads right, continuing to switchback up to the level of the teahouse and then levelling out on the side of Mt. Niblock until it reaches the 57 steps that ascend to the teahouse. The steep route branching left from Mirror Lake reaches the same destination by ascending directly and cutting across the base of the Big Beehive, but this trail is more difficult and is often wet and slippery. The left branch can also be used to pick up the Plain-of-the-Six Glaciers trail. The teahouse at the lake provides a novel incentive (bribe) for tired hikers.

The narrow lake is perched in a "hanging valley" which appears to be suspended in air high above Lake Louise and the Bow Valley. The lake itself is often covered with ice well into June and is cradled by Mt. Niblock (2,976 m) on the west, Mt. Whyte (2,983 m) and the Victoria Glacier to the southwest and Saddle (2,437 m) and Fairview (2,744 m) Mountains on the east.

Because of the presence of so many hikers and visitors to the teahouse, many picnic beggars will plead to share snacks. Lake Agnes abounds with whiskey jacks, Clark's nutcrackers, ground squirrels and chipmunks. Resist the temptation to feed them.

Hikers with extra energy can explore the Little and Big Beehives. The Little Beehive can be reached by hiking a ridge behind the teahouse for about 1 km. To get to the Big Beehive, continue along the length of Lake Agnes and then begin the winding trail to the top for a total distance of 1.6 km from the teahouse.

# Paradise Valley Loop

**Level:** Easy backpack or long day trip
**Loop:** 18.8 km
**Time:** 7 hours
**Elevation Gain:** 385 metres (800 feet)
**Maximum Elevation:** 2,105 metres (6,900 feet)
**Trailhead:** Parking area on W side of Moraine Lake Rd, 2.4 km S of the junction with the 1A highway to Lake Louise.
**Map:** 6 (pg 76)

Appropriately named, Paradise Valley is one of the most popular loop trails in the Lake Louise area and is an excellent introductory backpacking trip for children. Allowing several side trips and serving as a passageway to other trails such as the Saddleback or Sentinel Pass, this loop trail is continually populated with dayhikers. The population density of hikers is especially high as far as Lake Annette and by the Giant Steps but falls off considerably at the far end of the loop beneath the Horseshoe Glacier. Don't let the crowd deter a family hike here; hikers love this valley because it provides access to so much for only a minimal effort. It is a wonderful place.

As the trail wanders away from Moraine Lake Road, pay careful attention to the posted signs because there are many well-marked junctions for the first 5 km. From the parking lot, the trail meanders through a mature forest of alpine fir and spruce, which blocks most views. At 1.1 km, take the right branch of the trail; shortly after, at 1.3 km, take the left branch towards the valley. (The right branch heads west to Lake Louise.) Within three kilometres of the trailhead, the trail opens up to allow views of Mt. Temple (3,544 m) and the valley itself. Ignore a junction at 4.2 km. The left branch ascends the Saddleback; keep straight to remain in the valley. Further on, at 5.1 km, hikers must choose the direction in which they will travel the loop. Straight ahead, the trail continues up Paradise Creek to the Giant Steps and the campground; the left branch reaches these destinations within a similar distance but is a higher, more scenic trail.

Going left at 5.1 km, the trail ascends a short but steep route beside a creek until reaching Lake Annette at 5.7 km. This tiny blue lake lies embedded like a jewel in the rocks. It was named for Annette Astley, wife of the Lake Louise Chalet's first manager. The trail to the lake offers an unusual perspective on mountain streams because it leads directly past the outflow point of the lake where the flat, smooth lake water spills over its edge to tumble down into the creek. Beneath the massive north wall of Mt. Temple, Lake Annette makes a good destination in itself and is a great spot to picnic and watch for pika.

Continuing along the loop, either from the junction or Lake Annette, the trail climbs to 2,105 m along a rockslide area to the highest point on the valley trail. Here hikers will see a left-to-right concave panorama of Pinnacle Mountain (3,607 m), the Horseshoe Glacier at the end of the valley, the Mitre and Mt. Aberdeen (3,152 m) extending to the southwest, while a gaze to the northeast provides an excellent view of Mt. Temple. From this high point, the trail passes the Sentinel Pass turnoff on the left at 8.8 km. Keep straight ahead and descend to rocky areas and meadows beneath the Horseshoe Glacier. Within .3 km of the junction there is a lightly forested campground. The Horseshoe Meadows are filled with an abundance of wildflowers throughout the summer. The meadows do, however, tend to be a bit boggy well into the summer because of runoff from the glacier above.

After crossing a bridge, the main trail turns back down the valley towards Moraine Lake Road. A sharp left fork at 9.6 km leads away from the main loop trail to follow a wet and often scrubby trail 1 km to the Giant Steps. These large, flat limestone rocks do indeed look like steps. Although they lead nowhere, it is easy to imagine this area as a fantasy playground for dragons and ogres. It is a good playground for children and photographers, too, as they spend an afternoon exploring the levels of the orangish steps and cooling their feet in the water that skims in lively sheets over the square surfaces. The area is heavily visited and there are many trails leading to the upper and lower viewpoints of the Giant Steps.

After returning to the main loop by the most obvious path, the trail continues a straightforward, moderate descent through old forests towards the valley bottom. Several areas along this section of the trail are boggy or often littered with trees which have fallen during the winter. Trail crews clear most of these obstacles, but may not have reached them in the early season. By 13.0 km, the trail closes the loop and rejoins the original trail leading from the road.

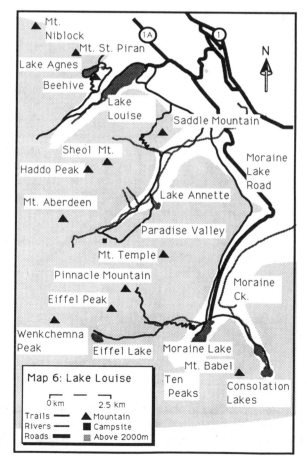

Map 6: Lake Louise

# The Plain-of-the-Six Glaciers

**Level:**  Moderate    caution on snow
**One Way:**  6.6 km
**Time:**  3 hours
**Elevation Gain:**  670 metres (2,200 feet)
**Maximum Elevation:**  2,410 metres (7,900 feet)
**Trailhead:**  W of the Lake Louise Chateau. Park in the Lake Louise parking lot and walk in front of the chateau to the trailhead at the NW side of the lake.
**Map:**  6  (pg 76)

Magnificent Lake Louise is the most-photographed beauty spot in the parks. The world-famous colour, common on all glacial lakes, is caused by tiny particles of glacial silt known as rockflour, which remain suspended in the water and reflect the wavelengths closest to their own size — the blue and green ones. To get a closer look at the sublime Victoria Glacier which hangs behind and melts into Lake Louise, a hike up to the Plain-of-the-Six Glaciers is well worth the effort.

First, a few words of warning: although the trail is completely safe if treated with respect, its deceptively easy beginning deceives hikers who do not take hiking seriously. Inadequate clothing can result in hypothermia; fooling around on the snow that often crosses the trail on open slopes can result in a quick, one-way trip to the valley bottom. Senior citizens, lured by the double temptation of an easy trailhead and tea at the top, also have been known to have heart problems on this trail.

Following along the northwestern shore of Lake Louise on a wide paved path, ignore the junction that leads up to Lake Agnes on the right and stay on the lower trail. The trail soon reverts to gravel but doesn't narrow until reaching an area of trees knocked over by snowslides during the winter at about 1.7 km. This blowdown area tangles the trail until it begins its ascent through a mature forest of spruce and alpine fir. Families are likely to share the trail with scores of other hikers and with strings of dudes grinning sheepishly from their leather-mouthed horses. Always yield to the horses, faster hikers and to hikers walking downhill.

Gradually, the trail begins its climb at 2.4 km and the forest gives way to the ashy-grey moraine slopes left behind by the backward and forward movements of the Victoria Glacier over the centuries. This barren scar of gravel continues to dominate the landscape, although a small stand of dwarfed and twisted trees has managed to survive near the teahouse. At 3.2 km, a trail from the Big Beehive/Mirror Lake area descends from the right to join the main trail and the remaining trail to the teahouse becomes steeper. The teahouse is reached within 5.3 km and an elevation gain of 365 m (1,200 ft). This is a great place to stop and refresh tired hikers and is a good destination in itself.

Beyond the teahouse, a glacial moraine extends along a crest. This crest

*On the trail towards the Victoria Glacier*

can be hiked cautiously until the trail disappears at its edge, 1.3 km beyond the teahouse. From this final viewpoint, mountaineers begin their trek up the retreating Victoria Glacier to the tiny stone hut on Abbot's Pass between Mt. Victoria (3,463 m) on the right and Mt. Lefroy (3,441 m) on the left. The pass was named for Philip Abbot, who died in 1896 while climbing Mt. Lefroy. Abbot was the first mountaineer killed in the Rockies. On the other side of the pass lie Yoho Park and the glaciated peaks above Lake O'Hara.

# Saddleback

> **Level:** Moderate
> **One Way:** 3.7 km
> **Time:** 2 hours
> **Elevation Gain:** 585 metres (1,950 feet)
> **Maximum Elevation:** 2,330 metres (7,650 feet)
> **Trailhead:** Lake Louise parking lot near Louise Creek and behind the boathouse on the SE side of the lake.
> **Map:** 6 (pg 76)

This popular hike is not as difficult as its elevation gain may suggest; four-year-olds have done it without complaining. The reward for your efforts is a magnificent view of square-jawed, glacier-capped Mt. Temple (3,544 m), open meadows of wildflowers, glimpses into Paradise Valley and the wide panorama of the Bow Valley ranges.

Leaving the masses swarming around Lake Louise behind by passing between the boathouse and the horse corral, the trail leads through a mature forest of alpine fir and spruce. At .3 km the trail reaches a junction; keep straight for the Saddleback trail. (Going to the right will lead along a mildly up-and-down trail to the Fairview Lookout for a sheltered view of Lake Louise which provides a look back at the chateau.) At .4 km, another junction leads left to skirt the eastern and northern slopes of Saddle Mountain and Mt. Temple to reach Moraine Lake. Keep straight and continue ascending along the southern flank of Fairview Mountain through the forest.

Once the trail crosses the first of several avalanche paths at 1.1 km, the forest begins to thin and the views of the precipitous north face of Mt. Temple and the Bow Valley get steadily better as elevation is gained. Leaving the forest behind, the Saddleback, an alpine meadow covered in a wide variety of wildflowers and larch trees, is finally attained. The Saddleback is actually a pass or shoulder between Fairview Mountain (2,744 m) and Saddle Mountain (2,437 m). Both of these low peaks can be climbed on easily found switchback trails, although the slightly higher Fairview Mountain offers better views of the Victoria Glacier.

Energetic families might decide to descend from the Saddleback down the other side into Paradise Valley instead of retracing the trail back along the slopes of Fairview Mountain. This option first leads beneath the austere and formidable cliffs of Sheol Mountain (named for the Judaic version of Hell) and then down into the wildflower meadows and forests of the valley. Upon reaching the valley, turn left to traverse beneath Saddle Mountain until rejoining the Saddleback trail. The loop distance for this option is 14.9 km.

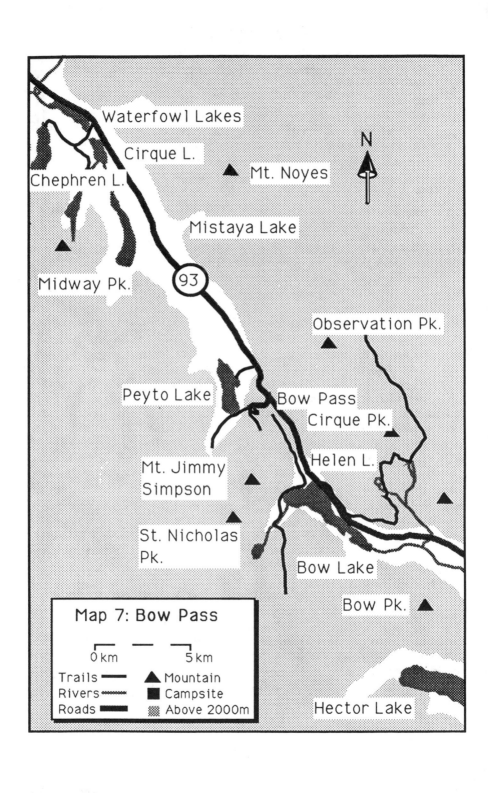

Map 7: Bow Pass

0 km     5 km

Trails —
Rivers ∞∞∞∞
Roads ▬

▲ Mountain
■ Campsite
▓ Above 2000m

Waterfowl Lakes
Cirque L.
Chephren L.
Mt. Noyes
Mistaya Lake
Midway Pk.
93
Observation Pk.
Peyto Lake
Bow Pass
Cirque Pk.
Helen L.
Mt. Jimmy Simpson
St. Nicholas Pk.
Bow Lake
Bow Pk.
Hector Lake
N

# Bow Glacier Falls

**Level:**   Easy
**One Way:**   4.3 km
**Time:**   2 hours
**Elevation Gain:**   150 metres (500 feet)
**Maximum Elevation:**   2,100 metres (6,900 feet)
**Trailhead:**   Parking lot behind Num-ti-jah Lodge on the Icefields
Parkway (Highway 93), 36 km N of the Trans-Canada
Highway junction.
**Map:**   7  (pg 80)

An easy trip through gravel outwash and up a narrow canyon to Bow Glacier Falls takes hikers on an interesting geological tour of the headwaters of the Bow River. Born in the receding Bow Glacier, the Bow River has carved its course from the Great Divide toward the prairies — a route that has been traced in more recent years by the railroad and the highway as the best way through the formidable barrier of the southern Rockies.

Beginning behind picturesque Num-ti-jah Lodge (Stoney for pine marten) located on stabilized delta silt, this hike begins very easily and pleasantly by moving toward and following the shores of Bow Lake. This large lake is truly spectacular on a calm, clear day when the reflections of the deep blue sky and the northern face of Crowfoot Mountain shimmer in the frosty blue waters.

After following the shore for 1.5 km, the trail moves toward an outwash area at 2.4 km where silt has been deposited by the Bow Glacier's meltwater. It is here that hikers begin to sense the awesome powers of erosion and its capacity to influence the landscape. As the delta grows each year, more slowly now than in the past when the glacier was larger, new rocks and silts pile up on old ones, the river changes its weaving course and most plants cannot find a permanent area to root.

Continuing up the right side of the river, the trail enters a very steep limestone canyon. The trail here is narrow and requires care. It is best hiked in dry weather, as it is dangerously slippery when wet. Near the end of the canyon at 3.2 km lies the natural bridge, a large limestone rock that has fallen across the sides of the canyon. The trail no longer goes over this bridge and it is advisable not to let anyone play on it, as it is narrow and the water rushing below is quite dizzying.

Upon emerging from the canyon at 3.4 km, the trail crosses a glacial moraine where the main outwash area and the falls, a further .9 km distant, can be seen. The Bow Glacier is part of the Wapta Icefield, which extends into Yoho Park and is noted for its smooth sea of ice punctuated by islands of tooth-like peaks, most notably St. Nicholas Peak (2,941 m) on its south side. It is possible to hike to the base of the falls, which cascade over a cliff from a small tarn just beneath the Bow Glacier. Simply find your own path through the moraine to get a closer look at the falls.

# Chephren Lake

Level:   Easy
One Way:   4.0 km
Time:   2 hours
Elevation Gain:   80 metres (250 feet)
Maximum Elevation:   1,755 metres (5,750 feet)
Trailhead:   Waterfowl Lake campground on Icefields Parkway
              (Highway 93), 58 km N of Trans-Canada Highway; trail
              begins at picnic area near Mistaya River.
Map:   7 (pg 80)

Easy access to fantastic high-altitude scenery and a good chance of seeing moose should entice families to this classic mountain lake. Chephren Lake (pronounced Keff-ren) lies beneath the horns of Howse Peak (3,290 m) to the south and Mt. Chephren (3,307 m) on the western shore. Mt. Chephren was originally called Pyramid Mountain by explorer Mary Schaffer in honour of its massive triangular shape, but was renamed after Chephren, the builder of the Egyptian pyramids, in 1918 because it was being confused with another Pyramid Mountain near Jasper.

The trail is easy and straightforward. After edging the Waterfowl Lakes campground, it crosses the Mistaya River at .5 km and gradually climbs through a marshy and forested area. Soon after the junction to Cirque Lake at 1.3 km, the trail opens up to meadows on the left and the peaks above come into view. The trail continues on to the lake but can be quite muddy and rooty. The view of Howse Peak is stunning. Frosted with snow and ice, the white limestone cliffs also cradle a small glacier and provide a dramatic contrast to the turquoise serenity of this lake. The peak was named for Joseph Howse, a fur trader working for the Hudson's Bay Company at the beginning of the nineteenth century.

# Cirque Lake

> **Level:** Easy
> **One Way:** 4.7 km
> **Time:** 2.5 hours
> **Elevation Gain:** 150 metres (500 feet)
> **Maximum Elevation:** 1,800 metres (5,910 feet)
> **Trailhead:** Waterfowl Lake campground on Icefields Parkway (Highway 93), 58 km N of Trans-Canada Highway; trail begins at picnic area near Mistaya River.
> **Map:** 7 (pg 80)

Cirque Lake is a smaller twin sister to Chephren Lake. In fact, the two lakes share the same mountains and peaks between them. Looking as if they are coated in icing sugar, Howse Peak (3,290 m), Mount Synge and Aiguille Peak rise above Cirque Lake to the west in a horned formation that separates the two lakes. The southern wall above Cirque Lake rises 800 m above the lake; the peaks are, starting from the south and left to right, Aries, Stairway and Midway.

The trail to Cirque Lake is longer and steeper than the marshy trail to Chephren Lake, but the view of the icy peaks against the still blue waters of Cirque Lake is worth the modest effort. This trail shares the Chephren Lake trail until the 1.3 km mark and then turns off to the left. After this turnoff, the trail becomes steeper as it gains elevation. Winding and narrow, the trail is almost a stairway of roots and rocks. It is not too difficult but is a bit slow because of the care required in selecting footing. Follow the trail along the stream through the subalpine forest until suddenly arriving at the lake.

Apart from the great views, Cirque Lake provides a popular fishing destination.

Which of these lakes is more beautiful? Decide for yourself by doing both Cirque and Chephren Lake trails on the same day, for a total distance of 12.8 km.

*Cirque Lake beneath the Great Divide*

# Dolomite Pass

> **Level:** Difficult
> **One Way:** 9 km
> **Time:** 4 hours
> **Elevation Gain:** 550 metres (1,800 feet)
> **High Point:** 2,500 metres (8,200 feet)
> **Trailhead:** Crowfoot Glacier viewpoint on Icefields Parkway, 7.7 km S of Bow Summit. Park opposite viewpoint on N side of the road.
> **Map:** 7 (pg 80)

The Dolomite Pass trail is appealing because it takes hikers on one of the highest dayhiking trails in the parks, reaching a windswept and impressive elevation of 2,500 m. This is the high country home of golden eagles, marmots and the occasional grizzly. Wildflowers, rockslides and barren ridges reward photographers with their displays. The yellow dolomite rock makes an interesting change from the usual grey colouring found in the front ranges.

The first 3 kilometres of the hike are the most difficult and unrewarding. Climbing through a mature subalpine forest of alpine fir and Engelmann spruce on a tightly switchbacked trail, hikers have little to look at but the trail rising in front of them. The views improve greatly once the trail breaks out of the forest and arrives at the open alpine meadows cradled on the steep ridges at 2.9 km. Now views of the Crowfoot Glacier and Bow Peak (2,868 m) behind and across the valley to the south, glaciated Mt. Hector (3394 m) to the southeast and nearby Dolomite Peak (2,972 m) make the climb worthwhile.

At 3.4 km, the trail switchbacks up Cirque Peak ridge to the edge of the treeline and circles around and beneath a rockslide at 4.5 km before entering a lovely meadow and coming upon little Helen Lake at 6.0 km. Children will be delighted with the antics of the hoary marmots among the rocks. Above the lake, a series of switchbacks takes hikers up a bleak, grey ridge to the high point of the hike at 2,500 m, 6.9 km from the trailhead. From here, there are good views to the southwest of the glaciers of the Waputik Icefield and down the ridge to Lake Katherine and, further along, Dolomite Pass.

Most families will likely turn around at this point because they will get no higher and the remaining trail requires a stiff, hard-on-the-knees descent to Lake Katherine and then a tough climb out again on the return. Continuing on depends on your energy and good weather. With lots of both, descend from the ridge to Lake Katherine at 8.1 km and then climb up to the summit of Dolomite Pass at (2,393 m). From Lake Katherine it is possible to see right down the length of Banff Park on a clear day.

The wide open meadows around Helen Lake are good for exploring, a game of ball or frisbee or a relaxing nap in the sun. The meadows are alive with wildflowers: Indian paintbrush, anemones, mountain avens, asters, sunflowers and moss campion, heathers and many others are in bloom at various times in the summer.

# Nigel Pass

**Level:** Moderate
**One Way:** 7.2 km
**Time:** 3 hours
**Elevation Gain:** 365 metres (1,200 feet)
**Maximum Elevation:** 2,195 metres (7,200 feet)
**Trailhead:** Gravel road on E side of Icefields Parkway 8.5 km S of Banff/Jasper boundary.
**Map:** 8 (pg 87)

This moderate trail takes hikers to relatively high alpine country with very little effort. Beginning at the access gate 200 m from the Icefields Parkway, the trail crosses Nigel Creek and begins a steady climb past several avalanche slopes littered with wildflowers such as fireweed and shrubby cinquefoil as well as avalanche debris. After crossing the river again, hikers reach Camp Parker at 2.1 km. Used as a base camp by explorers and outfitters for many years, and by the Natives long before that, Camp Parker is an interesting area to explore. Wander through the forest here and let children discover the carvings cut into many of the trees. Representations of faces, bottles and other icons of a past era can be found. Some date to early explorations of the area; many are less than fifty years old. One person's graffiti is another's art.

From Camp Parker, the trail heads northward and begins a steady and more difficult ascent up the Nigel Valley. Although walking through Engelmann spruce and alpine fir, hikers can see Nigel Pass before them as well as Mt. Athabasca (3,490 m) across the valley to the west for most of the way. Nigel Peak (3,211 m) can be seen to the west once sufficient altitude and distance have been gained. The trail continues to ascend and gradually breaks out into subalpine meadows scattered with trees and sun-loving flowers at 5.1 km. The ascent continues in a straightforward manner until reaching the pass at 7.2 km. Near the pass, hikers reach the krummholz zone of short, twisted trees. These shrubby trees survive the severe alpine climate and winds because of their low growth, which allows them to find shelter beneath the snow in winter. They indicate the upper edge of the treeline.

The pass lies on the Banff/Jasper boundary and affords excellent views north to the Brazeau River Valley, south to the icy summit of Mt. Saskatchewan (3,342 m) and directly above to the west to Nigel Peak. This trail leads to the Jonas Pass trail described in the next chapter.

# Parker's Ridge

> **Level:** Moderate
> **One Way:** 2.4 km
> **Time:** 1 hour
> **Elevation Gain:** 275 metres (900 feet)
> **High Point:** 2,270 metres (7,450 feet)
> **Trailhead:** 5 km S of Jasper/Banff boundary on Icefields Parkway;
> 42 km N of Saskatchewan River Crossing. Trailhead on N
> side of Parkway.
> **Map:** 8 (pg 87)

Few hikes in the Rockies rival Parker's Ridge for combining dramatic scenery, easy access and sobering environmental lessons. A short hour's hike up a switchback trail quickly takes you to spectacular panoramas of the Columbia Icefield, particularly the immense and moody Saskatchewan Glacier.

This popular trail begins right of the highway and zigzags through very fragile alpine terrain. The lower half of the trail travels through the highest reaches of the subalpine zone where the terrain varies between open meadows and small stands of dwarfish alpine fir. At 2,100 metres, you leave these windswept stands behind and enter the true alpine zone covered with tundra mosses, heathers and tiny alpine flowers. Upon reaching the crest, look around for loose rocks. In many of them you will find strange white circles that look like crystals. These are coral fossils formed million of years ago when this ridge was a seabed. To get the best view of the mighty Saskatchewan Glacier, descend along the trail to its end. Hikers should be able to feel the colder air blowing off the glacier. It's a good idea to bring extra warm clothing to put on at this stopping point. The crest can be cold and windy and the weather here is very changeable, quickly chilling hikers off from the hot work of climbing up the switchbacks. If stopping for lunch or a snack, try to find shelter from the wind behind one of the large rocks lying around. Be cautious on the ridge and discourage children from rock scrambling or straying off the trail. It damages the environment and can easily cause a fall or twisted ankle. Keep a sharp eye out for mountain goats and sheep.

This hike is particularly good because its open terrain affords magnificent views throughout the walk without the closed-in feeling you can get walking through trees for hours. Be sure to look back across the valley towards the White Goat Wilderness Area just outside of Banff Park. The trail also provides an opportunity to appreciate the subtleties of colour and the great variety of life in this precarious alpine environment.

Throughout the heavily used trail, notice bright orange signs warning hikers to keep to the trail and not to take shortcuts between switchbacks. Ignorant hikers have caused severe erosion on the trail by trying to save a few seconds going up or down. By doing this, they have destroyed many fragile plants which will take years to grow back in such a hostile environment. On this or any other trail, do not take shortcuts.

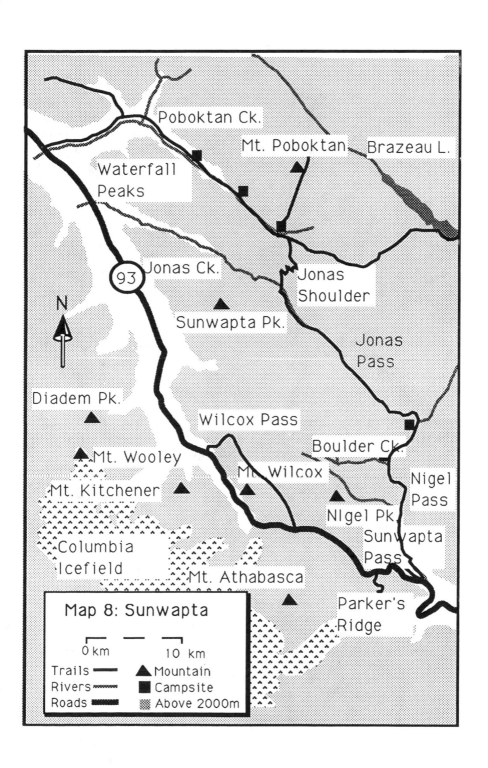

Poboktan Ck.

Mt. Poboktan

Brazeau L.

Waterfall
Peaks

93

Jonas Ck.

Jonas
Shoulder

Sunwapta Pk.

Jonas
Pass

Diadem Pk.

Wilcox Pass

Boulder Ck.

Mt. Wooley

Mt. Wilcox

Nigel
Pass

Mt. Kitchener

Nigel Pk.

Sunwapta
Pass

Columbia
Icefield

Mt. Athabasca

Parker's
Ridge

N

Map 8: Sunwapta

0 km          10 km

Trails ——          ▲ Mountain
Rivers ~~~~          ■ Campsite
Roads ▬▬          ▨ Above 2000m

# 7 // Jasper

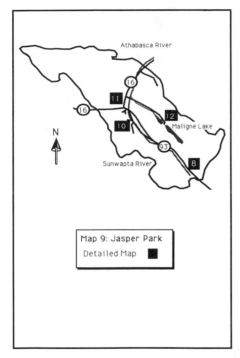

Map 9: Jasper Park
Detailed Map ■

Jasper National Park is the largest of the four adjacent Rocky Mountain parks, with an area of 10,878 square kilometres. Although it is the largest park, it is not nearly so heavily developed as Banff, perhaps because of its later inception and the minor role of winter activities.

Jasper might be a different park today had the original plans for the trans-continental railway been followed as proposed. Surveyors for the Canadian Pacific Railway originally chose the Yellowhead Pass as their route across the difficult Continental Divide to the ocean, but the Kicking Horse Pass in Yoho Park closer to the U.S. border was chosen instead to prevent competition from American railways. Without the railway, the Jasper area remained the haven of trappers and outfitters until the federal government realized that a second railway to the north could increase tourism. Jasper National Park was established in 1907 and the railway was completed in 1911. Almost ironically, Jasper is now a more important rail shipping route than Banff. The north-south Icefields Parkway between Jasper and Banff was built only in the late 1930s as a make-work project during the Depression, and the east-west Yellowhead Highway wasn't completed until 1968.

With more than a thousand kilometres of trails, Jasper is known for its long backcountry hikes along the extended ridges and valleys throughout the park more than for its wonderful dayhiking possibilities. Despite this trekking orientation, many wonderful opportunities for less demanding family hikes exist, particularly in the Maligne Valley, between Jasper townsite and Athabasca Falls, and near the townsite itself.

Bounded on the west by the Continental Divide and by Banff National Park on the south, Jasper is reached most easily via Icefields Parkway from Banff, and the Yellowhead Highway from either Edmonton to the east or Kamloops to the west.

# Jonas Pass

**Level:** Difficult backpack
**One Way:** 54.5 km
**Time:** Three–four days
**Elevation Gain:** 932 metres (3,058 feet)
**Elevation Loss:** 995 metres (3,262 feet)
**Maximum Elevation:** 2,470 metres (8,100 feet)
**Trailhead:** Icefields Parkway (Highway 93) 8 km S of the Banff/Jasper boundary and Sunwapta Pass. Park on gravel Camp Parker access road on northeast side of highway.
**Map:** 8 (pg 87)

Like so many of the trails in Jasper Park, the Jonas Pass trail requires strong hikers to trek several days through delicate alpine passes far above the treeline. This gorgeous hike is recommended only for families with older children who are very strong hikers because of the elevation gain and, particularly, because of the necessity of hiking 19.8 km from the Jonas Cutoff campsite to the Poboktan Creek campsite in one day. The trail also requires a car at either end of this one-way trek or a willingness for one person to hitchhike back to the Nigel Pass starting point. Despite this hike's logistical difficulties and its limited appeal for younger families, it is included in this book for rugged families who want to revel in the alpine glory of the mountains at their best. It is a truly fantastic experience to hike this trail.

Recommended as a late-season hike to avoid encounters with snow, this 54.5-km hike actually begins in Banff Park on the Nigel Pass trail. Beginning on a gravel road that was once part of the Banff/Jasper highway, the trail arrives at the Camp Parker cabin and horse corral. The trail crosses Nigel Creek and then rises moderately through open forest and meadow to the treeline at Nigel Pass (2,195 m) with Nigel Peak (3,211 m) on the west and with good views of Mts. Athabasca (3,490 m) and Saskatchewan (3,342 m) behind. See the Nigel Pass description for more details here.

Descending from Nigel Pass at 7.2 km toward the Brazeau Valley, the trail crosses the Brazeau River at 7.6 km and then again at 10.6 km. after a descent over rockslides and flower-filled meadows. The Boulder Creek campground lies just beyond the west side of the Brazeau River bridge. Boulder Creek is crossed at 11.4 km as the trail continues to descend through the forest. Four Point Campground is reached at 13.8 km, just prior to the Jonas Pass/Brazeau Lake junction. This is the last campground before the long hike over Jonas Pass and is usually crowded.

Take the left fork at 14 km and begin a stiff 2-km ascent of 210 m up switchbacks that climb through a mature forest. The switchbacks reach timberline at about 18.4 km. The hard part of the journey is now over as the trail levels out and opens up onto the beginning of the long and wide pass. Travelling up the left side of the shoulder, hikers pass through a wide variety of shrubs, such as shrubby cinquefoil and alpine willows as well as many wildflowers, before finally reaching the 2,320-m crest of the pass, about 23.8 km from the trailhead. The leisurely, gradually rising walk to the pass provides

*Tarns on Jonas Pass*

ample opportunity to count wildflowers and to enjoy the dramatic yet subtle open spaces of this alpine zone. Mountain goats, possibly grizzly and sometimes the rare caribou can be seen in this area, as well as the more common marmots and pikas. The pass itself makes a good picnic stop.

The northbound trail stays level until 25.3 km and then gradually descends toward the right before beginning a steep, dry climb up the bleak talus slope of Jonas Shoulder (2,470 m), which is almost 150 m higher than the pass. The early, rough section of the trail to Jonas Shoulder is clearly marked by rocky cairns. The final ascent cuts clearly toward the rocky ridge. From the shoulder, look back towards Jonas Pass and northward toward the Poboktan Valley.

The trail then descends steep switchbacks over the talus slopes toward a soggy meadow. Upon leaving the slope, the trail becomes quite indistinct, but head in the general direction of the treeline, picking up the distinct trail again and then descending into a gorge on its eastern side. Once among the trees, the trail crosses Poboktan Creek at 32.8 km and follows it another 1 km to the Jonas Cutoff and the Poboktan Pass trail. A wooded campsite is near this junction.

From here on out the trail is easy, generally descending through the spruce and alpine fir forest for about 20 km to the Sunwapta Warden Station. Two km below the campsite (at 35.7 km), the trail forks with a lower horse trail. Stay on the higher trail above the creek and continue the descent. After passing Waterfalls Warden Cabin at 40.1 km, a campsite is available halfway along the route out at the 42.1 km mark. A small waterfall here makes a beautiful picnic spot. Another campground is available at 46.6 km. Crossing the Poboktan Creek bridge here and again within 1 km, at the Poligne Creek bridge, the trail continues to descend through a boggy area which is bridged in the worst sections.

A final junction at the 47.8 km mark leads the trail left down the final descent to the highway. The right branch leads to Maligne Pass. The trail continues to follow Poboktan Creek for the remaining 6.2 km of the hike. Just before reaching the parking lot, hikers cross the final bridge at 53.9 km. The total distance for this three- to four-day hike is 54.5 km.

# Wilcox Pass

> **Level:** Moderate
> **One Way:** 4 km to pass
> **Return:** 3 hours
> **Elevation Gain:** 335 metres (1,100 feet)
> **Maximum Elevation:** 2,375 metres (7,800 feet)
> **Trailhead:** Entrance of Wilcox Pass Campground, 3.1 km S of Icefield
> Centre on E side of Icefields Parkway.
> **Map:** 8 (pg 87)

Home of bighorn sheep, grizzly bears and golden eagles, Wilcox Pass is deservedly popular as a moderate day hike because of its astounding views of the Columbia Icefield and its easy access to splendid wide alpine meadows above the treeline. Children are enthusiastic about this hike because the views are so spectacular that all effort is forgotten.

The Wilcox Pass trail rises immediately through a lodgepole pine and spruce forest, but the grade is moderate and the climb only 1 km before the trail breaks through the treeline and flattens out, making a winding, gradual ascent to the pass between Mt. Wilcox (2,884 m) and the flank of Nigel Peak (3,211 m). As soon as the trail leaves the treeline behind, the Icefield comes into view in all its glory. From this high, open vantage point, the trail looks down over the glaciers, allowing far better views of this 325-square-kilometre sea of ice than can be had from the Icefields Parkway. As the trail approaches the pass, alpine willows, shrubby cinquefoil and other shrubs get progressively smaller, gradually giving way to heathers and gorgeous rounds of moss campion, which also recede to make way for other mosses and lichens in the stony pass. Mountain avens, vetch, globeflowers, pussytoes and buttercups are just a few of the wonderful flowers that bloom as the snow melts. Between spotting flowers and gazing at the Icefield, it is easy to forget to look up to the right. The snowy tops of Nigel Peak and Tangle Ridge are less dramatic than the Icefields, but possess a majesty of their own.

Wilcox Pass parallels the Icefields Parkway for good reason. When this area was being explored at the turn of the century, the toe of the Athabasca Glacier was fully 1.6 km further east, covering where the Parkway now lies. To get around it, outfitters like Walter Wilcox took this high route through the pass and down Tangle Falls on the north side of the Icefields Centre location, 8 km from the trailhead. It is possible to follow this route the entire distance, although most hikers stop in the pass to avoid requiring a car at both ends of the trail.

The trail is less distinct in the pass and is often wet and partly covered with snow until mid-July. Please stay on the trail and avoid wandering the meadows. The flowers and shrubs here are very fragile and take many years to grow.

*Wilcox Pass with Columbia Icefield across the valley*

*Angel Glacier hanging from Mt. Edith Cavell*

# Angel Glacier/Cavell Meadows

| | |
|---|---|
| **Level:** | Moderate |
| **One Way:** | 3.8 km |
| **Time:** | 1 hour |
| **Elevation Gain:** | 370 metres (1,200 feet) |
| **Maximum Elevation:** | 2,135 metres (7,000 feet) |
| **Trailhead:** | Leave Icefields Parkway either at Athabasca Falls or 7.4 km S of Jasper near Wabasso Lake and take Highway 93-A 14 km N from the falls or 5.3 km S from the Wabasso Lake junction. Drive 14.5 km up Mt. Edith Cavell Road to its terminus. |
| **Map:** | 10 (pg 96) |

The hike in front of Mt. Edith Cavell (3,363 m) to view the cascading Angel Glacier is truly spectacular. The glacier, which extended the length of the valley during the Cavell Advance just 4,000 years ago, is receding quickly, but the 40-metre thick wings continue to grind into the quartzite amphitheatre into the east face of the mountain while the shortening body of the angel still hangs impressively over the cliffs.

The trail is paved for the first 0.6 km as it traverses glacial moraines, entirely buried in ice just 150 years ago, toward the best viewpoint for the glacier. Here the trail branches. To the right, the Path of the Glacier trail leads down to the foot of this massive mountain, once known as the White Ghost because of its snow-frosted appearance, but now named for a nurse executed during World War I for helping English, French and Belgian soldiers escape the Germans. The mountain is overwhelming in its imposing size and dominates the entire field of view. The closer view of the angel and of the round-topped Cavell Glacier to the south beside icy Cavell Glacier Lake are extra advantages of this branch, which loops back over 1.2 km through moraines and a regenerating forest of willows and spruce until returning to the parking lot.

The left-hand trail takes hikers almost 300 metres further up and away from most of the crowds taking pictures below. Switchbacking up lateral moraines and into an alpine fir and spruce forest, this trail reemerges above the trees to provide stunning views of the glacier at 3.2 km from the trailhead. From here, the trail wanders up higher in a loop through the Cavell Meadows, which bloom all summer long with a fantastic assortment of wildflowers. Stay on the trails within the meadows to preserve these easily damaged areas. The counter-clockwise direction of the loop is slightly easier than going clockwise.

# Geraldine Lakes

> **Level:** Moderate
> **One Way:** 3.8 km
> **Return Time:** 3.5 hours
> **Elevation Gain:** 200 metres (650 feet)
> **Maximum Elevation:** 1,725 metres (5,600 feet)
> **Trailhead:** Leave Icefields Parkway at Athabasca Falls junction and follow Highway 93-A 1.1 km to Geraldine Lookout Fire Road. Follow this dirt road 6 km to parking lot near lookout gate.
> **Map:** 10 (pg 96)

Views of isolated and rugged Mt. Fryatt (3,361 m) are the major attraction on this somewhat out-of-the-way hike. The trailhead is 6 km up a slow and bumpy but easily passable fire access road. There are actually four pretty lakes and one small tarn forming a 9.1-km stairway up the valley, but the recommended hike is just 3.8 km to the small tarn between the first and second lakes. Trail conditions beyond the first lake deteriorate and are almost impassable when the trail reaches the second lake. Few families will want to put themselves through the tedious extra effort required.

Beginning immediately with a moderate ascent along a wide path, the trail climbs gently but steadily, becoming a bit wetter and more rooty as it progresses. Views are limited, but glimpses of Mt. Fryatt ahead and Mt. Kerkeslin (2,956 m) back across the Athabasca Valley are regular and inspiring. The trail, dotted with lily-of-the-valley, horsetail, hellebore and columbines, descends quickly to reach the first of the three lakes in this chain at 1.8 km. The views of Mt. Fryatt here are well worth the trip.

The trail continues along the west shore of the lake for 1 km and then climbs up 90 metres over large rocks beside a waterfall. Passing through an expanse of big boulders, the easiest route is marked by cairns, which lead to a small tarn too tiny to be considered a lake. This tarn, at 3.8 km, provides a good viewpoint of the lacy waterfall descending from the second lake and is likely the best place to stop for lunch before returning to the trailhead.

For the more ambitious, cairns continue to guide hikers beyond the tarn and up the steep 150-metre climb over the ridge to gain views of the second lake at 5 km. Hikers wishing to camp overnight can do so at a primitive campsite at the south end of the second lake at 5.9 km, although they will have to negotiate considerable deadfall and poorly maintained trail to get there. Bushwhackers can continue to lakes three and four, but families should not consider this option, as there is no trail.

# Tonquin Valley

```
Level:    Moderate/Difficult backpack
One Way:    20.1 km
Time:    8 hours or 2 days to lakes
Elevation Gain:    445 metres (1,450 feet)
Maximum Elevation:    2,105 metres (6,900 feet)
Trailhead:    Cavell Lake outlet into Cavell River, 12.8 km along
              Mt. Edith Cavell Road from its junction with highway 93-A
              about 5 km S of the Jasper turnoff.
Map:    10  (pg 96)
```

The twin jewels of the Amethyst Lakes are truly magnificent, dramatically backed as they are by the peaks of the precipitous quartzite Ramparts, which rise a thousand metres above them in a splendour of ice and snow. A classic backcountry destination, this trip can be done as a long two-day backpack by strong hikers, but families would do well to break the trip up into a three- or four-day round trip, stopping at the old Horn campground 6.8 km or at Switchback campground 13.3 km along the trail. The trail is also best done in the late summer or early fall when the trails are dry and free of plaguing insects, such as the horseflies that follow the horses travelling the trail.

There are actually two routes that can lead hikers to the sublime Tonquin Valley: the 21.3-km Maccarib Pass route and the slightly shorter 20.1-km route along the Astoria River. While the former is more scenic because of the great views from Maccarib Pass of the Trident Range and the upper reaches of the Tonquin Valley, it is also longer and tougher than the route up the Astoria River Valley.

To take the Astoria River trail, park at Cavell Lake and cross the bridge over the lake's outlet and begin taking a southwesterly course gradually downwards along the valley beneath Mt. Edith Cavell. The trail reaches Astoria Creek and crosses to its northern side at 5 km. The Horn campground is encountered at the 6.8 km mark and makes a peaceful spot for camping among tall trees by the river if the family opts to tackle the hike in several stages. At 8.2 km, there is a junction. Keep straight for the Tonquin Valley or cross the river on the left and head for Chrome Lake and the Eremite Valley, a popular 6.5-km side trip which also loops back to connect up to the Tonquin Valley. While the Eremite Valley provides spectacular views of glaciers, the trail is often boggy and not too well maintained.

Beyond the junction, the trail begins to rise more steeply, switchbacking to the right up Old Horn Mountain until flattening out at 2,100 metres and meandering through flowering alpine meadows which offer increasingly superb views of the Fraser Glacier and the Tonquin Valley to the west as well as the closer Eremite Glacier and Valley and Thunderbolt Peak (2,682 m) to the south. The Switchback campground at 13.3 km makes a good base camp where you can leave your heavy gear and make a daytrip into the Tonquin Valley the next day. A junction at 16.8 km offers hikers the option of heading right into the Tonquin Valley, which can be seen in all its splendour from this point, or of heading straight to the Clitheroe campground .1 km further along. Beyond this campground, the Surprise Point campground can be found near the southern end of the lakes. The route to Surprise Point, which offers excellent views of the valley, takes hikers past the warden's cabin and through marshy areas to the lake's outlet. Both of these campgrounds make excellent base camps for exploring the valley.

To get into the middle of the Tonquin Valley, take the right fork at the 16.8 km junction above Clitheroe campground and follow the trail above the eastern shore of the southern lake, keeping high above the marshy shoreline. The trail passes beneath Mt. Clitheroe (2,750 m) and offers superb views of the ridge known as The Ramparts, running 5 km along and 1 km above the two connected Amethyst Lakes. The trail descends to Tonquin Valley Lodge at 19.0 km (a destination for trail riders) and through The Narrows between the northern lake and a small tarn until reaching the Amethyst campground at 20.1 km.

This wide valley offers ample opportunities for wandering, exploring, picnicking, rock scrambling and kite flying. Most hikers, tired out by the long trek in, are content to sit and absorb the unrivalled beauty of this spectacular area. The rare caribou are known to favour this valley for grazing.

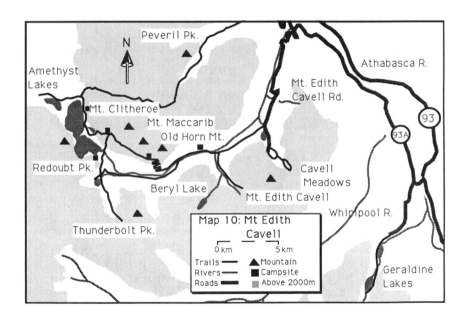

Map 10: Mt Edith Cavell

0 km — 5 km

| Trails | — | Mountain ▲ |
| Rivers | ～ | Campsite ■ |
| Roads | ▬ | Above 2000m |

# Lake Annette

**Level:** Easy    Wheelchair Accessible
**Loop:** 2.4 km
**Circuit Time:** 45 minutes
**Elevation Gain:** None
**Maximum Elevation:** 1,018 metres (3,766 feet)
**Trailhead:** Lake Annette parking lot on left side of Lodge Road, 1.5 km from junction with Maligne Lake Road. Turn onto Lodge Road immediately after crossing the bridge at the beginning of Maligne Lake Road, 1.7 km N of Jasper townsite.
**Map:** 11 (pg 98)

Close to Jasper townsite and popular as a swimming spot, Lake Annette also makes a perfect strolling and picnicking area on a hot afternoon. This flat trail around charming Lake Annette is entirely paved and is the only trail in Jasper that is completely wheelchair accessible. It serves as an easy introduction to hiking for very young children or for anyone with difficulties walking.

Beginning anywhere by the shore of the lake a short distance from the parking lot, this trail is a simple loop along the shore and through the succession forest of lodgepole pine, which began growing after a forest fire here in 1889. Hugging the shore for most of the hike, but occasionally heading through forests and meadows bright with brown-eyed susans and daisies, the trail gives good views of the mountains in the distance, particularly Signal Mountain (2,312 m) and Mt. Tekarra (2,694 m) to the southwest, Pyramid Mountain (2,763 m) to the northeast and The Whistlers (2,470 m) to the southeast.

Named for the wife of a park superintendent, this lake was created by melting glacial ice, but is not fed by glacial meltwater now. This means that the water doesn't have the same blue-green intensity as do the silty waters of glacial lakes, although some silts do enter the lake through underground channels from the Maligne Valley. More importantly, the lack of glacial meltwater entering the lake means that it is passably warm — up to 20°C — and is one of the few lakes that it is possible to swim in. A small beach has been added to the sandy shores to make swimming more pleasurable. Lake Annette is also known for its fine fishing. Rainbow and brook trout swim in its waters.

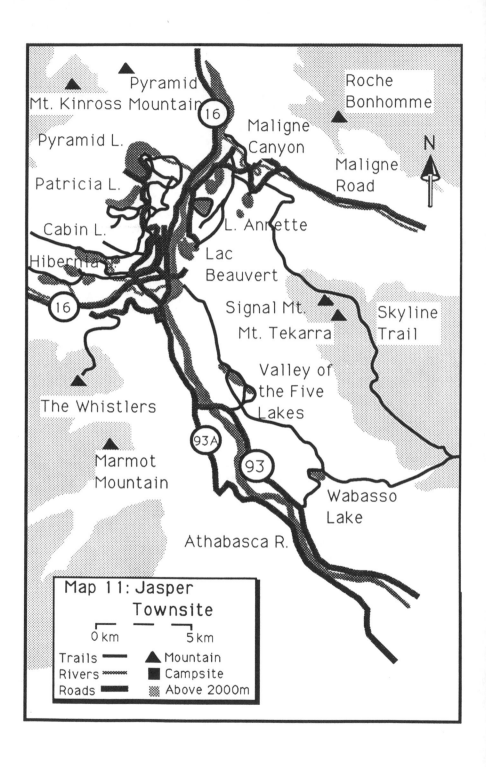

Map 11: Jasper Townsite

0 km      5 km

Trails ——
Rivers ×××××××
Roads ━━━

▲ Mountain
■ Campsite
▨ Above 2000m

# Maligne Canyon

**Level:** Easy
**One Way:** 3.7 km
**Time:** 90 minutes
**Elevation Loss:** 210 metres (690 feet)
**Maximum Elevation:** 1,240 metres (4,070 feet)
**Trailhead:** Maligne Canyon parking lot, 6.5 km along Maligne Lake
Road from its junction with the Yellowhead Highway.
**Map:** 11 (pg 98)

The longest and deepest limestone canyon in the Rockies, Maligne Canyon is so narrow in places that fallen boulders have formed precarious bridges. More water seems to flow out of the canyon than into it because, in addition to the waters flowing from Maligne Lake, an underground cave system serves as a mysterious escape channel for the waters of Medicine Lake, which spills over into an above-ground river only when its water level is exceptionally high.

From the interpretive signs at the parking lot, the paved trail descends immediately to the second of six bridges crossing the canyon. At 51 m, this is the deepest part of the canyon. The roar of the plunging water accompanies hikers descending from the rocky heights to mossy meadows and into a forest of Douglas fir and spruce. At the third bridge, just .6 km from the trailhead, the canyon depth is only 10 m and the cold misty spray spills over the bridge. Children are fascinated by this shower. Along the way, watch for potholes carved by circling water and channels that have been discarded in favour of less resistant routes. Notice ledges on the canyon which show signs of birds and rodents living on them. The fourth bridge is slightly further on at .8 km and it is here that most tourists stop. Between the fourth and fifth bridges, at 2.1 km, look for water seeping through the canyon walls. Some of this water comes from Medicine Lake, 15 km away. The trail flattens and the sixth bridge is encountered 1.6 km further along near the end of the trail.

Returning by the same route, it is all uphill, but benches are available for resting and viewing the chasm. Head above the second bridge to the first bridge to see the waters narrow and then begin their boiling descent through the canyon towards the Athabasca River.

Note that the chain fence ends at the third bridge and that all safety guards end at the fourth bridge. In the protected areas, the winding trail provides a lighthearted stroll that can be diverted by games of tag.

# Marjorie, Hibernia
# and Caledonia Lakes

**Level:** Easy
**One Way:** 5 km
**Time:** 2 hours
**Elevation Gain:** 100 metres (325 feet)
**Maximum Elevation:** 1,180 metres (3,870 feet)
**Trailhead:** W side of Jasper townsite on Pyramid Lake Road where it joins Cabin Lake fire access road just beyond a trailer park.
**Map:** 11 (pg 98)

Marked as trail #3, this quiet trail leads to three small but popular fishing lakes which offer possibilities for swimming and good views of The Whistlers (2,466 m), although most of the trail is enclosed in aspen, spruce and lodgepole pine.

Quickly passing a residential area and following a small, horsetail-flanked river on the right, the trail reaches an unmarked junction. Take either fork, for both turn toward an open, dry ridge where the trees have been blown or cut down. After traversing this ridge, the trail continues its way into a cool forest and gradually climbs beside a lush, green gully before reaching Marjorie Lake in 2.3 km. This lake makes a pleasant resting or fishing spot with a good view of The Whistlers.

The trail continues about .3 km along the north shore of the lake until it branches at the grassy western end. Continuing left, the trail arrives in 1.6 km at Caledonia Lake, the largest of the three lakes at 4.2 km from the trailhead. The branch to the right leads uphill to Hibernia Lake, 1 km distant.

Boats are for rent on all three lakes by prior arrangement with local tackle shops. The views and the fishing on each lake are equally good.

*Hibernia Lake*

# Mina-Riley Lakes Loop

| | |
|---|---|
| **Level:** | Moderate |
| **Loop:** | 9 km |
| **Circuit Time:** | 3 hours |
| **Elevation Gain:** | 180 metres (590 feet) |
| **Maximum Elevation:** | 1,240 metres (4,065 feet) |
| **Trailhead:** | Parking lot opposite swimming pool in Jasper townsite on Pyramid Lake Road near its junction with Pyramid Avenue. |
| **Map:** | 11 (pg 98) |

This pleasant trail takes hikers to two small lakes which are popular as fishing and birding spots and which both provide good views of Pyramid Mountain (2,763 m). Beginning opposite the swimming pool, the trail climbs quickly south up a hill known as the Pyramid Bench through a forest of lodgepole pine and aspen. Widening, the trail crosses the Cabin Creek fire access road at .8 km and continues on past a small pond and then reaches Mina Lake at 2 km. The trail follows the northern shore of the lake and saunters through the forest, beginning to curve back toward town.

At about 3.5 km the trail reaches a junction. The left fork goes up and down several small ridges for 1 km to the muddy shores of Riley lake. From Riley Lake it is possible to continue another kilometre to join trail #6, the Patricia Lake Circle. Returning from Riley Lake back to the main trail, the path continues through the forest, now dotted with Douglas fir and cottonwoods, for another 3.5 km, meeting the Cabin Lake Fire access road at about 7 km. Turn right here to return to the trailhead. Going left will take hikers on the long, winding trail #2, known as the Pyramid Lake Loop.

*Patricia Lake beneath Pyramid Mountain*

# Patricia Lake Circle

> **Level:** Easy
> **Loop:** 4.8 km
> **Circuit Time:** 90 minutes
> **Elevation Gain:** 60 metres (195 feet)
> **Maximum Elevation:** 1,210 metres (3,970 feet)
> **Trailhead:** Parking lot at Pyramid Lake riding stables, 3.5 km along Pyramid Lake Road.
> **Map:** 11 (pg 98)

This easy loop trail, designated #6 in the Jasper townsite area, occasionally shares its dusty, sawdust-covered path with horses, but provides quiet views of Pyramid Mountain from the lakeshore and bends around to survey the Cottonwood Slough, one of the prime areas in the parks for observing a wide variety of birds, as well as moose and beaver.

Beginning at the stables, the trail heads toward the Pyramid Lake Road, ignoring a junction with trail #2, which circles through the Pyramid Lake area. Crossing the road at .2 km and keeping straight ahead, the trail rises gently through aspens and spruce. It then joins an access road for a short distance and branches right to head downhill to the southern shores of Patricia Lake, 1.7 km from the trailhead. After edging along the length of the shore, which offers excellent views of stately Pyramid Mountain (2,763 m), the trail turns back into the forest and passes many charred Douglas fir, which have survived forest fires. The trail climbs gradually and passes two grassy ponds containing beaver dams. At the second pond, 3.2 km along, the trail splits. The right fork leads about 1 km to Riley Lake on trail #8. This side trip climbs three low ridges and can be somewhat wet and boggy, but provides more good views of Pyramid Mountain.

The Patricia Lake trail continues straight ahead to mount an open ridge that looks out over the marshes of the Cottonwood Slough and beyond to the Maligne Range across the Athabasca Valley. Keep straight to reach the Slough and enjoy the sights and sounds of the scores of birds that make this area their home, as well as the abundant pussytoes, buttercups and kinnikinniks on the open meadows of the ridge. The trail returns to the stables through the forest.

Patricia Lake was named for Princess Patricia of Connaught, daughter of the Duke of Connaught, the Governor General of Canada between 1911 and 1914.

# Valley of the Five Lakes

**Level:** Easy
**Loop:** 5.5 km
**Time:** 2 hours
**Elevation Gain:** 60 metres (200 feet)
**Maximum Elevation:** 1,095 metres (3,600 feet)
**Trailhead:** 9.5 km S of Jasper townsite on E side of the Icefields Parkway.
**Map:** 11 (pg 98)

This delightful circuit is the prettiest and most rewarding of any of the many easy day hikes to lakes in Jasper. Climbing immediately yet moderately over a low ridge sheltered by aspen and lodgepole pine, the trail soon descends to the lush green hills and marshes of the Prairie de la Vache at .8 km. A boardwalk carries hikers across the wetlands. Beaver lodges spot the grassy waters; this is a good place to watch for moose and waterfowl.

Across the water, the main trail meets another trail running perpendicular to the Five Lakes trail. It goes 10 km to the left to Old Fort Point or 6 km to the right to Wabasso Lake. Keep going straight for the Five Lakes. The trail ascends again and enters a lovely aspen forest with scarred bark obviously grazed by elk and a forest floor dotted with yarrow, roses, arnica and Indian paintbrush. Here, 1 km from the trailhead, the trail branches. The right fork takes hikers on a winding counter-clockwise circuit to the lakes, imaginatively named Five, Four and Three; the left fork descends quite directly between lakes One and Two.

Going right, the trail bops up, down and around small bumps and ridges until reaching the jade expanse of Lake Five. There are boats for hire and a tidy picnic site, complete with chopped wood and fire grate. Most of these lakes are dotted with these conveniences. The boats are locked up but can be rented for the day by making prior arrangements with private tackle companies in Jasper townsite. Continuing, the trail heads to the northeastern shore of the remaining lakes and cuts through the gentle slopes that dance with brown-eyed susans, wood lilies, heal-all, roses and many other delicate flowers. Despite the trail's low altitude, it offers wonderful views of Mt. Edith Cavell (3,363 m) to the southwest and the more westerly Trident Range.

The trail is clearly cut and obvious if you keep count of the lakes. The loop is closed by turning left between Lakes Two and One and crossing over a minor stream. This turn is not signed for counter-clockwise travellers, but thin Lake One is obviously the longest of the five. After cutting between the two lakes, the trail steeply ascends a ridge and returns to the junction. Children will enjoy following along the edge of Lake One a short distance, both to enjoy this beautiful, clear lake and also to bounce echoes off the rock cliffs on the opposite shore. The entire series of lakes provides an idyllic outing for picnicking, fishing and plain old relaxing.

# Wabasso Lake

**Level:** Easy
**One Way:** 3 km
**Time:** 1 hour
**Elevation Gain:** 45 metres (150 feet)
**Maximum Elevation:** 1,260 metres (3,700 feet)
**Trailhead:** 15 km S of Jasper on the east side of Highway 93.
**Map:** 11 (pg 98)

This pleasant trail initially parallels the Icefields Parkway and ascends a dry ridge to offer great views of Mt. Edith Cavell (3,363 m) and the Athabasca Valley to the west. Curving back into the forest, the trail follows an up and down course through a grassy aspen and lodgepole pine forest scattered with kinnikinnik, pussytoes, wood lilies and roses. After crossing a creek at 1.4 km, the trail branches left and rises over a dry, dusty ridge often dotted with brown-eyed susans and offering more wonderful views of the Athabasca Valley.

From the ridge, the trail descends into a cooler forest and curves to the left. A minor trail on the right leads to a small cascade which drops down a short gully. Winding through rocks and labrador tea to the left, the trail soon comes upon serene Wabasso Lake beneath Amber Mountain and the Maligne Range. Look for beaver and golden eagles around the murky green waters of this grassy, placid lake, which makes a great place for fishing or a picnic.

Most hikers return to the highway by the same trail they travelled in to the lake, but it is possible to skirt the lake to the north and join up with either trail #9, which leads north (left) 6 km to the Five Lakes, or with the steep Curator Mountain trail, which joins the Skyline Trail about 11 km to the east.

*Grassy Wabasso Lake*

# The Whistlers

```
Level:    Moderate
One Way:    1.4 km
Return Time:    90 minutes
Elevation Gain:    200 metres (650 feet)
Maximum Elevation:    2,466 m (8,100 feet)
Trailhead:    Upper terminus of the Jasper Tramway. The Tramway is
              located 4 km along Whistlers Mountain Road, which heads
              E from the Icefields Parkway 1.8 km S of Jasper.
Map:    11 (pg 98)
```

The hike to the summit of The Whistlers is one of the highest hikes easily accessible to casual hikers in the Rockies. The view at the top is a dazzling 360° panorama of the ice-capped mountains in every direction. Fortunately, the Jasper Tramway whisks hikers most of the way up in just seven minutes. The cost of the tramway is well worth it. Purists can hike the 7-km trail, which switchbacks up the mountainside, but no child will endure such brutal treatment while a tramcar slides effortlessly overhead every ten minutes.

The trail from the upper terminal lies entirely above the treeline and is almost barren of any vegetation. The route to the top is obvious: head up and follow the ant-like stream of people relaying to the summit and back. This well-signed and well-worn path does not offer solitude, but does give families a unique opportunity to get up into the highest of the high country. Most hikers stop at the first summit (2,394 m), but the trail continues to the east to the higher second summit (2,466 m). At the top, sign the guest register; it is also customary to place a rock on one of the stone cairns to record your visit.

Except on the cloudiest of days, the views are stunning. Most spectacular are the mountains to the south: Edith Cavell (3,363 m) in the distance and, closer, the Trident Range, including Terminal Mountain and Manx Peak. To the north are the Victoria Cross Ranges, to the west across the Athabasca Valley lies the Maligne Range and far to the east it is sometimes possible to see snow-shrouded Mt. Robson (3,954 m), 100 km away.

At best, the alpine zone is incredibly fragile. It can take up to twenty years before a moss campion can bloom; tiny trees below the upper terminal are estimated to be 250 years old. Needless to say, the heavy traffic in the area does a lot of damage to the moss campion, mountain avens, alpine willow and spring beauties that manage to grow on the sandstone and shale. Stay on the trail and watch your step.

# Bald Hills

**Level:** Moderate
**One Way:** 5.2 km
**Time:** 2 hours
**Elevation Gain:** 490 metres (1,600 feet)
**Maximum Elevation:** 2,165 metres (7,025 feet)
**Trailhead:** Terminus of Maligne Lake Road, past the lake's outlet and just prior to the dirt road leading to the Maligne Lake Warden Station. A parking lot is opposite the trailhead.
**Map:** 12 (pg 108)

Following a wide fire road for its entire distance, this spacious trail, despite ascending almost 500 metres, is a relatively easy way to introduce children to alpine meadows. The views are magnificent and the open freedom of the alpine zone is captivating.

Ignoring a left branch that heads to Moose lake at 200 m and a right branch at 3.2 km that leads toward the Skyline Trail, the fire road is a straightforward route up to the former site of the fire lookout. The wide road is easy to hike because of its gradual slope and openness. Wildflowers abound along the roadside. Halfway along the trail, spruce appear amid the lodgepoles and the forest gradually gives way to open meadows and the crooked krummholz zone of alpine fir and Engelmann spruce before abandoning trees for tundra and more abundant clusters of wildflowers.

Throughout the hike, the views are good, but, of course, they get better as the trail climbs and as the trees thin out. At the height of the trail, the hills afford a 360° view from the lookout area. Below lies the enormous turquoise stretch of Maligne Lake, and above it to the east lie the purple Opal Hills and the grey limestones of the almost vertical Queen Elizabeth Range, with Leah Peak (2,801 m) and Samson Peak (3,077 m) being the most prominent. To the south, Mt. Unwin (3,300 m) and Mt. Charlton (3,260 m) rise in icy blocks. To the northwest, the Maligne Range extends to Jasper townsite.

*Maligne Lake and the Queen Elizabeth Range from Bald Hills*

Take along lots of water on this dry hike. The hills are not too rocky and so any snow near the trails can entertain children as a slide. A reddish tinge in the snow comes from a common algae which is food for iceworms and other tiny critters. This is nicknamed watermelon snow.

# Jacques Lake

**Level:** Easy backpack
**One Way:** 13 km
**Time:** 4 hours
**Elevation Gain:** 90 metres (300 feet)
**Maximum Elevation:** 1,555 metres (5,100 feet)
**Trailhead:** Beaver Creek Picnic Area at the S end of Medicine Lake, on Maligne Lake Road, 28.3 km from its junction with the Yellowhead Highway.
**Map:** 12 (pg 108)

This rather long hike cuts between the Queen Elizabeth and Colin Ranges, offering an unusual perspective from behind their vertical grey faces. The trail also passes sink lakes with no visible outlet and crosses a watershed that sends water in two directions, yet the elevation gain is minimal and the trail is very easy.

The trail runs 4.8 km as a wide fire road, alive with butterflies, the occasional moose and mule deer, columbines, calypso orchids and labrador tea. The openness of the road allows good views of the sawtoothed Queen Elizabeth Range as the trail passes a stable near the trailhead and then Beaver Lake at 1.6 km. Long, green Beaver Lake is a popular fishing spot where boats can be rented. A picnic shelter and washrooms are provided.

The fire road ends at the First Summit Lake, which is usually the destination of mountain bikers who share the trail. The trail veers right and skirts through a forest of cottonwoods and lodgepole pine along the northwest side of the lake. The path gets wetter and lusher, bordered by bluebells and salmonseal and travelling over spongy mosses. Around the first and second lakes, the trail often crosses treed areas surrounded by a flood of dry gravel brought down from the fragile limestone slopes during heavy rainstorms or with spring meltwater. Both the first and second Summit Lakes are sink lakes with no visible outlet. The water escapes the lakes through underground channels in the limestone.

After the second Summit Lake, which is passed at 6 km, the trail zigzags across the narrow valley to offer good views of the Queen Elizabeth Range on the right and Mt. Sirdar (2,820 m) on the left. The trail becomes quite muddy for several kilometres, but is easily passable. Pinpointing the exact location of the watershed is an observation game children might enjoy playing. Where exactly does the water start flowing the other way? The change, which occurs imperceptibly near the third Summit Lake beneath the final edge of the Queen Elizabeth Range, is a hard one to catch, until hikers suddenly notice that the water is flowing downhill as they follow the left bank of a river. The trail soon leaves the river and heads gradually downhill through an enclosed forest until reaching a junction with the Merlin Pass trail, which heads up to the left at 12 km. Cross the bridge and follow the up-and-down trail to the right near the shores of Jacques Lake until passing through a gate and arriving at the primitive campground at 13 km.

The views from the campground looking back up the lake toward the hind end of the Queen Elizabeth Range are impressive, but they are even better just beyond the campground at the warden's station. As the first leg of the 176-km South Boundary Trail, Jacques Lake is nestled between three distinct and moody ridges, all visible from various viewpoints. If the warden is in, she/he can provide a wealth of information about the wildlife and trails. The horses, hobbled against running away and belled to warn away bears, are sure to enchant children.

A bearpole using pulleys is provided to store food away. Double bag all food and use an old canvas sack to hold everything: the poles are effective deterrents to bears, but helpless against the midnight attack of flying squirrels.

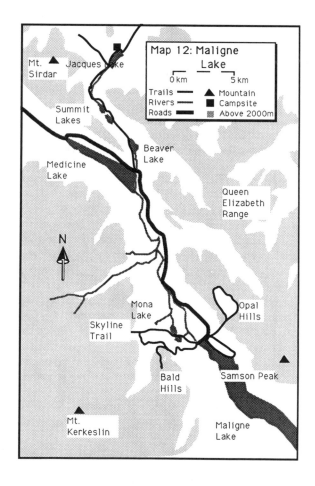

# Maligne Lake

**Level:** Easy
**Loop:** 3.2 km
**Circuit Time:** 1 hour
**Elevation Gain:** 10 m (33 feet)
**Maximum Elevation:** 1,680 m (5,460 feet)
**Trailhead:** Maligne Lake Chalet at the terminus of Maligne Lake Road.
**Map:** 12 (pg 108)

Known to the Natives as Chaba Imne, or Great Beaver Lake, and named Sorefoot Lake by disgruntled surveyor Henry MacLeod, this huge, beautiful lake got its name from its river. Jesuit missionary Jean de Smet named the river Maligne because of a difficult crossing near Jasper and eventually the name — French for evil — was applied to the valley and lake from which the river came.

Beginning at the chalet complex, the trail runs along the northwest shore of the lake past the historic boathouse, where canoes and rowboats can be rented, and past a grassy picnic site until reaching an interpretive site at Schaffer Viewpoint, which explains some of the human history of the area. This small point, named for Mary Schaffer, who rediscovered the lake in 1908 and who named most of the surrounding area, looks out towards the gleaming white Brazeau Icefield at the head of the lake and the twin peaks of Mt. Unwin (3,300 m) and Mt. Charlton (3,260 m). The view from here explains why so many people spend the money to take the two-hour boat tour down the lake.

Turning from the lake, the trail curves up a runoff stream and into a forest. A very minor uphill leads through a deadfall area and an enclosed forest with a mossy floor where red squirrels are often seen. Closing the loop in a counterclockwise circle, this part of the trail offers few views until reaching the junction with the Opal Hills trail, where these round and subtly-coloured hills can be seen. Returning to the lake by the path rather than cutting through the parking lot, the trail passes several "kettles" or depressions caused by broken chunks of glacial ice covered with gravel. When the ice melts, the gravel caves in to line the hollow below.

The best part of this trail is along the paved shore section, but the quiet circuit around to the kettles provides a brief glimpse of the geological variety of the mountains.

# Mona and Lorraine Lakes

**Level:**    Easy
**One Way:**    2.4 km
**Return:**    2 hours
**Elevation Gain:**    100 metres (325 feet)
**Maximum Elevation:**    1,780 metres (5,785 feet)
**Trailhead:**    Terminus of Maligne Lake Road, past the lake's outlet and just prior to the dirt road leading to the Maligne Lake Warden Station. A parking lot is opposite the trailhead.
**Map:**    12  (pg 108)

Fishing and a peaceful stroll are the major attractions at these serene lakes. These two small lakes are well known for their brook trout. The trail is also the beginning of the Skyline Trail, one of the most scenic high routes in Jasper. Despite the popularity of the trail, these lakes are tranquil respites from the crowds at roadside destinations.

Winding gently through a lodgepole forest, the trail passes by dry "kettles" or bowls left by broken chunks of glacier that have melted and left indentations in the moraine. The moderate uphill trail is quite easy, but offers only glimpses of the Bald Hills to the east and the Opal Hills to the west. At 2.1 km, a spur to the left takes you across two bridges over an island to a small peninsula on Lorraine Lake. The smaller of the two lakes, it offers a peaceful place for a picnic or an afternoon's fishing beneath partial views of the Bald Hills. After returning to the main trail, head further to Mona Lake, which is gained at 2.4 km following a spur trail to the right. Mona Lake is deeper and much larger than Lorraine and offers fine views of the Queen Elizabeth Range. Views through the forest are better on the return trip than on the way in.

*Lorraine Lake*

# Opal Hills

```
Level:    Moderate/Difficult
Loop:     8.2 km
Circuit Time:   4.5 hours
Elevation Gain:    460 m (1,500 feet)
Maximum Elevation:    2,200 m (7,150 feet)
Trailhead:    Uppermost parking lot at Maligne Lake at the terminus of
              Maligne Lake Road.
Map:    12  (pg 108)
```

This steep hike requires a lot of stamina to get to the top, but the spectacular views across Maligne Lake to the Bald Hills, the Brazeau Icefield, which feeds Maligne Lake, as well as the subtle purples of Opal Peak and the wildflowered hues of the alpine meadows make this a "grunt" worth doing.

Passing through a forest and a right fork at .2 km, the trail heads straight, skirting by a flat, grassy meadow. The easy beginning of this trail is deceptive. After the meadow, the route begins its stiff ascent through a thick lodgepole pine forest. It switchbacks up the slope for more than 1 km, often breaking off into many branches which are all attempts to find an easier ascent to the same destination. Around 1.2 km, the trail eases off but continues to climb until reaching a junction at 1.6 km. The loop begins here. To the right lies a quicker but steeper ascent to the hills, while to the left the loop route is slightly more gradual, but requires a longer wait before getting to the best scenery.

Heading right is the best option because hikers get above the treeline and into the scenery faster. It also makes the descent shallower, saving knees as hikers brace themselves down switchbacks. Once above the treeline within 2.6 km of the trailhead, the hard part is over and the hills are there to enjoy. Often spotted with snow into mid-summer, the purple hills are beautiful in their severity and their contrast with the green heathers and mosses hugging the meadows. Moose and grizzly bears can sometimes be seen in this gorgeous area. The summit is reached at 3.2 km. From here there are superb views of the Bald Hills, the double peaks of Mt. Unwin (3,300 m) and Mt. Charlton (3,260 m), and the Brazeau Icefield.

The trail continues across a gully and then onto the flat meadows between Opal Peak on the east and a large hill on the west. Curving around this knoll, the trail begins its moderate descent into the forest at 4.7 km until rejoining the trail at the 1.6 km junction. The remaining descent is quite steep until levelling off at the meadows.

There is no water on the trail except for a minor runoff stream in early summer at the gully just after emerging above the treeline. Be sure to take lots of water along on this thirsty hike. This hike is best done in the late summer and fall to avoid the famously vicious mosquitos that swarm here.

# 8 // Yoho

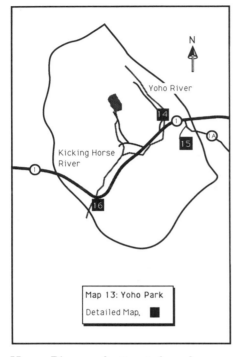

Map 13: Yoho Park
Detailed Map.

"Yoho" is a Native expression of wonder. Although Yoho National Park is the smallest of the four contiguous parks with an area of only 1,313 square kilometres, its dramatic peaks, turquoise lakes, white waterfalls and massive icefields help the park live up to its name.

Like Banff and Jasper parks, Yoho's history is linked to the Canadian Pacific Railroad. The precipitous Kicking Horse Pass, named for an incident in which James Hector, the discoverer of the pass, was almost killed by a horse, was chosen as the preferred route over the Continental Divide instead of the northern Yellowhead route in 1881, even though the initial grade was the steepest ever built for a commercial railway. The railway was completed in 1884. The small town of Field was established near the flat alluvial fan of Kicking Horse River and attracted explorers and railway workers. In 1886, sixteen square kilometres were set aside as the Mount Stephen Reserve, substantiating claims that Yoho is Canada's second national park, even though it didn't achieve national park status until 1911.

Although Yoho Park has only 400 km of trails, it is one of the prime hikers' destinations in the four parks. There are many steep trails too difficult for children, but family hikers will find plenty of options in this intimate park. The most popular trails focus on the Yoho Valley and the Lake O'Hara area. Hikes in the Emerald Lake area connect with Yoho Valley hikes, and other popular hikes leave from the Trans-Canada Highway, which cuts through the park.

Yoho is also known as the site of the Burgess Shale. This area was made a World Heritage Site to mark the significance of the rare soft-bodied fossils found in this shale and at the Stephen Fossil Beds. Research on these areas is still being conducted by paleontologists, and access is restricted. Hikers are permitted in the fossil beds only with qualified guides.

Field is the only town in the park. Primarily a residential town for park residents, it is currently almost undeveloped and offers only a few essentials such as information, gas and light lunches. Development in this town is rumoured to be lurking in the near future. Already, there is an excellent visitors' centre, complete with playground, to lure families off the highway.

# Emerald Lake

> **Level:** Easy
> **Loop:** 5.2 km
> **Time:** 2 hours
> **Elevation Gain:** 10 metres (30 feet)
> **Maximum Elevation:** 1,312 metres (2,740 feet)
> **Trailhead:** The Emerald Lake Road is 2.6 km W of Field on the Trans-Canada Highway. Take this road right and follow it until it ends at the Emerald Lake parking lot, where the trail begins at the N end.
> **Map:** 14 (pg 115)

This jewel of a lake is one of the most aptly named in the parks. These gorgeous waters take their emerald-green colour from the silt and rockflour washed into the lake by the meltwater of the Emerald Glacier. Quiet and sheltered, this trail is very popular with day hikers, particularly because of its proximity to the picturesque Emerald Lake Lodge. The trail is also shared at several points with strings of trail riders on horseback. Rented canoes dot the lake.

The 5.2-km circuit around Emerald Lake is almost flat and curves closely around the entire shore of the lake. Going in a counter-clockwise direction, this trail is paved for .5 km until it reaches the first avalanche slope on the dry western shore of the lake. Thereafter, the trail is very flat with a surface of small gravel; it should be wheelchair accessible until reaching the Emerald Basin junction on the north shore at 2.3 km. From the western shore there are good views back toward the lodge and to Wapta Mountain (2,788 m) and Mt. Burgess (2,599 m). The trail continues past roses, low shrubs and slender trees until reaching a junction with the Emerald Basin trail at the beginning of the alluvial fan found at the north end of the lake, just 1.6 km from the trailhead. Hikers heading around the lake keep right.

The fan, comprised of gravel and debris brought down from the Emerald Glacier, is alive with willows, asters, daisies, harebells and shrubby cinquefoil. The fan offers good views of the President Range to the north and Mts. Wapta and Burgess to the east. The area is often flooded, particularly early in the season and after heavy rains, but the well-built and bridged trail avoids most of the water. At the eastern end of the fan, the Yoho Pass trail leaves the main circuit at 2.3 km by heading left up through the forest between Mt. Wapta and Michael Peak. Here also, an unusual silt delta is building up over the gravel alluvial fan.

Closing the loop, the trail heads onto a narrow, rooty footpath which takes hikers into the wet forest on the eastern side of the lake. This protected forest of cedar, hemlock, Douglas fir and spruce has a slightly boggy floor covered in mosses and horsetails, a marked contrast to the drier western shore. In June and July, look for at least four species of rare orchids that grow in this damp area. The trail winds slightly up and down as it heads toward the lodge. The Burgess Pass junction heads upwards to the left at 4.0 km and the trail reaches the lodge by descending a flight of stairs at 5.0 km. It returns to the parking lot after meandering through the lodge facilities.

This easy hike is one of the most delightful in Yoho Park. It is highly recommended as a casual stroll for novice hikers who want to see the mountain lakes at their best. Less crowded than Lake Louise and more hikeable than Moraine Lake, this little gem epitomizes the splendour of the mountains. Dolly Varden, char, and brook and rainbow trout swim these icy waters and the fishing is quite good here. Trail riding and canoeing are other options families might like to try.

The lake derives its name from its colour. Lake Louise originally held the name, but when it was renamed to honour Princess Louise, the name was given, most appropriately, to this lake. Emerald Lake could once be seen on the back of the Canadian $10 bill.

*Emerald Lake looking toward Emerald Park and Mt. Carnarvon*

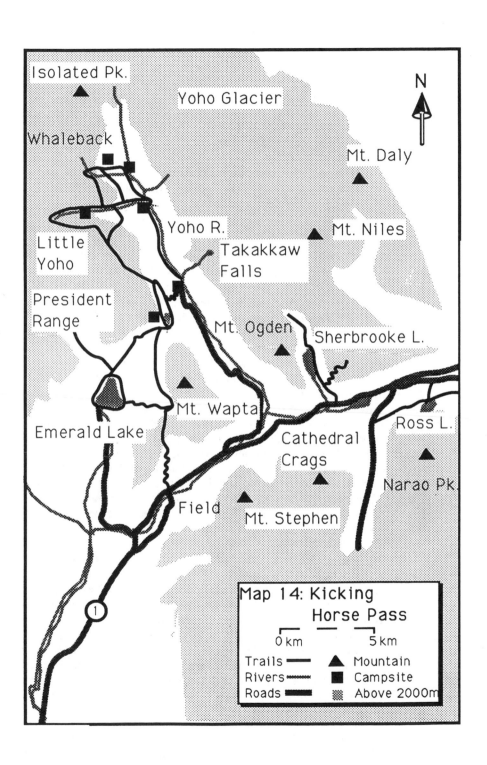

Isolated Pk.

Yoho Glacier

Whaleback

Mt. Daly

Little
Yoho

Yoho R.

Takakkaw
Falls

Mt. Niles

President
Range

Mt. Ogden

Sherbrooke L.

Emerald Lake

Mt. Wapta

Ross L.

Cathedral
Crags

Narao Pk.

Field

Mt. Stephen

N

**Map 14: Kicking
Horse Pass**

0 km          5 km

Trails ———       ▲ Mountain
Rivers ∾∾∾∾∾     ■ Campsite
Roads ▬▬▬       ▨ Above 2000m

1

# Iceline

**Level:** Difficult
**Loop:** 21.8 km to Little Yoho Valley and back
**Time:** 8 hours
**Elevation Gain:** 695 metres (2,280 feet)
**Elevation Loss:** 135 metres (450 feet)
**Maximum Elevation:** 2,220 metres (7,280 feet)
**Trailhead:** Whiskey Jack Youth Hostel, 12.5 km along the Takakkaw Falls road from its junction with the Trans-Canada Highway. Hostel on W side of road.
**Map:** 14 (pg 115)

This dramatic hike passes so high onto the shoulders of Vice President Mountain that hikers get exhilarating panoramic views of the most spectacular glaciers and mountains in Yoho, the Waputik Range. More than this, the hike glides directly beneath the imposing Emerald Glacier and enables hikers to see the terrain above the parks' highest waterfall, Takakkaw Falls, as its meltwater flows from the Daly Glacier on the opposite side of the Yoho valley. Much of the trail is exposed above the treeline in an area notorious for bad weather. This is a fair-weather hike only.

The Iceline trail is only a few years old now. Built to give the overused Highline and Skyline trails a much needed rest from heavy-treading hikers, the Iceline lives up to its name and traverses an awe-inspiring moonscape of worn rock and scattered glacial moraine. The very bleakness of this lifeless environment is impressive, especially considering that it is a barrenness created not by people, but by the sheer power of nature. It is an unparalleled aesthetic experience. The vivid contrasts between the bare gravel hills, the looming blue ice of the Emerald Glacier immediately above you, the open blue sky and the green meadows are unforgettable. The area is so huge that distances are deceptive; however, the up-and-down gravel trail is easy to follow and well marked with stone cairns. Be sure to look across the valley, where you can see the Daly Glacier which feeds Takakkaw Falls.

The trail begins at the Whiskey Jack Youth Hostel parking lot and switchbacks steeply up beneath Michael Peak through a heavily shrubbed track dotted with columbines, asters, strawberries and sunflowers. Continue right at the 1.1 km junction; the left fork goes .3 km to the Hidden Lakes. At 1.3 km, a second junction allows hikers to shortcut right for the Iceline or go straight ahead for a loop around Yoho Lake, which emerges again further along the Iceline trail. Keep right. The trail continues to rise steadily. Watch Takakkaw Falls across the valley; eventually hikers can see above the top of the falls and get a good view of the Daly Glacier. At 2.5 km, the Yoho Lake trail intersects the Iceline trail again. Keep right and ascend the avalanche slopes onto the moraines of the Emerald Glacier.

From this junction, the most difficult section of the trail is finished and the truly spectacular part of the hike begins. Leaving vegetation behind, the trail climbs over the moraines to pass beneath the crusty and rounded toes of the Emerald Glacier. The wind blows coldly off the glacier rising immediately above the trail, even on warm days, so be sure to take along warm clothing. The trail

*Crossing a snow bridge on the Iceline*

continues to climb up and over the rocky landscape of glacial leftovers on an easily followed trail marked by cairns. Across this bleak slope, the hiking goes quickly because of children's enthusiasm for being in such high places. Few obstacles are encountered. You may need to hop across runoff streams at 4.6 and 5.6 km. There may also be snow to traverse, even late in the season. None of this should prove difficult even for smaller children.

At 5.7 km, a trail connecting to the Highline and Twin Falls trails branches downhill to the right. If intent on backpacking in the Little Yoho Valley, keep ascending to the left until reaching the highest moraine at 2,210 m, 6.4 km from the trailhead. As on most of this alpine stretch, the views above to the President Range and across the valley to the Waputik Icefield are excellent here. Mt. McArthur and Isolate Peak (3,015 m) on the Glacier des Poilus of the Wapta Icefield are also easily viewed at this high point.

From here the trail descends across moraines to a small lake at 7.4 km before heading west and reentering the forest by following the old Skyline trail to its end at the Little Yoho River, 10.2 km from the trailhead. Cross the river here and head a further .2 km up the valley to reach the Little Yoho campground. Returning to the trailhead from the campground, follow the Little Yoho Valley trail down the river 5.5 km to Laughing Falls and then a further 4.9 km to Takakkaw Falls. See the Twin Falls and Little Yoho Valley trails for more detailed descriptions. From Takakkaw Falls, hike a further 1 km along the road to return to the Whiskey Jack Hostel. The total distance for this loop is 21.8 km.

For strong day hiking families or those wishing to camp at either Twin or Laughing Falls, return to the 5.7 km junction from the Iceline summit and head right down a switchbacking trail that connects to the abandoned Highline trail. Within 4.5 km, this trail works its way through mossy, damp forests, past Lake Celeste and crosses the Little Yoho trail. At this 10.2 km junction, either follow the river downstream for 2.1 km to find Laughing Falls and the 4.9-km hike out to Takakkaw Falls or continue straight for a further 3 km past diminutive Marpole Lake to reach the Twin Falls campground. The total distance for the Laughing Falls option is 18.2 km, including the 1-km hike from Takakkaw Falls to the Whiskey Jack Hostel. The total distance for the Twin Falls loop is 23.7 km.

# Little Yoho

> **Level:** Moderate backpack
> **One Way:** 9.7 km
> **Time:** 4 hours
> **Elevation Gain:** 550 metres (1,775 feet)
> **Maximum Elevation:** 2,135 metres (7,000 feet)
> **Trailhead:** Terminus of Takakkaw Falls road.
> **Map:** 14 (pg 115)

The Little Yoho Valley is a classic hike leading to lovely subalpine meadows lying in a bowl between the icy peaks of the President Range in the south and the Glacier des Poilus to the north.

The first 4.9 km of this trail are identical to the Twin Falls trail. See the preceding trail description for further details. By camping at Laughing Falls, it is possible to do both hikes by making forays in either direction on different days, or to connect the two hikes in a loop.

From the Laughing Falls campground, the trail climbs steeply through a heavy subalpine forest by ascending switchbacks on the northern banks of the Little Yoho River. The first junction making a loop to Twin Falls is encountered 6.4 km from the trailhead. Stay left; the right fork heads to Twin Falls via a low route. Three hundred vertical metres above Laughing Falls at the 7.0 km mark, hikers come across another junction. The right fork leads over the Whaleback, which has a summit of 2,210 metres, and then down switchbacks to Twin Falls. The Whaleback is often covered in snow late into the summer and is a route recommended only for families with older, strong children. Just beyond the Whaleback junction, at 7.1 km, is a junction with the southern section of the Highline trail, which heads left to Lake Celeste.

The trail continues to climb up the valley and gradually becomes more open, revealing better views of the Vice-President (3,602 m) and the President (3,124 m). At 10.1 km, the trail reaches an open meadow and an ACC hut known as the Stanley Mitchell Hut. Reservations at the hut can be made by phoning the Alpine Club of Canada in Banff at 762-4481. The campground is just .3 km beyond the hut. There is also a warden's cabin nearby, but this is only for the use of park personnel.

The meadows offer opportunities for relaxing and exploring, animal watching and games of tag. Strong hikers can cross the bridge beyond the campground and ascend Kiwetinok Pass. The trail to the pass is only 2.5 km, but gains 375 metres in elevation to an icy and windy 2,450 metres for a fine view of the Little Yoho Valley to the east and the Kiwetinok valley to the southwest.

# Paget Lookout

Level: Moderate/Difficult
One Way: 3.5 km
Time: 3 hours
Elevation Gain: 520 metres (1,700 feet)
Maximum Elevation: 2,135 metres (7,000 feet)
Trailhead: Wapta Lake picnic area, halfway between the Great Divide and the Spiral Tunnels on the Trans-Canada Highway, near Wapta Lodge.
Map: 14 (pg 115)

Fires caused by lightning strikes, railway construction and careless camping have all taken their toll on the beauty of the parks. Before modern methods of aerial surveillance were available, the only way to have an early warning system for forest fires was to post people at strategically placed lookout towers or cabins throughout the parks. Great for people who like to read, this job was lonely and monotonous, but necessary to protect the parks. The Paget Lookout, at a high altitude of 2,135 m, was one of these isolated outposts. Many of these towers have been torn down, but Paget Lookout remains as a window on a bygone era.

The first 1.4 km of this hike follows the trail to Sherbrooke Lake up a moderate climb through alpine fir, lodgepole pine and Engelmann spruce. At the junction, take the right-hand trail, which meanders flatly across treed meadows rife with wildflowers before beginning a moderately steep ascent over some avalanche slides and up into the subalpine zone on the south side of Paget Peak. Climbing east and west up the slope into the subalpine zone, notice the dwarfed and twisted alpine fir and whitebark pine of the krummholz zone. There are also several Douglas fir trees, which usually grow at lower, damper elevations.

The trail gets steeper toward the top, but the views become increasingly good as hikers gain altitude. Upon reaching the lookout (which is open), the effort to get there will be rewarded by a magnificent panorama. To the west lie the pale turquoise waters of Sherbrooke Lake, banked by the precipitous scree slopes and cliffs of Mt. Ogden (2,550 m). To the north are the gleaming white Waputik and Wapta Icefields; to the far east lies the Bow Valley to Mt. Richardson (3,086 m) in the Slate Range in Banff Park; across the Kicking Horse Valley to the southeast stands magnificent Cathedral Mountain (3,189 m) and the peaks of the Lake O'Hara area and, far to the west, the lower mountains of the Van Horne Range. This 360° panorama is well worth the extra push needed to get up to this altitude. On top of all this, the lookout site is usually dotted with wildflowers and often frequented by mountain goats.

# Ross Lake

**Level:** Easy
**One Way:** 1.3 km
**Time:** 30 minutes
**Elevation Gain:** 90 metres (300 feet)
**Maximum Elevation:** 1,735 metres (5,700 feet)
**Trailhead:** Highway 1A, 2 km E of its junction with the Trans-Canada Highway and just west of the Great Divide. Parking lot opposite trailhead.
**Map:** 14 (pg 115)

This pretty little lake is an easy, picturesque destination for young families, especially those who fancy fishing for the abundant brook trout that swim in its shallow waters.

Beginning on a narrow, somewhat stony fire access road, the trail makes a rather straight course beside a stream through an old subalpine forest of lodgepole pine, alpine fir and spruce rising above the forest floor, which is patched with abundant montane and subalpine flowers: columbines, labrador tea, strawberries, mountain avens and calypso orchids. The climb is very gradual. Halfway to the lake, the trail narrows to a footpath and becomes more rooty as it curves to the left and arrives, surprisingly soon, at the lake.

*Ross Lake below Mt. Niblock*

The lake is a shallow cirque carved by receding glaciers 10-20,000 years ago. To the west lies the round and flat northern ridge of Narao Peak (2,974 m), while Mt. Niblock (2,976 m) thrusts upwards more dramatically to the east.

Just before reaching the lake, the trail branches right and can be followed to the Lake O'Hara fire road, but the trail is rather unrewarding. Most people take the shuttle bus up. At the lake, the trail crosses a boardwalk (partly removed because of vandalism) over the lake's outlet and then continues a rather level 8-km route parallel to the 1A Highway flanking Mt. Niblock to reach Lake Louise eventually. This trail is seldom used by hikers because it is almost entirely enclosed in forest, but is often used by cross-country skiers in the winter.

# Sherbrooke Lake

> **Level:** Easy
> **One Way:** 3.1 km
> **Time:** 90 minutes
> **Elevation Gain:** 185 metres (600 feet)
> **Maximum Elevation:** 1,800 metres (5,900 feet)
> **Trailhead:** Wapta Lake picnic area, halfway between the Great Divide and the Spiral Tunnels on the Trans-Canada Highway, near Wapta Lodge.
> **Map:** 14 (pg 115)

This narrow lake is one of the largest in Yoho. Fed by the Waputik Icefield above it, this trail is a relatively easy day hike which gives hikers good views of Cathedral Mountain (3,189 m) across the Trans-Canada to the southwest and of the nearby rockwall of steep Mt. Ogden (2,550 m) to the west.

This straightforward trail climbs steadily from the parking lot past the picnic site. It veers sharply left at .2 km, where it meets a spur trail running up from the nearby lodge. Because this area is both moist and sunny, it is densely covered with ferns, strawberries, hellebore, buttercups, bunchberries and other flowers, particularly in July.

At 1.4 km, hikers reach a junction. The right fork heads flatly toward the moderate switchbacks leading to the Paget Lookout. Straight ahead, the trail continues to Sherbrooke Lake. At this junction, most of the elevation to the lake has been gained, but the trail still continues easily upward. The trail was formerly very boggy and wet, but has been recently bridged. Just prior to the lake, the gravel trail passes through a blowdown area, which formerly hindered hikers from approaching the lake, but has now been cleared for easy access. The lake is reached at 3.1 km and offers many small shoreside stopping spots for picnicking.

For families with extra time and energy, the icy-blue glacial lake can be skirted on its east side along its entire length of 1.4 km. The view back along the lake toward the Cathedral Crags is worth the modest effort. At the northern end of the lake, the trail scrambles over some moraines and then climbs along a canyon and waterfall to open alpine meadows wonderful for hunting flowers and for getting a closer view of the many waterfalls that plummet from the surrounding mountains. The distance from the northern end of the lake to the far end of the meadows is approximately 3 km. No trail goes along the western scree slopes that slide into the lake from Mt. Ogden.

The lake was named for the Quebec town of Sherbrooke, which was named after Sir J.C. Sherbrooke, Canadian Governor-General between 1816 and 1818.

# Twin Falls

```
Level:    Moderate
One Way:    8.5 km
Time:    4 hours
Elevation Gain:    300 metres (975 feet)
Maximum Elevation:    1,800 metres (5,900 feet)
Trailhead:    Takakkaw Falls parking lot at the very end of the Yoho
              Valley Road, which branches from the Trans-Canada
              Highway at the bottom of the Kicking Horse Pass.
Map:    14  (pg 115)
```

Slender and graceful, the Twin Falls spill over a high flat cliff in two snow-white arms which join hands again in the white crash of water eighty metres below. Although this waterfall does not rival the raging Takakkaw Falls for height and power, its distinctive doubleness makes it one of the most beautiful waterfalls in the parks. The scenic destination, the relative flatness of the trail, which stays in a valley bottom, and the wealth of side trips and optional loops combine to make this one of the best introductions to overnight camping in the Rockies.

This is a noisy and usually wet hike. Beginning opposite the foamy roar of Takakkaw Falls, which drops 380 metres into the Yoho River Valley below, the trail leads through a lovely walk-in campsite left mossy and damp in the mist at .3 km. At .5 km, a boardwalk travels most of the way across glacial deposits left behind by the meltwater of the Emerald Glacier. The bleakness of this chalky white alluvial fan is quite out of character with the rest of the lush, green hike and shouldn't dampen spirits or deter progress. After leaving the boardwalk, the trail continues on its flat course along a wide trail until it narrows at the 2.2 km junction to Point Lace Falls and the Angel's Staircase. As these falls are only short distances from the main trail, they both make quick and worthwhile side trips.

The trail narrows and climbs quickly and steadily up its only major hill through a dense, wet spruce and pine forest, passing Duchesnay Lake at around 3.6 (a .4-km spur leads to the lake) and then leading into a flat section of the valley bottom, highlighted by the gurgle of Laughing Falls at 4.9 km. This first section of the trail is relatively open and scenic, affording fine views of the Vice-President (3,063 m) on the left and Trolltinder Mountain (2,917 m) and the Wapta Icefield ahead and to the right. A small campground suitable for a few tents is perched on several islands of gravel outwash. It is a great place to camp for young families, those who have gotten a late start or families that intend to do a longer loop around the Yoho Valley. If imaginative family members have ever wondered what it would be like to cling to a rooftop in the midst of a flood, the fast-rushing water surrounding this damp campsite does its best to simulate that adventure during peak runoff seasons. The trail this far also serves as an entrance to Little Yoho Valley. See Little Yoho description.

*Twin Falls*

Beyond the Laughing Falls campsite, the trail branches to the left for the Highline, Iceline and Skyline trails. Unless taking these steep options over into the Little Yoho Valley, continue northward on the trail and cross Twin Falls Creek. Enclosed in forest, the trail is not especially scenic until the Twin Falls come into view. Half a kilometre before the Twin Falls campsite at 6.7 km, the first views of the falls appear suddenly through the trees. At 7.0 km, the trail branches to the right towards the Yoho Glacier, an interesting side trip to moraine fields some 3.8 km distant. Continue on the main trail to the left and down three switchbacks until reaching the campsite by the river. This campsite itself doesn't offer the best view of the falls, but provides a convenient riverside stopping place from which to make daytrips.

For the best view of the falls, continue past the campground and up steep switchbacks for another 1.3 km and 150 vertical metres to the Twin Falls Chalet. Opened by the CPR in 1923, the chalet continues summertime services and offers snacks and lodging for small parties. Watch for packhorses carrying in supplies for the hut in traditional trail riding style. Hikers can also continue on up beyond this 8.5 km turn-around point on the trail to a small campsite located on the flat limestone shelf close to the lip of the falls at an elevation of 1,980 metres and 2.7 km further. This last option is not recommended for families with young children who are prone to explore or wander. The cliff is an unforgiving precipice. Several people have slipped into the swift meltwater streaming from the Glacier des Poilus and have been carried over the edge. This is an area for extreme caution.

This is definitely a hike that will require rain gear. Being so close to the Continental Divide, this is one of the wettest areas in the parks. It is also an immensely popular trail, so expect lots of company.

# Lake O'Hara

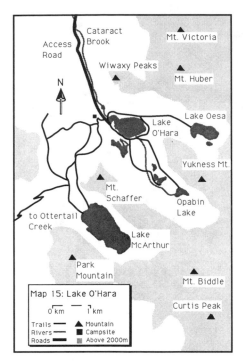

Map 15: Lake O'Hara

Cataract Brook

Access Road

Mt. Victoria

Wiwaxy Peaks

N

Mt. Huber

Lake Oesa

Lake O'Hara

Yukness Mt.

Mt. Schaffer

Opabin Lake

to Ottertail Creek

Lake McArthur

Park Mountain

Mt. Biddle

Curtis Peak

0 km          1 km

Trails ——        ▲ Mountain
Rivers ····       ■ Campsite
Roads ——        ▨ Above 2000m

The Lake O'Hara area is one of the most famous in the Canadian Rockies. With thirty trails extending 80 kilometres to more than twenty-five lakes, it is impossible to do the area justice. The three trails described here are just a sampling of the many hikes that can be done as isolated half-day trips or extended to link up with other trails radiating through this heavily used area. For more information, consult *The Magic of Lake O'Hara* or *The Wonder of Yoho*, both by Don Beers, as well as the area map published by the Lake O'Hara Trails Club.

Access to the lake is somewhat restricted. Few families will want to walk the 12-km fire access road or Cataract Brook trail to reach the area. The only other option is to reserve seating on a bus that travels the restricted road. Reservations can be made up to one month in advance by phoning (604) 343–6433 in Field. The cost is $5 per adult, $2 per child each way. Reservations for the 30-site campground can be made by phoning the same number and are highly recommended in this immensely popular area. Accommodation at Lake O'Hara Lodge can be arranged by phoning (403) 762–2118 or (604) 343–6418; reservations for the ACC-run Elizabeth Parker Hut can be made by phoning (403) 762–4481 in Banff. All of these facilities are booked up well in advance.

# Lake McArthur

Level:  Moderate
One Way:  3.5 km
Time:  1.5 hours
Elevation Gain:  310 metres (1,025 feet)
Maximum Elevation:  2,345 metres (7,700 feet)
Trailhead:  Lake O'Hara warden cabin, on W side of access road.
Map:  15 (pg 124)

Lake McArthur remains one of the most popular hiking destinations in the Lake O'Hara area because it is both the bluest and largest of the lakes. Its deep colour is the result of the lake's 85-metre depth. Dropped beneath the Hungabee Glacier on Mt. Biddle and accented by stands of larch which turn a brilliant orange in the fall, Lake McArthur is an exceptionally picturesque destination.

The trail to the lake rises only a modest 310 metres, but it takes hikers to one of the higher day hiking elevations in the area. It is also a trail that requires attention, as it intersects many junctions which lead to other destinations. Starting at the warden's cabin, the trail climbs moderately, ignoring a left-branching fork known as the Big Larch route to Schaffer Lake at .3 km. Continuing right, the trail enters the area known as the Alpine Meadow at .6 km. At the ACC-operated Elizabeth Parker Hut, head left for the lake and begin a steep uphill ascent through a dense subalpine forest. Just before reaching Schaffer Lake, the Big Larch route rejoins the Lake McArthur trail on the left at 1.5 km, and the Odaray Plateau route forks to the right beyond the bridge of the Schaffer Lake outlet. Keep left at Schaffer Lake, 1.6 km from the trailhead, ignoring both the right-tending Odaray Plateau and the McArthur Pass trails.

Beyond these junctions, the trail heads left around the shore of Schaffer Lake and then switchbacks up a larch-bordered stone stairway and edges along a rockslide on Mt. Schaffer. Another junction at 2.4 km offers hikers a choice of taking the more scenic high route to the lake over boulders and ridges or the less exposed route over McArthur Pass. If snow remains in the area, or if the weather is poor, take the lower route. The high route climbs steeply to a maximum elevation of 2,345 m at 3.0 km and then descends through meadows alive with Indian paintbrush, moss campion, pasque flowers and pussytoes toward the larch-fringed lake almost 100 m below and .5 km from the summit, 3.5 km from the trailhead. The lower trail breaks from the main trail at 2.4 km and heads northwest toward the forested shoulder of McArthur Pass between Odaray and Park mountains. The trail loops toward McArthur Lake .3 km west of the pass.

The lake was named for J. J. McArthur, who discovered this lake and much of the O'Hara region.

*Lake McArthur from Mt. Schaffer*

*Lake Oesa beneath Mt. Victoria and Mt. Lefroy*

# Lake Oesa

**Level:** Moderate
**One Way:** 3.2 km
**Time:** 90 minutes
**Elevation Gain:** 240 metres (785 feet)
**Maximum Elevation:** 2,275 metres (7,460 feet)
**Trailhead:** Outlet of Lake O'Hara near warden cabin.
**Map:** 15 (pg 124)

This clog-shaped lake is frozen much of the year, thus deserving its Stoney name, Oesa, which means ice. Tucked beneath Abbot's Pass (2,922 m) and Mt. Lefroy (3,423 m), which both also serve as the backdrop to Lake Louise to the east, and flanked on the north by Yukness Mountain (2,847 m) and Mt. Huber (3,368 m) in the south, turquoise Lake Oesa is one of the most popular hikes in this sublimely beautiful area. The lake also serves as an access route for climbers attempting Abbot's Pass, so watch for climbers on the peaks above the lake.

Beginning at the outlet bridge of Lake O'Hara, less than .2 km from the warden cabin, head northward along the shore as if circling the lake counter-clockwise. The high alpinist route to Lake Oesa heads away from Lake O'Hara to the left at .2 km. This route provides spectacular views of the entire area, but demands that hikers achieve an elevation of 2,530 m at Wiwaxy Gap, and its exposed scree slopes remain dangerously covered in snow late in the summer. Avoid this route unless all family members are strong, agile hikers and unless weather conditions are excellent. Continuing eastward along the shore, hikers will reach the Lake Oesa junction at .8 km. Here the trail leaves Lake O'Hara behind and begins a short series of switchbacks up a rocky ledge. The grade eases once the height of this ledge has been reached. From this minor summit, the trail rises in a series of smaller ledges as it progresses towards Lake Oesa. Along the way, the trail passes Lake Yukness at 1.8 km, Lake Victoria at 2.5 km, and Lefroy Lake at 2.8 km. Each of these small jade lakes is smaller than the one before. Just before reaching Victoria Lake, at 2.4 km, hikers will note a plaque commemorating Lawrence Grassi, a trail-builder and warden here during the 1950s. At Lake Victoria, continue straight to Lake Oesa, ignoring the right forks heading toward Yukness Ledge.

The high point of the trail overlooks Lake Oesa at 3.0 km. At this junction the left trail heads to Abbot's Pass and the Wiwaxy Gap, while the right heads south to Yukness Ledge via alpinist routes. The shores of Lake Oesa are bleak and rocky. As such, the lake offers ideal opportunities for bouldering through the talus slopes, picnicking and watching the marmots and pikas, which prefer this nearly barren terrain.

# Odaray Plateau

> **Level:**    Moderate
> **One Way:**    3.4 km
> **Time:**    1 hour
> **Elevation Gain:**    280 metres (920 feet)
> **Maximum Elevation:**    2,315 metres (7,600 feet)
> **Trailhead:**    W side of the access road across from warden cabin.
> **Map:**    15  (pg 124)

The panorama of the Continental Divide as seen from the prospect on Odaray Plateau trail is justly famous, and entices many hikers up this short but steep climb. Starting at the warden cabin as many other hikes do, this trail shares the access route leading to other areas until reaching the Indian paintbrush, columbines and asters of the Alpine Meadow. The trail begins to climb moderately, ignoring the Big Larch fork heading left to Schaffer Lake at .3 km. Continuing right, the trail enters the Alpine Meadow at .6 km.

Turn right at the ACC-operated Elizabeth Parker Hut at .6 km, cross a stream in the meadow and then head left at .7 km to begin the steep switchbacks through a thick forest up to the prospect. The right branch at this junction heads to the Morning Glory Lakes, which can be viewed from the prospect. At 1.4 km, another junction is encountered. Keep right to reach the prospect rather than taking the direct route up to the plateau. The trail curves through the forest for .8 km and then cuts back left to the south to climb up to the prospect at 2.6 km.

Below the 290-metre cliff of the prospect lie spectacular views of the Morning Glory Lakes and the spires of Cathedral Mountain (3,189 m) beyond them to the north, Lake O'Hara and the stunning backdrop of Mt. Victoria (3,459 m) and Mt. Lefroy (3,423 m) as well as the other peaks of the Continental Divide.

The prospect holds the best views of the trail, but families wanting to go higher can head south along the Odaray Plateau to reach the 2,315-metre elevation, 30 m above the prospect and .8 km distant. It is likely best to ignore the spur trail, which climbs 1.1 km west to 2,530 m onto Odaray Grandview Ridge. The views are superb, but the route is easily lost on this exposed scramble. From the 3.4 km mark, hikers can descend on the bottom half of the Grandview route back to the Alpine Meadow or continue to head south towards McArthur Pass and Lake McArthur.

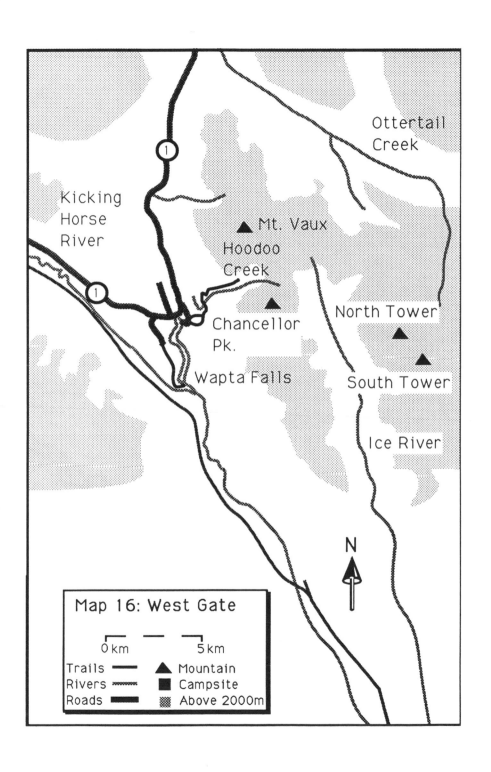

Ottertail
Creek

Kicking
Horse
River

▲ Mt. Vaux

Hoodoo
Creek

▲

North Tower

Chancellor
Pk.

▲

Wapta Falls

South Tower

Ice River

N

Map 16: West Gate

0 km          5 km
Trails ———      ▲ Mountain
Rivers ~~~~~    ■ Campsite
Roads ▬▬▬      ▨ Above 2000m

# Leanchoil Hoodoos

> **Level:** Moderate
> **One Way:** 3.2 km
> **Time:** 90 minutes one way
> **Elevation Gain:** 455 metres (1,500 feet)
> **Maximum Elevation:** 1,585 metres (5,200 feet)
> **Trailhead:** Hoodoo Creek Campground, 7.2 km east of the West Gate
> and 22.5 km west of Field. Park outside the campground gate.
> **Map:** 16 (pg 129)

Named for a Scottish manor, the Leanchoil Hoodoos (pronounced lee-Ann-coil) are the best-preserved hoodoos in the four national parks and are among the best examples in the world. Unlike those in other places, notably Banff, most of these tall, relatively recent sentinels still have their caps to protect them from the eroding forces of wind and rain.

The remains of limestone glacial till that has eroded away around the protected columns, these hoodoos can be reached directly from the campground or by following the flat gravel circle road about 1.6 km from the campground gate to Hoodoo Creek. Starting from the gate, this flat road accounts for half of the hike's distance and seems to contradict the steep climb ahead. Children's imaginations are captured by these strange pillars, making the tough climb worthwhile.

Crossing the wooden bridge over Hoodoo Creek, notice the immense amount of gravel that has been washed down by this minor river. The gravel and the yellow gorge above are testimony to the fierce eroding power of water and the crumbling properties of limestone. After crossing the creek, the trail immediately begins its steep, unrelenting ascent to the hoodoos, 1.6 km distant. Switchbacks carry hikers quickly up the necessary elevation gain, keeping the gorge to the right and offering good views of both the gorge and Chancellor Peak (3,277 m). Look for dogwood and juniper bushes among the lodgepole pine and white spruce. Calypso orchids and strawberries also border the trail. Small families of mountain goats might be seen along the gorge in the early season. After levelling out in a dry forest area, the trail branches into two trails that go above and below the hoodoos. The best views are above the hoodoos, so head up the steep switchbacks as far as you want. The trail will take you right beside and eventually above these towers in a short distance. Exercise caution near the cliff edge; the ground gives way easily and the drop is sheer.

Even in the early season, this is a dry trail, so take along water. Rough benches have been built in strategic locations for those needing a rest.

# Wapta Falls

**Level:**   Easy
**One Way:**   2.4 km
**Time:**   90 minutes
**Elevation Loss:**   30 metres (100 feet)
**Maximum Elevation:**   1,120 metres (3,700 feet)
**Trailhead:**   Parking area 2.0 km up Wapta Falls Road. This turnoff is poorly signed, but is 4.8 km east of the Yoho West Gate, and 1 km W of the Chancellor Peak campground on the S side of the Trans-Canada Highway.
**Map:**   16  (pg 129)

Unlike most hikes in the Rockies, this short nature hike goes down to its destination rather than up. Short by park standards, Wapta Falls is a very impressive waterfall because it is more than twice as wide as it is high. Falling only 27 metres, the falls are a broad 61 metres wide. Almost all of the meltwater from Yoho Park passes over Wapta's lip as the Kicking Horse River leaves the park. During the peak runoff times in the summer, about 255 metres a second flow over its edge.

Driving in to the trailhead, note the Leanchoil Marsh with its beaver dams on the left. There is a good chance of seeing moose and blue heron here also. The wide, flat trail faces toward the Beaverfoot Range outside of the parks and parallels an old access road now covered with progressively thicker and taller spruce and lodgepole pine. About 1.1 km from the trailhead, the wide gravel path and its many flowers are left behind and the trail curves to the left and into a lush, cool forest on a narrow track.

The waterfall can be heard for a long time before it is reached at the fenced upper viewpoint, where the roar of the water is intense. The best views can be had below the falls. Follow the long switchbacks down to the grassy beach. In the past, many people have taken shortcuts along the edge of the cliff, causing erosion problems and risking serious injury on the steep, slippery slopes. Avoid these and keep to the trail.

Once down at the bottom, notice the distance that the waterfall has receded upstream as it has eroded the cliffs of the Kicking Horse River and left angular islands in its path. You can get close enough to the falls to feel mist on your face. The flat beach is a great place for picnicking or for whiling away an afternoon by skipping stones and floating sticks in the turbulent water or hunting for rare orchids.

# 9 // Kootenay

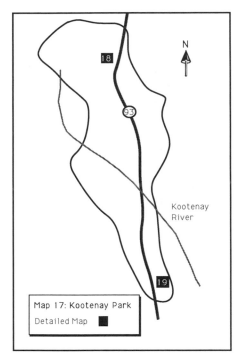

N

18

93

Kootenay
River

19

Map 17: Kootenay Park
Detailed Map ■

Kootenay National Park began as a commercially motivated venture to link the upper Columbia valleys to the Bow Valley in an effort to provide transportation routes for fruit and produce. The construction project ran out of money and was bailed out by the federal government on the condition that 8 kilometres on either side of the 94-kilometre highway be reserved as parkland. Under these conditions, Kootenay Park was established in 1920; the Banff-Windermere Highway, the only one in the park, was completed in 1924.

This 1,406-square-kilometre park, named for an Indian tribe (also spelled Kootenai), remains little-known as a hikers' destination. Perhaps it is overlooked because it offers only 200 km of trails and because the only town, Radium Hot Springs, lies outside park boundaries, tempting people to travel through the park rather than stopping there. Kootenay is indeed a small park, but it is incredibly diverse: where else in Canada can you find cactus and alpine meadows in the same area?

Hikes in Kootenay Park range from rugged backpacking trips to casual day hikes. Families will find that the northern area of the park near Vermilion Pass and the Continental Divide, and the area around McLeod Meadows offer the most suitable dayhiking trails. Most hikes in the Radium vicinity, apart from the Juniper Trail, go up drainage creeks and offer little scenic appeal, and so are excluded from this book.

Bounded by Yoho National Park on the north, Banff National Park, the Continental Divide and Mt. Assiniboine Provincial Park on the east, Kootenay Park is accessible from the Trans-Canada Highway at Castle Junction in Banff to the northeast and from Invermere on Highway 93 to the south.

# Stanley Glacier

```
Level:          Moderate
One Way:        4.5 km
Time:           2 hours
Elevation Gain:     365 metres (1,200 feet)
Maximum Elevation:      1,950 metres (6,150 feet)
Trailhead:      3.5 km W of the Alberta/B.C. border on Highway 93 or
                2.5 km N of the Marble Canyon information centre; parking
                lot in the midst of an obvious burn on south side of road.
Map:    5  (pg 68)
```

Most visitors shudder and drive faster upon seeing the immense burn that scars the Vermilion Pass at the north end of Kootenay Park. From the highway, this burn area seems to be an appalling, lifeless blight on the beauty of the Rockies. Twenty-four square kilometres of forest were burned here during a fire caused not, as might be expected, by human stupidity, but by lightning in 1968. Now, more than twenty years later, the skeletons of the blackened trees remain to remind everyone of the destructive power of forest fires.

The shocking ugliness of the area as seen from the road is deceptive. The hike through the burn towards Stanley Glacier is actually one of the most lovely and educational in the parks. This is now a naturally regenerating forest. Because the trees and their shady branches have been burned away, sunlight is able to brighten and warm the forest floor, allowing myriad wild flowers to grow. Fireweed, columbines, buttercups, arnica, Indian paintbrush and many more sun-loving flowers flourish here, especially in early summer. The trees are also reestablishing themselves. Soon after the fire, lodgepole pines (which need heat to open their cones and disperse seed) began to grow on the sunny mountainsides, and have become well established as a twenty-year-old forest.

The trail begins by immediately crossing a bridge over the Vermilion River. It then ascends eastward up the valley on moderately steep switchbacks, which weave through the charred spikes of the old forest and the hopeful flowers and fast-growing young trees that will constantly surprise and delight naturalists in the family. Listen to the dead trees as they creak and sway in the breeze. (Avoid hiking this area in strong or gusty winds, which can blow the dry, dead snags over without warning.) On the right side of the trail, look for the imposing limestone cliffs beneath Stanley Peak (3,165 m) which, especially in the spring and after heavy rains, leak countless small waterfalls from their 450-metre height.

After about 2.5 km, the trail crosses Stanley Creek, which flows from the glacier ahead. Here the trail rises above the creek away from the burned area and towards the imposing views of the Stanley Glacier. As you get higher by walking along the creek bank trail for another kilometre, the views improve and the forest thins out. Here you will notice a patch of older trees. These are alpine fir and spruce that were missed by the fire. Emerging from this section of the trail, the path becomes far more arduous and poorly defined. Within 4 km of the trailhead, hikers will find that the path has almost entirely disappeared upon reaching a spur that extends out above the glacier-carved valley. Simply choose your own path to the tip of this spur, trying to avoid stepping on plants and flowers. The view of the glacier is superb. Enjoy a picnic lunch to the music of the pikas and marmots calling across the bouldered meadow.

*Floe Lake beneath the rockwall of the Vermilion Range*

# Floe Lake

**Level:** Difficult backpack
**One Way:** 10.5 km
**Time:** 5 hours
**Elevation Gain:** 730 metres (2,400 feet)
**Maximum Elevation:** 2,040 metres (6,700 feet)
**Trailhead:** Trail sign on west side of Highway 93, opposite a highway camp, 22.5 km S of the Alberta/B.C. boundary or 72 km N from Radium Hot Springs. Turn off highway at sign and follow access road about 400 m to gate.
**Map:** 18 (pg 136)

One glimpse of the imposing mountains of the Vermilion Range on the western border of Kootenay Park will entice almost any family into the Floe Lake area. This 40-km ridge of limestone, that rises about 1 km above the lake and extends north and south, is known as the Rockwall. It rivals the more famous scenic areas in the Rockies for sheer drama and imposing grandeur.

Curving south from the parking lot, the trail descends gradually through forest and meadows to meet the Vermilion River at .4 km. After crossing the river by bridge, the trail begins its ascent above the river towards Floe Creek. At 1.7 km, the trail crosses the creek on a suspension bridge typical of Kootenay Park's attention to trail-building and then climbs steeply on switchbacks up the forested valley. The switchbacks get steeper but the trail finally eases off around 6 km. As hikers gain elevation, the views of the Rockwall ahead get better, as do the views behind to the Ball Range, which provides the boundary between Kootenay and Banff parks.

A campground at 7.8 km can be used as a base camp by hikers too tired to lug their gear up the steep switchbacks ahead to the lake, but camping at Floe Lake, with its magnificent views, is preferable for most families. Beyond the campsite, the trail climbs very steeply for 2.3 km and then eases off as the lake comes into view. From here, the terrain is easy until reaching the lake and campground at 10.5 km.

The powerful aesthetic appeal of this lake makes it a popular backpacking destination. Children can wander the shores, count the ice floes that have broken off from the glacier hugging the bottom of the Rockwall and observe the lagoon created by the glacier's terminal moraine. The larch trees that fringe the lake turn a brilliant orange in the fall, making a stunning contrast to the icy-blue water and the grey limestone of the Rockwall. A possible day hike from Floe Lake would be to head 2.7 km north to Numa Pass, an elevation gain of 315 m above the lake.

Hikers can gain access to the Rockwall area by taking this hike or by entering along Numa Creek or Tumbling Creek. All are equally demanding hikes. As a family hike, the Floe Lake entrance was chosen because the campground is closest to the hike's destination, allowing the most convenient access for exploration. Ambitious hikers can join this trail to the Numa and Tumbling trails to create a 54-km trek that could be easily done in four days. This hike, however, does not maintain its elevation once it has been gained, but requires climbing and descending Numa and Tumbling Passes.

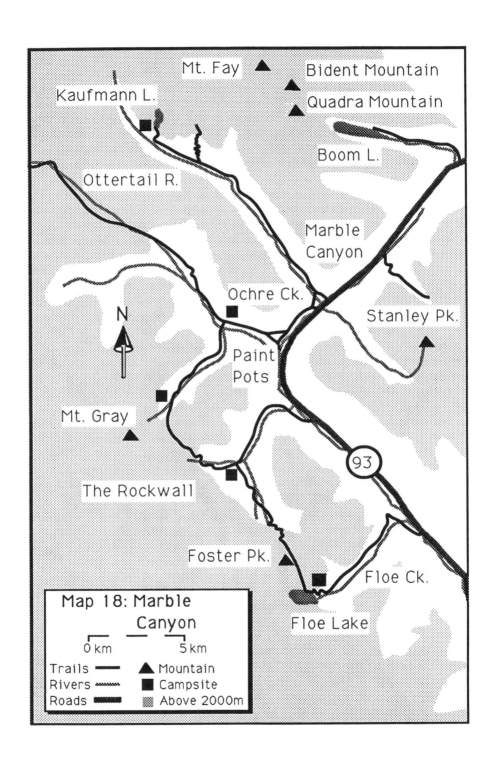

Mt. Fay

Bident Mountain

Kaufmann L.

Quadra Mountain

Boom L.

Ottertail R.

Marble
Canyon

N

Ochre Ck.

Stanley Pk.

Paint
Pots

Mt. Gray

93

The Rockwall

Foster Pk.

Floe Ck.

Floe Lake

Map 18: Marble
Canyon

0 km      5 km

Trails ▬
Rivers ∿∿∿
Roads ▬▬

▲ Mountain
■ Campsite
▨ Above 2000m

# Kaufmann Lake

```
Level:    Moderate backpack
One Way:   15 km
Time:     6 hours
Elevation Gain:   565 metres (1,850 feet)
Maximum Elevation:   2,060 metres (6,750 feet)
Trailhead:   Marble Canyon parking lot, 6.6 km from the Alberta/B.C
             boundary on Highway 93.
Map:    18  (pg 136)
```

The destination for this overnight hike is the lovely and secluded Kaufmann Lake which is ringed by the same mountains that make the Moraine and Consolation lakes so spectacular — the Wenkchemna or Ten Peaks. The trail is relatively flat for most of its length as it follows Tokumm Creek along the bottom of Prospector's Valley to the lake. The energy saved while covering the bulk of the trail will be much needed on the final 2 km of the trail, which are very steep. This last push is a formidable uphill grunt which will have the fittest hikers leaning forward and gasping for breath to climb about 400 metres of vertical distance to the lake and campsite.

The trail begins by climbing up an old access road that runs above but parallel to the Marble Canyon nature trail. At about 1.6 km, the real trail begins as it narrows to a footpath extending beneath an enclosed spruce and pine forest which offers few views. The trail opens up at about 3.2 km when it reaches the valley bottom and parallels Tokumm Creek on its northern bank. The trail is moderately uphill along the creek and crosses many open meadows and avalanche slopes blooming with asters, daisies, fireweed and Indian paintbrush. Hikers will encounter bridged tributaries at 8.5 and 10.3 km, but the trail remains certain.

The only junction in the trail occurs at 10.4 km, just after a bridge. The right fork leads up a very steep 2.4-km ascent to Fay Hut, once owned by the Alpine Club of Canada, but now operated by the parks. Free camping is available at the hut, but it requires a permit and a seemingly vertical ascent of about 700 metres. The hut is used mostly as a base by climbers.

Continue straight along the main trail through a landslide area at 12.2 km and then across several small but bridged streams. At about 13.5 km, most of the distance and all of the easy hiking is over. Here, the trail begins its gruelling climb up to the lake. Just before reaching the lake, the trail will level off to offer some relief.

This secluded lake shimmers in subtle shades of blue and white beneath the ice and scree slopes of the lofty Wenkchemna Peaks, particularly north to south (left to right) Deltaform Mountain (3,424 m), Mt. Tuzo (3,249 m) and Mt. Allen (3,301 m). A little hiking can be done along the lakeshore, but there are few other opportunities for wandering and exploring. Kaufmann Lake is a wonderful place to be still. Towards evening and in the early morning, hikers are quite likely to see mule deer and porcupines near the lake. Put all shoes and leather items inside the tent to prevent the porkies from devouring them.

# Marble Canyon

**Level:** Easy
**Loop:** 1.5 km
**Time:** 45 minutes
**Elevation Gain:** 40 metres (130 feet)
**Maximum Elevation:** 1,530 m (4,872 feet)
**Trailhead:** Marble Canyon parking lot, 6.6 km from the Alberta/B.C. boundary on Highway 93.
**Map:** 18 (pg 136)

Marble Canyon is a narrow, moderately deep gorge cut by the waters of Tokumm Creek as they plummet furiously downward to join the Vermilion River. Crossed by half a dozen bridges on a well-maintained path, the trail offers hikers an easy stroll up to the canyon's lip, where the water drops most sharply. Children have fun on the many bridges that cross over the canyon. Hikers can enjoy the cool forest and rushing water on this trail, but shouldn't expect to find any real marble. The canyon is cut through grey and white dolomite limestone, which vaguely resembles marble in colour.

Beginning at the Marble Canyon parking lot, the trail starts tamely enough at the lower reaches of the canyon, where the water is curving to meet the Vermilion River. However, the canyon gets more exciting as the trail climbs easily over slopes and stairs up towards the lip. Successively, the trail's bridges cross deeper and deeper sections of the canyon until reaching the final bridge at the far end of the loop at about .8 km, where the water drops 39 metres. In places, the canyon is exceptionally narrow and there are several natural bridges, left behind when the rushing water found an easier route downwards. These natural bridges are made of chunks of limestone, which were more difficult to erode than the rock beneath them, either because of natural properties in the rock or a flat-faced structural orientation perpendicular to the flow of the water. Throughout the hike, look for fossils in the dolomite and for the potholes left behind by miniature whirlpools.

Hikers can return to the parking lot by retracing their trail along the canyon or by looping back on a cool trail running above the canyon and sometimes used as an entrance route to the Kaufmann Lake trail.

# Paint Pots

**Level:**   Easy
**One Way:**   1 km
**Time:**   45 minutes
**Elevation Gain:**   15 metres (50 feet)
**Maximum Elevation:**   1,465 metres (3,613 feet)
**Trailhead:**   Paint Pots parking lot, 3 km S of Marble Canyon information centre or 9.5 km S of the Kootenay/Banff boundary on Highway 93.
**Map:**   18  (pg 136)

This well-signed and historic hike is fascinating because of vibrantly coloured soils in the area and the glimpse that it offers into the human history of the Rockies. The Paint Pots are three springs with a high iron content bubbling up in the midst of a clay bed. The iron oxides left behind in the clay as the water seeps through it account for the bright vermilion hue of the surrounding soils, which are known as ochre. The Native peoples baked the ochre into a powder and mixed it with fish oil or animal grease to create dyes for skin, clothing and other possessions. This dye was a highly valued commodity for trade and was a catalyst for much of the Native exploration of the mountains. For a brief time, ochre was mined here by white entrepreneurs in a failed venture.

The hike begins by descending to the Vermilion River which gets its name from the ochre colouring on many of its rocks. A bouncy suspension bridge carries hikers over the river. On the far bank, the trail butts into a T-junction. The right fork leads northeast to Marble Canyon, an optional starting point for this trail; the left fork leads toward the Paint Pots. Heading left, the trail passes a large, sparsely grassed field of ochre and then passes some rusty, abandoned equipment used in the mining operations at the turn of the century. Narrow mounds of ochre near these relics suggest that the last shipment of ochre was never removed from the site.

The relatively flat hike now begins its minor climb up the red-stained Ochre Creek to the grass-fringed Paint Pots. Here the water bubbles up through the clay, building their three bowls higher and higher as the iron oxides solidify around them. The Paint Pots trail ends here, although hikers seeking access to Tumbling and Wolverine Passes will continue west along Ochre Creek. Return to the parking lot by reversing the trail and enjoy the view across the valley to the east of the Ball Range above the Egypt Lake area in Banff. Throughout, the trail is well signed to provide scientific and historic information about this unusual area.

# Cobb Lake

| | |
|---|---|
| **Level:** | Moderate |
| **One Way:** | 2.7 km |
| **Time:** | 1 hour |
| **Elevation Loss:** | 105 metres (340 feet) |
| **Maximum Elevation:** | 1,370 metres (4,500 feet) |
| **Trailhead:** | Small parking lot 14.6 km N of West Gate on Highway 93. Signed from W, but not N side of trailhead. |
| **Map:** | 19 (pg 140) |

The hike to Cobb Lake is one of the nicest in the southern end of Kootenay Park, leading as it does to a beautiful lake in the midst of a river, rather than merely following a drainage system as so many of Kootenay's other trails do. This is a good hike to do on hot days because the forest canopy keeps hikers cool as they descend into the valley beneath Mount Sinclair (2,550 m) to the southwest.

The trail on this hike is quite straightforward, switchbacking downwards into the valley bowl rather than climbing up a mountain slope. While this 105-metre descent through roses, thimbleberries, salmonseal and columbines makes an easy beginning to the hike, the effort lies ahead for hikers, who will

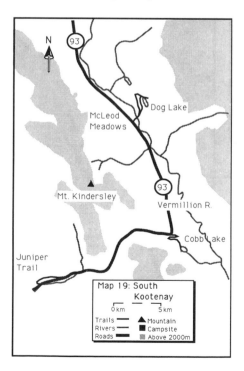

have to climb out of the bowl on their return journey. The switchbacks continue past charred Douglas firs which have managed to survive forest fires because of their thick, fire-resistant bark, until reaching Swede Creek at 1.6 km. After crossing the creek, the trail continues south on a gradual incline until reaching Cobb Lake. This pretty lake, surrounded by a mixed forest of Douglas fir, lodgepole pine and spruce, is calm and glassy in its sheltered valley. Several small grassy areas along the shore provide families with fine areas for picnicking, fishing and simply enjoying this peaceful respite from the world.

# Dog Lake

**Level:**  Easy
**One Way:**   2.7 km
**Time:**   1 hour
**Elevation Gain:**   60 metres (200 feet)
**Maximum Elevation:**   1,220 metres (4,000 feet)
**Trailhead:**   N end of the McLeod Meadows Picnic area, near the kitchen shelter; 26.4 km from Kootenay West entrance on Highway 93.
**Map:**   19 (pg 140)

This low-lying trail runs entirely within a heavy coniferous forest and is conveniently close to the McLeod Meadows campground. Offering only glimpses between the trees of the Kootenay River valley, the main attraction of this hike is a close-up look at beaver dams and waterbirds nesting in the grasses that edge the shore. The prospect of an afternoon of peaceful fishing also makes this lake popular with families.

The well-marked trail is best done as a straightforward out-and-back hike, but can also be done as a loop. Beginning at the picnic shelter at the roadside pull-off south of the McLeod Meadows campground, the trail heads through a meadow and across a bridge before skirting through the campground. Upon crossing the bridge, head immediately right, emerging from the campground by the campground theatre. Continue straight and cross the Kootenay River on two suspension bridges. On the opposite shore, at .9 km, the trail intersects a fire access road running north-south. Cross the fire road and head left through the thick forest. The trail climbs a long, moderate ridge through the mossy forest. Upon reaching the crest of the ridge, the trail flattens and veers right before descending the eastern slope of the ridge to Dog Lake.

The lake is barely visible until hikers actually reach its shores. The trail formerly led across a beaver dam, but now crosses the outlet stream by bridge just beneath the remains of the dam. The trail continues to wander the northern shore and gives access to the slowly foresting gravel flats, which provide good views of the lake and Mt. Harkin (2,982 m), named for "Bunny" Harkin, the superintendent of the Rocky Mountain Parks most responsible for the parks' emphasis on the preservation of wildlife and the natural environment.

The return trip retraces the rose-lined route to the lake. Another option is to continue north from Dog Lake beside the outlet stream until meeting the fire access road, .8 km from the lake. Then double back along this road for 2.2 km until meeting the trail again, .9 km from the trailhead and just before crossing the Kootenay River on the way back through the McLeod Meadows campsite. The total distance for the loop trail is 6.6 km, while the out-and-back distance is 5.4 km.

*Dog Lake beneath Mt. Harkin*

*Sinclair Creek flowing beneath Sinclair Canyon*

# Juniper Trail

**Level:** Moderate
**Loop:** 4.6 km
**Time:** 2 hours
**Elevation Gain:** 150 metres (500 feet)
**Maximum Elevation:** 1,185 metres (3,900 feet)
**Trailhead:** Parking lot immediately W of Sinclair Canyon on the N side of the road, .3 km from the park's West Gate.
**Map:** 19 (pg 140)

This moderate hike offers the greatest variety and scenic reward of any of the hikes in southern Kootenay Park.

Beginning immediately west of Sinclair Canyon, the trail travels on switchbacks down into the valley bottom, reaching it in .4 km. Notice the trail's progression from being arid and sparsely forested near the parking lot toward being a near rain forest by the banks of the creek. The lush, cool creekside is a refreshing change from the severe rockface. By breaking away from the main trail on the valley floor and heading upstream a short way, hikers can get an excellent view of Sinclair Falls as it chutes out of the canyon. Sinclair Creek carved the canyon, but has been contained within a tunnel running beneath the highway to tame this once forbidding area and make it an accessible transportation route.

The trail crosses the creek and then leaves the creekbed behind as it zigzags up the opposite side of the valley, which is even drier than the descending slope. Although treed, this dusty knoll is eroding heavily, as is the trail hikers follow. At 1.3 km, the trail curves around to reach the edge of the canyon's lip, where hikers can look for birds' nests on the opposing cliff face and catch glimpses of the cars travelling below. The trail continues to climb and reaches the summit of the canyon at 2.1 km. Look west to see the Columbia River in the Rocky Mountain Trench and the low, low ridge of Steamboat Mountain. Immediately to the north lies Mt. Berland and behind that Mt. Kindersley (2,697 m). Redstreak Mountain lies across the canyon to the south.

The trail continues east from the summit and gradually descends to the Aquacourt and Radium Hot Springs Lodge at 3.2 km. The trail officially ends here, but hikers must, after a relaxing dip in the 40°C pool, hike 1.4 km down the highway and through the sunset-orange canyon back to the parking lot where the trail began, making a 4.6-km loop.

Sinclair Canyon, its falls and creek, as well as Mt. Sinclair and Sinclair Pass, were all named after James Sinclair. Sinclair guided 120 Manitoban settlers through this area to Oregon in 1841 to strengthen England's claim to sovereignty in that disputed area.

# 10 // The Great Outdoors

## // Mountain Biking

Most mountain bikes in the parks never leave the main drags of Banff and Jasper. Their owners perhaps prefer to be seen seeing the sights instead of heading for the hills. But there are many biking opportunities in the parks for families with lots of enthusiasm and energy. Many paved roads near the townsites are quiet and suitable for family biking, skateboarding and even rollerblading. Mountain biking is permitted on many fire access roads and some trails, making many wilderness destinations accessible.

Most designated mountain biking roads and trails require a degree of strength and agility beyond the abilities of the youngest children. In this case, trailers can be rented to carry children unable to bike themselves along the trails. Most older children will find that they can manage the moderately graded inclines. Their progress will likely be slow but steady. Restraint is necessary on the way down to prevent children from going too fast and losing control. Obstacles such as roots, rocks and hikers make most biking trails quite challenging and safe only for bikers who can keep control of their bikes at all times.

Because mountain bikes can damage the fragile environment of the parks, biking is restricted to specific trails and fire roads within the parks, as well as all paved roads. They are never permitted off the trails. Some of these trails and roads offer wonderful cycling possibilities for your family:

**Banff**
- most trails in the Banff townsite and Lake Louise areas
- Johnson Lake Loop Trails — 12 km
- Pipestone Trail to old campground — 6.3 km
- Cascade fire road; Bankhead to Stoney Creek — 9 km
- Vermilion Lakes Drive
- Mt. Norquay Road
- Tunnel Mountain Road
- Bow Valley Parkway (Highway 1A)
- Lake Louise Drive from the Trans-Canada up to the lake is bikeable but not recommended for family cycling. The road is narrow and, windy, with a constant and heavy flow of traffic.

**Jasper**
- Palisade fire road — 10.8 km
- Geraldine fire road — 5.5 km
- Whirlpool fire road — 8.5 km

**Yoho**
- Tally-Ho Trail; 1 km west of Field to Emerald Lake Road — 3 km
- Amiskwi fire road to river crossing — 24 km
- Emerald Lake Road
- Takakkaw Falls Road

*Biking by the Bow River*

### Kootenay
- West Kootenay fire road; Crook's Meadow to Kootenay Crossing Warden Station — 10 km
- Kootenay Crossing Warden Station to boundary — 12.8 km
- Dog Lake/McLeod Meadows — 2.7 km

For a complete list of trails, see the brochure "Trail Bicycling in National Parks in Alberta and British Columbia."

Bikers are subject to all of the same rules and recommendations as hikers. Additionally, they are advised to wear helmets, travel slowly and carefully, and to equip their bikes with bells. Because bicycles can travel so swiftly and quietly, they are unexpected by hikers and wildlife. Using bells as warning signals, especially when approaching corners, will help avoid collisions.

Mountain bikes can be rented from several locations, including:

- Sports Rent — 208 Bear Street, Banff
- Wilson Mountain Sports — Samson Mall, Lake Louise
- Jasper Park Lodge — Lodge Road, Jasper

## // Trail Rides

Trail riding offers families a memorable adventure along scenic trails without the effort and time required by hiking. Usually restricted to adults and children over eight, trail rides operate out of Banff, Lake Louise, Jasper and Radium Hot Springs. Rides hired can vary in length from several hours to several days. Costs vary, but range from $14 per hour to $24 per half-day to $75–100 per day for longer treks. Among the many companies offering trail rides are:

- Banff Springs Corral — Banff Springs Hotel, Banff, (403) 762-2848
- Martin Stables — Birch Avenue, Banff, (403) 762-2832

*Dudes on the trail*

- Warner and MacKenzie Guide and Outfitting — 132 Banff Avenue, Banff, (403) 762-4551
- Timberline Tours — Deer Lodge, Lake Louise, (403) 522-3743
- Num-ti-jah Lodge — Icefields Parkway at Bow Lake, (403) 761-7020
- Jasper Park Riding Academy — Jasper Park Lodge, Jasper, (403) 852-3301
- Pyramid Riding Stables — Pyramid Lake Road, Jasper, (403) 852-3562
- Emerald Lake Riding Stables — Emerald Lake Lodge, (604) 762-4551

## // Fishing

Although hunting is strictly forbidden in any of the national parks, limited sport fishing is permitted. Only permit-holders may fish for the trout, whitefish and grayling that can be found in the lakes and rivers of the Rockies. Children under sixteen may fish on an adult's permit, but their catches must be included in the catch limit of the permit holder. Children are entitled to permits of their own, and each is allowed the full catch limit. Permits are available at information bureaus throughout the parks.

Because the fish are protected to ensure their continued strong population, catches are limited to possession of a total of five fish, with a maximum of five grayling, two whitefish and two trout in the full catch. Fishing is permitted primarily between Victoria Day (May 24 or the first Monday before May 25) and Labour Day (first Monday in September), although certain areas have extended fishing seasons. Fishing is prohibited between two hours after sunset and one hour before sunrise. Jasper and Banff parks have reserved several waters where no fishing is permitted at any time.

Fishing techniques are limited within the parks. Motorboats (except on Minnewanka, Pyramid and Maligne Lakes), netting, multiple hooks or lures and baiting with live fish or fish parts are among the fishing methods forbidden within the parks. Outside the parks, provincial regulations apply. For a complete list of open waters, fishing seasons and regulations, consult the pamphlet "Fishing Regulations: Mountain National Parks in Alberta and British Columbia." This pamphlet is available at all information centres.

## // Water Sports

Both the turbulent, fast-flowing waters that foam through the mountain valleys and the many placid, jade lakes can provide a new perspective on the magnificent mountain scenery. The more adventurous can raft down several of the major rivers for several hours or days; however appealing, this is a limited option for most families because most rafting companies restrict participants by a minimum weight of 40 kilograms or age sixteen. Apart from Jasper Park, most rafting in the parks is limited because of natural hazards such as waterfalls. Costs between companies depend upon demand and trip length. Check around before committing yourself. Families with small children may want to content themselves with a peaceful paddle through calm lakes. Rafting companies include:

- Alpine Rafting Company — Banff, (403) 762-5627
- Brewster Transportation and Tours — Banff, (403) 762-2241
- Hydra River Guides — Banff, (403) 762-4554
- Rocky Mountain Raft Tours — Banff, (403) 762-3632
- Jasper Raft Tours — Jasper, (403) 852-3613
- Maligne River Adventures — Jasper, (403) 852-3370
- Glacier Raft Company — Golden, (604) 344-6521
- Kootenay River Runners — Radium, (604) 762-5385

Canoes can be rented at most popular lakes, including Lake Louise, Moraine Lake, Maligne Lake, Emerald Lake, Pyramid Lake, Lake Minnewanka. Prices range from $12 to 15 per hour.

In Jasper, fishing boats can be rented on most lakes by prearrangement with Currie's Tackle company, 622 Connaught Drive, (403) 852-5650. Prices are about $20 per day for a small rowboat. The boats are padlocked to chains, but the keys can be picked up at the tackle shop.

Whatever water sport your family enjoys, ensure that everyone, including the adults, is wearing a life jacket. The glacially fed waters in the parks rarely rise above about 4°C in most of the lakes and rivers (apart from a few in Jasper); people swimming in or falling into this icy water can be rendered numb and unconscious quickly and become unable to save themseves.

## // Educational Tours

The naturalists working in the parks will share their knowledge of the park animals, flowers and geography. You can find them giving presentations or leading hikes somewhere in each park every day, usually several times a day. All of these services are free and are directed towards family audiences and general levels of interest. Children's questions are always welcome.

Naturalists give slide shows and other presentations at the public campgrounds, usually every second evening. The programs are scheduled and the contents vary, so you can learn new things at each presentation you go to. These talks are oriented toward children primarily, but they are entertaining and informative for everyone. The schedule of presentations can be found at the campgrounds or at information centres.

Families can also take in guided walks along some of the nature trails

*Flower-gazing*

near the towns and campgrounds. These hikes are designed to be slow and leisurely, while a naturalist answers your questions about nature's wonders. Lasting from one to six hours, these hikes are ideal walking classrooms where the whole family can learn together. Take your lunch along on longer trips. Hikes are offered at various locations seven days a week. Consult the information centres for hiking schedules. Also, watch for roving interpreters who wander various nature trails, ready to answer your questions.

Access to the world-famous Burgess Shale fossil beds is restricted. Anyone wishing to hike up to this World Heritage Site must do so as a member of a guided tour. Contact Rosemary Power, (604) 343-6470, to arrange a licensed, guided tour of this area. Cost is negotiated on an individual or group basis. The parks service attempts to schedule its own hikes to the area, but has difficulty finding qualified guides. Contact (604) 343-6324, ext. 24, for information about the availability of free hikes. It is illegal to visit the Shale without a guide, or to deface or remove any of these fossils.

At the Athabasca Glacier on the Icefields Parkway, Peter Lemieux offers three- to five-hour Athabasca Glacier Icewalks daily at 12:30 at the "Toe-of-the-Glacier" parking lot. Reservations can be made through Jasper Central Reservations, (403) 852-4242.

## // Wildflower Watching

Wildflowers can be seen in abundance anytime from spring to early autumn in the mountains, but are particularly spectacular between mid-July and mid-August on the sun-drenched meadows in the alpine and subalpine areas. These meadows will be ablaze with colour from glacier lilies, Indian paintbrush, buttercups, stonecrops and hundreds of other delicate blossoms. Often these displays are fleeting. Glacier lilies, for example, may bloom only a few splendid days before fading. Where and when to find plants depends on their type, elevation, weather, site and shelter. The sun-loving flowers tend to bloom on the western slopes and open valleys first, ascending later in the season to the alpine regions and eastern or northern slopes as the weather gets warmer. By early September, the first frosts kill off most of the remaining flowers. Mushrooms will be found in the wetter areas and the wetter, cooler seasons: early spring and fall.

Take a guidebook to mountain flowers along with you on your hikes so that you can identify the flowers as you go. Seeking out and identifying these beautiful gifts of nature is a wonderful pastime for children. Effortlessly, they will learn to respect the fragility of nature while they appreciate its beauty. Apart from viewing flowers on the trail, there are many spectacular flower-viewing locations that are accessible by car:

- Norquay Meadow — a viewpoint halfway up Norquay Road
- Icefields Parkway, particularly Nigel Pass, Parker's Ridge area, Bow Summit and Athabasca Summit
- Sunshine Meadows
- burns, such as those at Stanley Glacier/Vermilion Pass area
- ski slopes near Lake Louise
- Bald Hills and Opal Hills above Maligne Lake
- Peyto Lake area near Bow Pass
- most campgrounds

## // Animal Watching

Seeing wildlife close-up is a thrill for young and old alike. Fortunately for wildlife seekers, finding wildlife is easy. Unfortunately for many of the animals, it is too easy. Much of the best animal watching is done from the roads and campgrounds, as many animals come to these areas in search of food. Some, like bears, are seeking human food or salt from the roadside, but others are in these areas because they are located in the valley bottoms where there is an abundance of food.

While this conjunction makes it relatively easy to see wildlife, it also risks animal/human confrontations. Enthusiastic picture-hunters or children can get too close to these animals, most of which are unpredictable and will bite, kick or ram if they feel threatened. Feeding the animals is illegal, but many do get fed and become ill or eventually die because of the disruptions to their natural diets. Many animals are killed because they venture onto the roads and are hit by cars. Accidents are also common when tourists suddenly jam on the brakes upon suddenly seeing an animal they wish to watch.

Most of the larger animals are best seen at dawn and dusk, when they do their feeding. Be particularly alert while driving during these times. When watching wildlife from the road, come to a stop gradually and pull well off to the side of the road. Stay in your car or keep well away from the animals. Use a telephoto lens to get close-up photographs, but don't approach the animals. The parks are not a zoo and the animals are wild, even if they look calm and tame. Never try to feed or pet the animals.

Some of the best roadside viewing areas are:

- Lake Minnewanka Road for bighorn sheep
- Icefields Parkway for sheep, goats, grizzly bears, black bears and moose
- Bow Valley Parkway for mule deer, coyotes and sheep
- Vermilion Lakes Drive for elk, eagles, osprey, moose and deer

- Mt. Norquay Road for sheep
- Takakkaw Falls Road for porcupines
- Lake Louise area near Skoki for grizzly bears
- all Banff campgrounds, Kicking Horse, Takakkaw Falls and McLeod Meadows campgrounds for black bears
- Bow Summit on the Icefields Parkway for marmots
- Moraine Lake for pika
- all campgrounds for Clark's nutcracker, crows
- Trans-Canada Highway, Banff airport, McLeod Meadows, Whistlers campground for elk

See the wildlife section of **A Sense of Place** for more information about where to find specific animals in the Rockies.

## // Picnics

All of the parks have many designated picnic sites along the roadsides and near especially scenic areas. Many are located near nature trails to make an ideal hike/picnic combination. These sites are easily accessible and are equipped with picnic tables and washroom facilities, as well as bear-proof bins for garbage disposal. Families are likely best to picnic efficiently, getting their food out, eating it and packing it and any garbage away again, to prevent scavenging by birds and animals. If you do leave your food on a table while you wander around, keep it stored in a cooler. Be warned that some animals, like bears and raccoons, can open coolers easily and others will chew through coolers made of unprotected styrofoam.

Birds, squirrels and chipmunks descend upon picnickers in an attempt to scavenge food. At first they are cute, enthralling children especially with their closeness and apparent tameness, but they soon become nuisances. Be deaf to the pleas of children and do not feed these wild creatures.

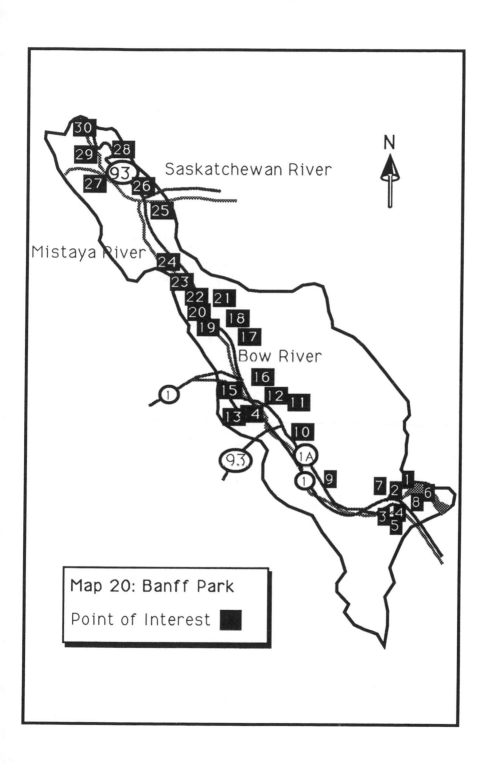

Saskatchewan River

Mistaya River

Bow River

N

Map 20: Banff Park

Point of Interest

# 11 // From The Road

Sometimes it is hard to get children excited about hiking. Fortunately, many natural wonders can be seen without the efforts of hiking or backpacking and even without straying far from your car. These points of interest can be missed if you don't know to watch for them. Pointing them out to your children may help draw them into an enthusiasm for the area that will encourage their desire to get out on the trail.

## // Banff

### 1. Cascade Falls

One of the first sights on entering Banff from Calgary, Cascade Falls plummets in a thin, wispy spray down Cascade Mountain and is diverted from Lake Minnewanka into lakes and canals that flow through the Cascade Power Station, which provides power for the Banff area. Cascade Mountain (2,998 m) was named Minnehappa by the Stoney Indians. Minnehappa means "mountain where the water falls." Explorer James Hector of the Palliser Expedition anglicized the name in 1858.

### 2. Buffalo Paddock

Accessible from the Banff/Minnewanka overpass north of Banff townsite, the paddock contains a small herd of bison — North America's largest mammal. Once there were up to 60 million bison roaming the woods and plains of North America. Unfortunately, they were slaughtered to near-extinction by farmers, settlers and Natives during the last century. Wood bison, native to the Rockies, became extinct here in 1858. Plains bison were introduced to the parks in 1897, but were replaced by the native wood bison in 1981. These wood bison were brought from the herds of Wood Buffalo National Park. Their descendants are now the only animals in captivity within the parks. The paddock is located near the original site of Banff's train station, Siding 29. Families can drive around the paddock by car.

### 3. Banff Townsite

First called Siding 29 by CPR employees who were laying the track for the national railway, Banff was given its present name in 1883. The name comes from Banffshire, a district in northern Scotland where George Stephen, a director of the CPR, was born. Established primarily as a tourist centre, Banff is the largest and oldest town in the national parks. The population is approximately 4,000.

### 4. Bow Falls

This beautiful, wide falls within Banff townsite can be viewed either from Glen Avenue on the south side of the Bow River or from the base of Tunnel Mountain Drive on the north side of the river. Here, the Bow River has cut a course through a limestone bedrock between Mt. Rundle and Tunnel Mountain. Once

*Bow Falls*

the water flowed over a series of cliffs; however, these have been worn down by thousands of years of erosion. The Bow River derives its name from a Cree word for "bow," because the Natives made bows from wood growing near the river. The headwaters of the Bow River are 90 kilometres to the north in the Wapta Icefield.

### 5. Tunnel Mountain Drive

This short loop begins in Banff townsite on the west side of the bridge across the Bow River, where Banff Avenue and Buffalo Street intersect. Following the Bow River east, the road provides great views of the Banff Springs Hotel and of Bow Falls before heading up Tunnel Mountain Drive for a view of the Bow Valley. The drive butts into Tunnel Mountain Road. Go right past the campground to the hoodoos lookout. After admiring the hoodoos, turn left to return to Banff townsite. Tunnel Mountain was familiar to the Natives as Sleeping Buffalo Mountain because of its shape, but its modern name is derived from a surveyor's plan to gain access to the Bow Valley by cutting a 275-metre tunnel through the mountain. The tunnel was never built and an easier way was found into the area along the valley bottom, but the name held.

### 6. Lake Minnewanka

Beautiful Lake Minnewanka offers a wide variety of family activities: canoeing, power boating, tour boat riding, scuba diving, fishing and picnicking. It is a pleasant place to hang out between hikes. Enlarged by two dams built in 1912 and 1941, the 22-kilometres-long lake is now 8 kilometres longer and 25 metres higher than when used by Sir George Simpson, governor of the Hudson's Bay Company, as an entrance to the Rockies on his whirlwind east-west tour around the world. The Native campsites and trails that skirted the original lake are now submerged, as is Minnewanka Landing, a small resort town once on the shore. This large reservoir/lake is located north of Banff townsite on Lake Minnewanka Road. A two-hour cruise in a glass-enclosed boat is available. Adults $17, children $8.50, four and under free. Tours: (403) 762–3473.

### 7. Mt. Norquay Lookout

Mt. Norquay Drive, just north of Banff townsite, switchbacks up this mountain famous for its winter skiing. Near the top, a viewpoint provides a great view of Banff, the Bow Valley and its many peaks, as well as Mt. Rundle. The viewpoint meadow is a great place to have a picnic and pretend to be in *The Sound of Music*. Watch for mule deer and bighorn sheep. If in operation, a gondola at the ski area takes visitors to a restaurant near the summit of Mt. Norquay (2,515 m).

### 8. Bankhead

This abandoned coal mining town is located on the Lake Minnewanka Road north of Banff. One of several collieries in the Rockies, Bankhead was established in 1904 and was a town of about 1,000 people at its height. Its non-smoking semi-anthracite was used by the CPR to fuel its locomotives and was in high demand until the early 1920s, particularly during World War I. Although it boasted a skating rink, library and tennis court, all that remains of this formerly thriving town are a monument, patches of rhubarb, a few foundations, scraps of iron and the slag heaps from the mining operations.

Mining was encouraged in the early days of the national parks because it brought the federal government royalty revenues. Not until 1930 was new industrial activity banned from the parks by the National Parks Act. Bankhead closed down in 1922 because of labour disputes and the low demand for coal. The lead-silver mines near Field were the last to close, in 1952.

### 9. Bow Valley Parkway

The original road through the Bow Valley when it was built in 1920, this secluded section of the 1A highway winds between Banff and Lake Louise and then heads into Yoho Park — all away from the noise and rush of the Trans-Canada Highway. Beginning 5.5 kilometres west of the Mt. Norquay overpass, the highway makes its way past Johnston Canyon and beneath Castle Mountain before turning toward Lake Louise. Children should be on the watch for coyotes, moose and mule deer, which are often sighted along this road. This low-speed route was likely used by Natives to get through the valley and is currently a favourite with cyclists.

Near the Mt. Norquay overpass is the Back Swamp, a wetland filling up with decomposed and carbonizing vegetation known as peat. Slightly further along is Muleshoe, a small fishing lake cut off from its feeding river by the railway and filling in with vegetation. Both areas are favourite habitats for moose, beavers and waterbirds. Moose Meadows, opposite Johnston Canyon Resort further down the Bow Valley Parkway, is a grassy area also favoured by moose.

### 10. Silver City

A railway boomtown that once had a population of 2,000 people, Silver City existed near what is now Castle Junction for only two years, from 1883 to 1885. There never was any silver, only poor-quality copper and lead on nearby Copper

Mountain. Little evidence remains of this city which was bigger than Calgary during its heyday. A small exhibit south of Castle Junction marks the open field that was once Silver City. A brief stop is all that is needed here.

### 11. Castle Mountain

Briefly known as Mt. Eisenhower in honour of a former American president, unmistakable Castle Mountain lives up to its more romantic name, especially when it becomes a ruddy gold in the early evening alpenglow as the sun sets. Unlike the front ranges, which are made of layers of sedimentary rock thrust upwards on a steep angle (such as the classic Mt. Rundle), Castle Mountain's layers are relatively flat and have been eroded into turrets and towers. These flat layers were created when a sheet of rock was pushed into place onto younger rock about 600 million years ago. The mountain has two prominent cliffs and is constructed like a sandwich. The top cliff is limestone and the bottom cliff is dolomite. Between the two lies a thin ledge of shale. This landmark mountain is located near the Lake Louise junction and can be viewed from the Trans-Canada or from the Bow Valley Parkway. The name Mt. Eisenhower now applies only to the southern tower of Castle Mountain.

### 12. Morant's Curve

This popular viewpoint was made famous by CPR photographer Nicholas Morant. Often seen on postcards, this viewpoint provides a wide-angle view of the Lake Louise peaks, including Mt. Temple, at 3,544 metres the third-highest mountain in Banff Park, and the Wenkchemna Peaks above Moraine Lake. This scenic curve is located south of the Lake Louise junction on the Bow Valley Parkway.

### 13. Moraine Lake

This is the lake on the back of the Canadian $20 bill, but it is far prettier in real life. The lake was discovered and named by climber and explorer Walter Wilcox in 1893. Wilcox named this entire area Desolation Valley because of its stark contrast to Paradise Valley, lying beyond Sentinel Pass to the north. Once thought to have been gouged out by a glacier, it is now believed that this lake was created by a landslide — likely from the Tower of Babel to the south — which dammed the flow of water. Another theory suggests that the rockpile came from further up the valley and was carried to its present location by an advancing glacier.

The lake is famous for its view of the sawtoothed mountains popularly known as the Ten Peaks but officially named the Wenkchemna Peaks in 1979. Wenkchemna is the Stoney word for ten. These peaks rise 1,200 metres above the lake in a 15-kilometre ridge.

Located at the end of Moraine Lake Road off to the left of the 1A highway as it ascends to Lake Louise, Moraine Lake is a starting point for several easy day hikes and boasts a pleasant lodge and restaurant. Canoeing, watching for marmots and comparing the view with the $20 bill will amuse children here.

### 14. Mt. Temple

Magnificent, solid Mt. Temple, 3,544 metres high and comprising an area of 15 square kilometres, inspires the awe befitting its name. This easily recognized

*Lake Louise*

mountain in the Lake Louise vicinity is one of the largest in the Rockies because of its area. It is the eleventh-highest in the national parks and the third-highest mountain in Banff. Named for Sir Richard Temple, the leader of an 1884 scientific expedition, Mt. Temple's glacier-capped peaks are popular with mountaineers. The most difficult and hazardous technical route is up the north face of the mountain. Unfortunately, mountaineering accidents are not unusual on this 1.6-kilometre vertical ascent.

### 15. Lake Louise

No trip to the Rockies is complete without a trip to Lake Louise, the photogenic turquoise lake seen on seemingly every second postcard sent from Banff. Discovered by Tom Wilson in 1882 while he was working for CPR surveyors, the lake quickly became a tourist mecca for mountain exploration. Fed by the Victoria Glacier, 8 kilometres away on Mt. Victoria (3,464 m), the lake's famous colour is caused by silt, known as rockflour, which is suspended in the water and reflects back the blue-green wavelengths in the light spectrum. The lake is 2.4 kilometres long, 500 metres wide and 90 metres deep. It is usually frozen from November to June and never manages to get above 4°C because of the glacial origin of the water.

The lake was originally known by the Indian name of The Lake of Little Fishes and was named Emerald Lake by Wilson. It was renamed Lake Louise after Princess Louise, a daughter of Queen Victoria and wife of the Marquis of Lorne, who was Governor General of Canada between 1878 and 1883. More than 70 kilometres of trails lead from the lake to the surrounding mountains; canoes can be rented and trail rides on horseback can be arranged.

The chateau itself is worth a family stroll while you are in the area. It is one of a series of magnificent hotels built across the country by the CPR to encourage tourism among the wealthy. The first log chalet, built in 1890, burned down in 1893. It was replaced with a succession of increasingly lavish buildings. The first rendition of the present chateau was a twelve-person chalet. Wings and additions were added periodically in an eclectic mix of styles. The wooden wings of the chateau burned down in 1924 and were replaced with concrete wings in 1925. The chateau changed little for almost sixty years until its severe, blank facade was resurfaced in 1984-85. In 1986 a major and controversial development project began. A new 150-room wing was built, as were a large parkade and retail area. A convention facility will also be added in the future.

### 16. Lake Louise Ski Area

Located opposite Lake Louise townsite on the east side of the Bow Valley, the Lake Louise Ski Area made the Rockies — and Banff Park in particular — famous for winter skiing. This encouraged year-round use of the park and led to the park's comparatively intense development of facilities and trails. The downhill runs are clearly visible from the road. Behind this area, but too arduous for most family hikers, lies mythical and mystical Skoki Valley. Explored by mountaineers and members of the Alpine Club of Canada, alpine Skoki Valley is central to many of the mountain legends associated with the early years of the national parks.

### 17. Icefields Parkway

This spectacular highway between Lake Louise and Jasper runs northwest to southeast close to the Continental Divide and beneath some of the most spectacular icefields in the world. The route now known as the Icefields Parkway was gradually established by Natives and early explorers, who could travel easily in the open valleys. The road itself was constructed during the depression of the 1930s as a make-work project to join Lake Louise and Jasper, some 230 kilometres apart. A prime area for seeing wildlife, particularly mountain goats and mountain sheep, the parkway provides easy access to many of the most interesting and scenic spots in the Rockies.

### 18. Mt. Hector

James Hector was one of the most important explorers of the Rocky Mountains. Credited with discovering the Kicking Horse, Bow and Vermilion Passes, as well as extensive areas throughout the Rockies, Hector was a physician and geologist who served on the Palliser Expedition from 1857 to 1860. Imposing Mt. Hector (3,394 m), on the east side of the Bow Valley north of Lake Louise, was named in his honour in 1884. Hector was the man kicked and almost killed by a horse in 1858, an incident remembered in the name Kicking Horse Pass.

### 19. Crowfoot Glacier Viewpoint

Part of the Wapta Icefield, the Crowfoot Glacier on Crowfoot Mountain is a cliff of ice close to the Icefields Parkway just south of Bow Lake. Named for its shape, the Crowfoot once had three toes, but the third toe has disappeared in the last century as the glacier has receded.

### 20. Bow Lake

Bow Lake lies just south of Bow Summit and is fed by the Bow Glacier of the Wapta Icefield. The glacier is the source of the Bow River, which provided a transportation route through the southern part of Banff Park. Creamy blue because of high quantities of rockflour in the water, this large lake once had its delta where picturesque Num-ti-jah Lodge now stands. The delta gradually moved to its current location, likely because of the change in sediment flow caused by the retreat of the Bow Glacier. Num-ti-jah Lodge was built in 1923 by outfitter and guide Jimmy Simpson, who had run an outfitting camp in the area since the early 1900s. The unusual octagonal shape was chosen because Simpson wanted to build his lodge using the short trees that grew nearby. The name is a Stoney word for pine marten.

### 21. Bow Pass

The summit of Bow Pass (2,088 m) is the highest point on the Icefields Parkway. A great spot for seeing alpine wildflowers, a short stroll to a viewpoint crosses alpine meadows and offers truly breathtaking views of the Waputik Range to the west and Observation, Cirque and Dolomite (2,972 m) peaks to the east. The meadows here are covered with glacier lilies, mountain avens and anemones as the snow melts in June.

### 22. Peyto Lake

The short trail from Bow Summit to the Peyto Lake viewpoint is well worth a side trip from the Icefields Parkway. Winding through the krummholz zone of stunted Engelmann spruce and alpine fir, the trail heads to a viewpoint high above this oddly shaped and deeply turquoise lake. This is the best and most easily accessible aerial view of any lake in the Rockies. It is possible to hike down to the lake, but the view is far better from above. The lake was named for "Wild" Bill Peyto, an early outfitter and later a park warden famous for eccentric behaviour and strange practical jokes, such as frightening a friend by dressing up in a fresh grizzly carcass.

### 23. Howse Peak

Located just south of the Waterfowl Lake Campground, 57 kilometres north of the Lake Louise junction, the Howse Peak viewpoint provides the best panorama of the Continental Divide. The view spans seven high mountains linked in a ridge 9 kilometres long. The highest and most northern of these mountains, Howse Peak, is 3,290 metres high. From Howse Peak, the Continental Divide, which separates waters flowing to the Pacific and Atlantic Oceans, veers west and doesn't come so close to the highway again for 150 kilometres, at Yellowhead Pass. Moose are often seen in this area.

### 24. Mt. Chephren

Mt. Chephren (3,307 m) is a fine example of a horn mountain (a steep-sided mountain that has a horn shape, like the Matterhorn) created by downward glacial erosion. Glacial cirques have been carved into the valleys on either side of this mountain and are accessible to dayhikers (see hiking chapters). The mountain was originally named Pyramid Mountain by Mary Schaffer, but the name was changed to Chephren (keff-ren) in honour of the son of Cheops, architect of Egypt's Great Pyramid.

### 25. Saskatchewan River Crossing

The wide valley of Saskatchewan River Crossing is the lowest point on the

Icefields Parkway and is 700 metres lower than Bow Pass, just 37 kilometres to the south. The North Saskatchewan River is fed by the icefields from the Continental Divide and heads east for more than 1,200 kilometres before joining the South Saskatchewan River. Crossing the Saskatchewan River was one of the most difficult challenges facing outfitters and explorers in the area because of its wide, deep and fast waters.

The valley is unusually arid for the mountain regions. Dry air and high winds tend to sweep into the river valley from the prairies, minimizing rain and snow and making the ecosystem here more typical of front-range foothills than of mountain valleys. The area is a favourite wintering ground for mountain sheep, goats and deer because of the easier climate.

### 26. Howse River Viewpoint

The many-channelled Howse River, which feeds into the North Saskatchewan River, leads upstream to the Freshfield Icefield, one of the largest icefields in the parks with an area of 70 square kilometres. The icefield's name has nothing to do with water quality, but honours Sir Douglas Freshfield, a prominent British scientist and explorer. The icefield has sixteen peaks exceeding 3,050 metres in elevation.

### 27. Graveyard Flats

The bleak gravel bed near the junction of the Alexandra and North Saskatchewan Rivers was actually a welcome sight to explorers because it offered easy travel on horseback compared to the difficult Bow Valley. The area was named by explorer Mary Schaffer because of the many animal skeletons she found in the area. The abundant and stark driftwood scattered over the area contributes to the spooky atmosphere summoned up by the name.

### 28. Weeping Wall

This rockwall on the east side of the Icefields Parkway lies 17 kilometres south of the Banff/Jasper boundary. It derives its name from its appearance: scores of large to tiny waterfalls cascade down its side, especially during the late spring and early summer when the snow melt is at its peak. The water emerging from the wall comes from seeps on Cirrus Mountain (3,215 m). The area is an ice-climbing mecca in the winter.

### 29. The Big Bend

Just before climbing 360 metres to Sunwapta Pass, the Icefields Parkway loses 100 metres elevation and curves abruptly to the west instead of climbing the pass directly and without losing elevation. Road builders had to take this route to construct the road at a moderate grade and to stay above the Nigel Creek canyon. However aggravating for cyclists, the elevation loss and extra distance make the route easier and safer than other options. The Big Bend is to the Icefields Parkway what Craigellachie is to the Last Spike of the national railway, for it is here that the road crews from Lake Louise met those from Jasper and finished the parkway in 1939.

### 30. Sunwapta Pass

Pass from summer to winter by driving up this 2,023-metre high pass. It serves as the boundary between Banff and Jasper Parks and is near the high point

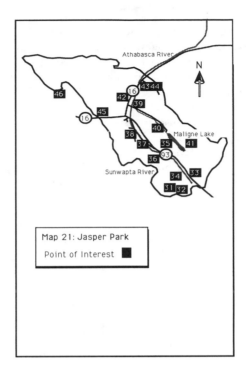

Map 21: Jasper Park
Point of Interest ■

of the Columbia Icefield, although it is second to Bow Pass in height. It is also the watershed divide between the Atlantic-draining North Saskatchewan River and the Sunwapta River, which eventually drains into the Arctic Ocean. Geology professor and explorer A.P. Coleman named the area Sunwapta in 1892. Sunwapta is a Stoney word meaning turbulent river.

## // Jasper

### 31. Columbia Icefield

The immense Columbia Icefield straddles the Continental Divide and covers 389 square kilometres. As the largest sheet of glacial ice in North America, excluding the Arctic, this icefield is the major remnant of the glaciers that dominated the mountains between a million and 20,000 years ago. The cool temperatures at the high elevation of the Continental Divide, as well as heavy snowfall, keep these glaciers large, although some, like the Athabasca Glacier, are receding. Water from the Icefield reaches the Arctic, Atlantic and Pacific Oceans.

### 32. Athabasca Glacier

One of the most majestic of the sights on the Parkway, the Athabasca Glacier descends from the massive Columbia Icefield on the Continental Divide. Just north of Sunwapta Pass on the Parkway, this receding glacier can be walked to over the moraine it has left behind. Signs along the path indicate the location of the toe and show how remarkably fast the glacier is receding.

Many families climb about on the toe of the glacier. The temptation is great, but do so with care. The glacier is very slippery and even the lower reaches of it contain crevasses that are a long, cold fall down. Ninety-minute SnoCoach tours of the glacier can take you right onto the glacier on a five-kilometre guided trip. Reservations can be made through Brewster Transportation and Tours [(403) 852–3332]. Naturalist Peter Lemieux also offers three- to five-hour Athabasca Glacier Icewalks daily at 12:30 from the Toe-of-the-Glacier parking lot. Reservations can be made through Jasper Central Reservations [(403) 852–4242)]. The Icefield Interpretive Centre also provides free information, slide shows and exhibits about the Icefield.

Just to the north of the Athabasca Glacier is the Snow Dome (3,520 m), from which water drains in three directions to the Arctic, Atlantic and Pacific Oceans.

### 33. Sunwapta Canyon

This unusual canyon is cutting through a 50-metre rockslide that has fallen from Mt. Kitchener (3,505 m), just north of the Icefield Centre and on the western side of the Icefields Parkway. Whereas most canyons in the parks cut through bedrock, this one is being formed as the river erodes the limestone boulders that have fallen in its path. The Kitchener Rock Slide is the third-largest measured slide in this area.

### 34. Stutfield Glacier

Carving the amphitheatre between Mt. Kitchener and Stutfield Peak, the Stutfield Glacier is one of the most dramatic in the Columbia Icefield area. It was named for Hugh Stutfield, a mountaineer and explorer. With his colleague, John Norman Collie, he wrote the classic *Climbs and Explorations in the Canadian Rockies* in 1903.

### 35. Endless Chain Ridge

Named by explorer Mary Schaffer, this 20-kilometre ridge is one of the finest examples of an overthrust mountain range. Heavily tilted, these mountains were thrust upwards by compression when they were formed. The southwestern slope tilted upwards at a steep angle as the sheets of rock were forced upward over the sheer northeastern cliffs. Mt. Rundle in Banff and the Queen Elizabeth Ranges in Jasper are other good examples of this formation.

### 36. Sunwapta Falls

A fifteen-minute walk from a short road off the Icefields Parkway 55 kilometres south of Jasper, Sunwapta Falls is a steep canyon that is eroding through a crack in the limestone bedrock. The river, which has been heading northwest, suddenly heads southwest to get around a moraine left behind by the Columbia Glacier. More waterfalls can be viewed downstream before the river resumes its northerly course.

### 37. Athabasca Falls

Unlike most waterfalls in the Rockies, Athabasca Falls has been cut into Gog quartzite, not limestone. This type of quartzite is one of the hardest and most common rocks in the parks. Very resistant to erosion, the rocks have nevertheless been cut away gradually by the Athabasca River. Walkways leading over and beside the falls reveal many potholes where the circular flow of water has eroded the round shapes. There are also several channels that have been abandoned for easier routes.

### 38. Mt. Edith Cavell

Visible for long distances along the Icefields Parkway, Mt. Edith Cavell (3,363 m) is truly one of the most impressive mountains in Jasper. Known to the Natives as the "White Ghost" and to fur traders as "the mountain of the great crossing," this massive mountain was named for a British nurse executed in 1915 by the Germans for helping British, French and Belgian soldiers across the frontier. It can be viewed up close by driving heavily switchbacked Edith Cavell Road from Highway 93-A to its base. A memorial service for Cavell is held annually in the fall and a cross in her honour has been placed at the summit of the mountain.

### 39. Maligne Canyon

The narrow, 55-metre-deep Maligne Canyon has been worn away by the frothing waters of the Maligne River as it flows from Maligne Lake to join the Athabasca River. Plummeting 23 metres through the canyon, the river has eroded a deep, narrow gorge in the limestone and dolomite bedrock. Located about 6 kilometres from the beginning of the Maligne Lake Road, this dramatic canyon is bridged six times, making it easily accessible and hikeable. For more details, see hiking chapters.

### 40. Medicine Lake

Thin Medicine Lake, on the Maligne Lake Road, is an unusual lake because of its continually changing water levels. It was considered a "magic" lake by the Natives, because the water level sinks. The cause will be a mystery to children, as it has been to adults for many years. Despite constantly receiving water from spring runoff and glacial melting, the lake gets full enough for the water to overflow the banks and head down the valley by river only every few years. At its lower water levels, the lake seems to have no outlet; the water flows to the northeastern shore and then disappears in the gravel. Most of the water drains into sink holes and then into a system of caves. These underground channels can carry as much as 57 cubic metres of water per second. The water reemerges at the fourth bridge of Maligne Canyon, 15 kilometres away and about twenty hours later. Some water may also find its way into lakes near Jasper townsite. The underground drainage in the limestone bedrocks of Medicine Lake and other smaller lakes in this area is known as karst topography.

### 41. Maligne Lake

Fed by the Brazeau Icefield, jade-coloured 22.3-kilometre Maligne Lake is the longest and largest natural lake in the Canadian Rockies. Known to the Stoney Indians as Chaba Imne, or Great Beaver Lake, it was also called Sore-Foot Lake by a weary surveyor. The lake was given the name Maligne — French for evil — by Jesuit missionary Jean de Smet because of a difficult crossing over the river that flows from it.

Maligne Lake is renowned for its tranquil beauty beneath the sawtoothed peaks of the Queen Elizabeth and Maligne ranges. Unlike other major lakes in the parks, Maligne Lake still has its pristine beauty intact because park authorities have refused to develop it beyond allowing boating and tour boats on the lake. However, it is one of the few lakes, along with Pyramid and

Minnewanka, to allow power boats. Two-hour boat tours cost $26 per adult; $13 per child aged 6-12; and $75 per family. A day-use chalet is situated near the shore of the lake.

### 42. Jasper and Talbot Lakes

North of Jasper townsite, the Yellowhead Highway heads in a northeasterly direction toward the prairies and into a dry terrain containing many wetlands. Jasper Lake, north of the townsite, dries up in the winter and its sandy bottom is blown by the wind and deposited in sand dunes. One such dune has separated Jasper Lake from Talbot Lake and forms a natural causeway on which the highway runs. As the Athabasca River erodes a deeper riverbed, the summer filling of Jasper Lake will cease and the lake will dry up altogether. The dunes are held in place by low-growing shrubs and roses and provide a windbreak for the wetlands of Talbot Lake, which are a popular home for waterfowl and bighorn sheep.

### 43. Pocohontas

Coal was discovered on Roche Miette (2,316 m) in 1908 and mining began near the town of Pocohontas, named for a Virginian mining town, in 1910. The mine was initially prosperous, with 100,000 tonnes of coal extracted and 120 employees in 1912. A spur of the Grand Trunk Pacific Railway line ran to the mine, making shipping easy until the railway was moved to the other side of the Athabasca River when it joined the Canadian Northern Railway. A series of accidents and labour disputes coupled with the decline of the coal market after World War I forced the mine to close in 1921. The ruins of the mine can be seen a short distance from the entrance to the Miette Hotsprings Road. Nearby, the Pocohontas Ponds provide an excellent spot for birdwatching, especially during the summer and fall migrating seasons.

### 44. Punchbowl Falls

Just beyond Pocohontas on the Miette Hotsprings Road is a small but pretty waterfall known as Punchbowl Falls. This falls has eroded through a natural concrete known as the Cadomin Formation. The falls gets its name from several punchbowl-like basins that have been worn into the rock.

### 45. Yellowhead Pass

The Yellowhead Pass, at 1,125 metres, is the lowest of the mountain passes. First chosen by Sir Sanford Fleming of the CPR as the railway's route to the Pacific, it lost out to the far more difficult Kicking Horse Pass, which was chosen to ward off competition from northern American railways. Thirty years after the CPR built its southern railway, the Yellowhead Pass was crossed by the tracks of the Grand Trunk Pacific Railway in 1911 and those of the Canadian Northern Railway in 1913. Originally known as Leather Pass because of the leather trade passing through the area, the name was changed to honour Pierre Bostonais, a blond Iroquois trapper and guide known as Tete Jaune, French for Yellowhead.

### 46. Mt. Robson

Eighty kilometres west of Jasper on Highway 16, Mt. Robson is the tallest of the Canadian Rocky mountains at 3,954 metres. A 3,100-metre difference

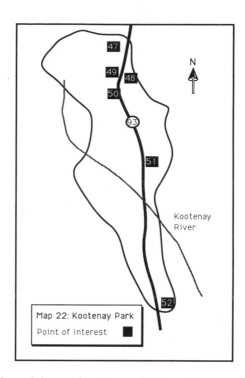

Map 22: Kootenay Park
Point of Interest ■

N

Kootenay
River

between the peak and base elevations of this colossus makes Robson the biggest (not highest) mountain in both the Canadian and American Rockies. (The highest Rocky mountain in the U.S. is Mt. Elbert in Colorado at 4,399 metres; the biggest U.S. Rocky mountain is Pikes Peak, which has an elevation gain 800 metres less than Mt. Robson.) Although located in Mt. Robson Provincial Park, blocky Mt. Robson, with its heavily glaciated peaks, is visible from the Yellowhead Highway and is well worth a side trip.

## // Kootenay Park

### 47. Vermilion Pass

Like the Yellowhead and Kicking Horse passes, Vermilion Pass crosses over the Continental Divide. Vermilion Pass is the highest of the three at 1,651 metres, although the gradual incline on either side makes it appear to be lower. It was discovered by James Hector in 1858. Hector also discovered the Kicking Horse and Bow passes that year. Vermilion Pass is noted for the bad weather that is pushed through it by the prevailing southwest winds.

### 48. Vermilion Pass Burn

In 1968, lightning started a fire in the Vermilion Pass area at the north end of Highway 93, burning 2,400 hectares of forest in four days. This forest is now regenerating, primarily with lodgepole pine, and is abundant with wildflowers.

However, the grim spikes of the dead trees still standing are a sobering lesson on the devastating effects of any forest fire, whether caused by human carelessness or natural events. Forest fires are one of the greatest hazards to the parks because of their rapid devastation and the difficulty of controlling them. This burn is one of the only major fires to occur in the parks in the last fifty years after the initial devastation in the Bow Valley during the construction of the railway. However, the absence of forest fires has led to many over-mature forests, which are waiting to burn like the massive fires that burned in Yellowstone Park in 1988. The parks are initiating an experimental program to conduct controlled burns in specific areas to prevent Yellowstone's catastrophe from occurring in the Rockies.

### 49. Marble Canyon

One of several canyons close to the roadside in the Rockies, Marble Canyon provides an interesting hike or diversion for families. Actually made of white and grey dolomite, not marble, the canyon is narrow and cool. Accessible via stairways and six bridges over its lip, the canyon proves fascinating to children, who are mesmerized by the rush and surge of the plunging water.

### 50. Paint Pots

Located near Marble Canyon on Highway 93, the Paint Pots are springs that deposit ochre, red and orange oxides onto the clay soil. Carried by the cooling water of the springs, dissolved iron crystallizes on the surface as iron oxides and colours the ground surface. This coloured clay was baked and powdered for use as pigments for clothing and face paint by the Stoney and Kootenay Indians. They were a major item of trade among the Natives and were later mined by white entrepreneurs.

### 51. Animal Licks

Halfway between Vermilion and Kootenay Crossings, there is an animal lick on the eastern side of Highway 93. A surface deposit of mineral salts, this lick is frequented by mule deer, moose and elk, which crave the salt and ignore their audience.

### 52. Sinclair Canyon

Sinclair Canyon provided a route for James Sinclair to guide 200 Metis through the mountains from Manitoba to Oregon in 1841. The settlers were taken to Oregon to bolster the British claim to the area. Highway 93 passes right through the canyon as it travels to Radium Hot Springs. The canyon bottom has been paved for the highway and the creek runs underground. The dolomite cliffs have been damaged during highway construction, but remain dramatic because of their winding narrowness and deep brownish-orange colouring.

## // Yoho Park

### 53. The Great Divide

The Continental Divide separates the waters flowing to the Pacific and Atlantic Oceans. At the Great Divide on the Great Divide Parkway, the 1A from Lake Louise to the Trans-Canada Highway in Yoho, you can actually see the waters dividing. Divide Creek branches at this point and heads for two oceans separated by 4,500 kilometres of land. This spot also marks the Alberta/British Columbia boundary, and cairns commemorate James Hector, discoverer of the Kicking Horse Pass, and the surveying crews working in the area.

### 54. Kicking Horse Pass

The Kicking Horse Pass straddles the Continental Divide, the watershed that

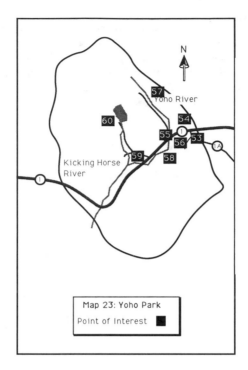

Map 23: Yoho Park
Point of Interest

determines whether water reaches the Atlantic or Pacific Ocean. Named "kicking horse" to immortalize the incident when surveyor Dr. James Hector, an explorer with the Palliser Expedition, was kicked by his horse in 1858, the pass rises 110 metres moderately from Lake Louise to its elevation of 1,630 metres, then plunges 390 metres down to the gravel flats of Field in a dramatic descent. The western slope is steeper because of heavier glaciation and the short distance from the divide to the Pacific Ocean, which results in a steeper, more erosive descent for rivers on the western slope. Going west down the pass, notice the spectacular views of the Waputik Icefield and, further west, the President Range on your right. On the left, look for the aptly named Cathedral Mountain, with its pinkish dolomite cliffs and spires. This mountain is particularly beautiful just before sunset, when alpenglow turns it a stunning gold.

### 55. Spiral Tunnels

The Spiral Tunnels, built in 1909 just west of the Kicking Horse Pass, are an amazing feat of engineering. They can only be truly appreciated when you see a long train enter the tunnel and then come out like a snake in a 270° rotation over the top of its tail, which is still entering the mouth of the tunnel. The tunnels were built to reduce the grade that the trains had to climb or descend to get through the Kicking Horse Pass. Trains had been crossing the pass since the CPR built its original route to the Pacific in 1884, but this route was terrifyingly steep and plagued with avalanches. The tunnels haven't solved every problem. Water seeping into the tunnels causes ice buildup during the winter, making it difficult for the trains to travel through. Between twenty and thirty trains use the tunnels each day. It is just a matter of time before one rolls by.

*Takakkaw Falls*

## 56. Meeting of the Waters

West of the Spiral Tunnels, the Yoho and Kicking Horse Rivers join at the Meeting of the Waters. At this junction, the Yoho River is actually larger, but it is considered a tributary to the Kicking Horse River. The muddy water from the Yoho River is distinguishable from the clearer Kicking Horse River's waters. The difference between the waters is unusual because both rivers are glacially fed. The Kicking Horse River is clearer at this point because much of its silt has settled out in Sherbrooke and Wapta Lakes.

## 57. Takakkaw Falls

The highest falls in the parks at 380 metres, Takakkaw Falls is a must-see destination on any trip through the Rockies. Fed by the Daly Glacier in the Waputik Icefield, the frothing falls plummet over a cliff down to the Yoho River. During heavy rains or extra warm temperatures, the amount of water going over the falls increases dramatically and carries more silt and stone with it, often turning the white plume into a muddy brown torrent. The falls can be reached by taking Yoho Road on the right of the Trans-Canada Highway at the bottom of Kicking Horse Pass. A signed, paved walkway travels right to the base of the falls from the parking lot.

Motor homes are not permitted on this road. You will see why when you reach two tight switchbacks near the end of the road. Tour buses do make it up, however, becoming an attraction in themselves when they reverse up or down the lower switchback.

### 58. Monarch Mine

This ore mine on Mt. Stephen closed in 1952, the last of many mines in the parks to cease operations. Worked first by explorer Tom Wilson, but operated by many companies in its seventy-year history, the mine produced lead, zinc and silver, and showed traces of gold. At one point, a tramway was used to bring ore from the mountain to the roadside. Other mines operated in the area of Mt. Field and near the Kicking Horse campground. Small holes in the mountains are still visible from the road, but all of the mines have been permanently sealed.

### 59. Natural Bridge

The Natural Bridge is located near the entrance of the Emerald Lake Road, 3 kilometres west of Field. The Kicking Horse River has eroded its way through the limestone bedrock to create its channel. At the Natural Bridge, it encountered a flat block of resistant limestone. At first, the water went over this rock, forming a small waterfall, but gradually wore away the limestone beneath it, eventually leaving it behind as a bridge. The bridge is submerged during peak flows of water, especially during the spring when the ice and snow are melting. An animal lick of mineral salts is nearby and attracts many animals, particularly elk.

### 60. Emerald Lake

This classic, glacier-fed lake is one of the most beautiful in the mountains. Located at the end of 8-kilometre-long Emerald Lake Road, this lovely gem beneath Emerald Peak and the President Range is well worth a side trip. The lake was discovered in 1882 by Tom Wilson, who also found Lake Louise that same year. The original lodge, Emerald Lake Chalet, was built by the CPR in 1902, but was rebuilt in 1986 under private ownership. A trail around the lake can be hiked and boats can be rented for $12 per hour. Daily trail rides are also available. Emerald Lake Lodge is a cosy spot for lunch or a cup of tea.

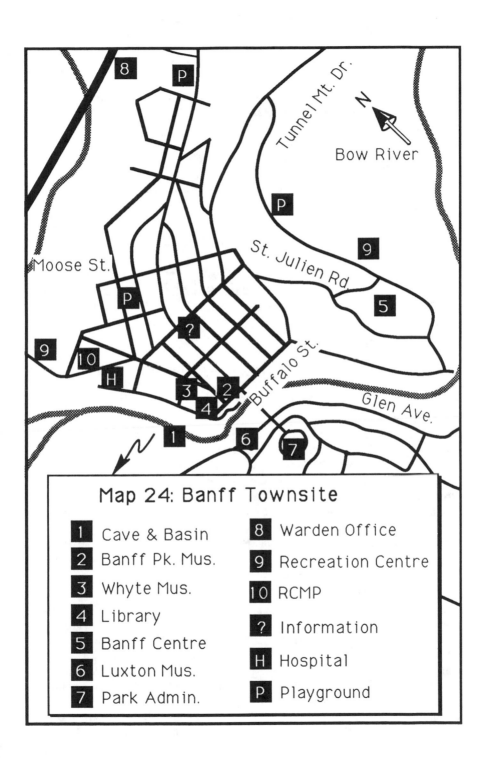

## Map 24: Banff Townsite

| | | | |
|---|---|---|---|
| 1 | Cave & Basin | 8 | Warden Office |
| 2 | Banff Pk. Mus. | 9 | Recreation Centre |
| 3 | Whyte Mus. | 10 | RCMP |
| 4 | Library | ? | Information |
| 5 | Banff Centre | H | Hospital |
| 6 | Luxton Mus. | P | Playground |
| 7 | Park Admin. | | |

Bow River

Tunnel Mt. Dr.

N

St. Julien Rd.

Moose St.

Buffalo St.

Glen Ave.

# 12 // Rainy Days And Relaxation

Sometimes, bad weather or the need for a rest from hiking leaves families in the predicament of circular conversations:

"What can we do?"

"What do you want to do?"

"I don't know. What do you want to do?"

"I don't know . . . " And so on . . .

For these days and for the sake of family sanity, here is a list of entertaining townsite activities and places to visit.

## Banff

### // Places to See

□ The Banff Centre

With an international reputation, The Banff Centre is a hub of cultural activity, offering an idyllic setting for writers, dancers, actors and artists of all kinds to learn and explore their craft. The buildings of this centre on St. Julien Road blend into the natural setting and make a comfortable background for a pleasant stroll. More importantly, the centre offers a wide array of concerts, poetry readings and exhibitions during its summer-long Festival of the Arts. Most of these are more appropriate for adults or older children, but some will appeal to younger members of the family. Phone (403) 762–6300 for a schedule of events.

□ Banff Park Museum

When hunting was permitted and even encouraged in the early days of the national parks, many wildlife specimens were collected and preserved. This impressive collection of animals and birds is on permanent display at the Banff Park Museum on Banff Avenue, just before the avenue crosses the Bow River. Built in 1903 of Douglas fir, the museum building is notable for its pagoda-style roof, which allows a maximum amount of natural light to brighten the warm orange-red wood interior. This unusual Victorian building — and its stuffed occupants — will delight families for at least an hour of looking and wondering. Open daily from 10 am to 6 pm. Free admission. Wheelchair accessible on first floor.

□ Banff Springs Hotel

The directors of the CPR realized early on that drawing tourists to the mountains could increase the railway's revenue greatly. The idea made great economic sense, and the first log-frame Banff Springs Hotel, the first of many CPR hotels across Canada, was opened in 1888. Halfway through construction, it was discovered that the guest rooms were facing away from the best views, which the kitchen staff would enjoy instead. A viewing area on the kitchen side of the hotel was hastily added to correct this error. The present hotel, built of concrete, faced with siltstone and facing the right way, was built between 1904 and 1928. Free tours are offered Friday to Tuesday at 3 pm.

*Cave and Basin*

## // Swimming Pools

▫ Cave and Basin Centennial Centre

Recently renovated, the Cave and Basin Centennial Centre on Cave Avenue, south of the Bow River, can provide families with up to half a day of entertainment. The discovery of the hot springs here in 1883 provided the momentum needed to convince government and railway officials to preserve the wilderness around them as Canada's first national park. Bathhouses were built here in 1887, and the present stone building, with its arches inspired by Scottish manors and French chateaux, was built in 1914. Swimming in the naturally heated pool (29–32°C) is, of course, the main attraction for children. The pool is open from mid-June to Labour Day between 10 am and 8 pm. Admission for adults is $2, and $1.25 for children aged three to sixteen. As a fun alternative, bathing suits of the style worn in 1914 can be rented for $1 each.

In addition to the pool, there are displays, video presentations and self-guided interpretive trails available at no charge year-round. Wheelchair accessible.

▫ Upper Hot Springs Pool

This naturally heated pool on Mountain Road is warmed by the sulphur springs of Sulphur Mountain. The smell of sulphur is sometimes quite strong, but this pool is popular because it averages 38°C, a full six degrees hotter than the Cave and Basin pool. Open year-round, the pool is open June to October from 8:30 am to 11 pm. Adults $2, children $1.25.

## // Museums

▫ Luxton Museum

This small museum at 1 Birch Avenue will be of interest to children intrigued by history and the culture of the Indians of the Northern Plains and the

*Banff Park Museum*

Canadian Rockies. Open year-round; May to October, 10 am to 6 pm. Adults $2, children under 12 free.

▫ Natural History Museum

This small museum features displays and videos on the geological and biological evolution of the mountains. Open year-round. July and August, open 10 am to 10 pm; May, June, September, open 10 am to 8 pm. Adults $2, children $1, under 10 free. 112 Banff Avenue, (403) 762-4747.

▫ Whyte Museum of the Canadian Rockies

This quiet museum at 111 Bear Street can offer families several enjoyable hours of viewing an extensive collection of mountain paintings and photographs. With a large archival collection, three galleries, several historic homes and a heritage collection, the exhibits at this museum change monthly. Open year-round. Victoria Day to Thanksgiving, 10 am to 6 pm. Adult $2, seniors/students $1, children under 12 free. (403) 762-2291 for exhibition information.

▫ Walter J. Phillips Gallery

Located in Glyde Hall of the Banff Centre on St. Julien Road, this gallery is noted for its exhibitions of contemporary art. It is likely of interest only to older children. Open year-round. In summer, open noon to 5 pm. Free admission. (403) 762-6283 for exhibition information.

## // Gondolas

▫ Lake Louise Gondola Lift

Used for skiers during the winter, this gondola provides summer visitors with incredible views of the Victoria Glacier and Lake Louise across the Bow Valley, as well as the Slate Range to the east. The lift ascends to the 2034-metre mark of Mt. Whitehorn. Wildflowers abound here, and there are hiking trails through the mountain meadows. A restaurant, outdoor terrace and gift shop are found at the

*Banff Springs Hotel*

upper terminal. Open daily, 9 am to 6 pm from mid-June to late September. Adults $8, children 5-12 $4, under 5 free. Lake Louise Ski Area Road. (403) 522-3555.

◻ Sulphur Mountain Gondola Lift
From its base on Mountain Avenue, this gondola lift takes families up to a 2,285-metre elevation in eight minutes, to the summit of Sulphur Mountain, and offers a 360° panoramic view of Banff and the Bow Valley area. It is a very popular outing for children, and is close to Banff townsite. A restaurant, cafeteria and gift shop are located near the observation deck. Seasonal hours. Adults $8, children 5-11 $3.50, under 5 free. Recorded information: (403) 762-5438.

◻ Sunshine Village Gondola
This five-kilometre gondola ride is supposed to operate in both summer and winter, but service has been sporadic. When operating, it takes visitors to the lovely alpine Sunshine Meadows beneath the icy Monarch Ramparts. A free chairlift takes visitors even further to a viewpoint and the starting point for several hikes in the area. Located at the end of Sunshine Road which leaves the Trans-Canada Highway 8 kilometres west of Banff. June to September, 9 am to 8 pm. Seasonal rates. Information: (403) 762-6500.

## // Playgrounds

◻ Banff Avenue by Marmot Centre.
◻ Squirrel Street between Moose and Elk Streets.
◻ Tunnel Mountain Campground.
◻ Picnic area in Central Park on Buffalo Street, behind Parks Canada Museum.
◻ Banff Recreation Grounds – Cave Avenue, east of Luxton Museum – picnic and playground facilities, two ball diamonds, soccer field and track; permits: (403) 762-1229.
◻ Soccer field by Banff Springs Hotel.

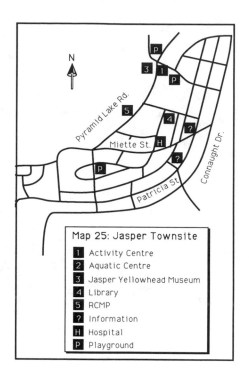

Map 25: Jasper Townsite
1 Activity Centre
2 Aquatic Centre
3 Jasper Yellowhead Museum
4 Library
5 RCMP
? Information
H Hospital
P Playground

## // Cinema

- □ Lux Cinema Centre – Bear and Wolf Streets, (403) 762-8595.

## // Recreation Centres

- □ Banff Community Fitness Centre – 335 Beaver Street (in high school), (403) 762-1229.
- □ Banff Recreation Centre – Mt. Norquay Road, (403) 762-4454.
- □ Douglas Fir Resort/Waterslide Complex – Tunnel Mountain Road, (403) 762-5591, $7 per day.

## Jasper

## // Places to See

□ Jasper Park Lodge

Built by the Canadian National Railway in imitation of the successful lodges constructed by the Canadian Pacific Railway, Jasper Park Lodge was built in 1922 as the world's largest log building. Guests stay in surrounding log cabins and can order room service delivered by bicycling waiters. The recently renovated present lodge was built in 1952 to replace the original structure, which burned down that year.

There is a lot for families to do here. In addition to touring the lodge and its facilities, kids can go wild here. Canoes, row boats, sailboats and paddle boats can all be rented for a day's entertainment. Lodge guests can take advantage of a children's recreation and daycare program daily between noon and 5 pm. There is also a riding stable, and bike rentals are available. (403) 852-3301.

## // Swimming Pools

□ Miette Hot Springs

Three springs feed the pool here and make it the warmest one in the Rockies at an average of 40°C. This is definitely a hot pool. Kids love it. Located 60 kilometres north of Jasper townsite on Highway 16, the springs are open daily, mid-June to Labour Day, from 8:30 am to 10:30 pm. The surrounding grounds make a nice spot for a picnic dinner. Adults $2, children $1.25.

## // Museums

□ The Den

More than 100 specimens of wildlife can be found at The Den, an exhibit at Whistlers Hotel, Connaught Drive and Miette Street, (403) 953-3361.

□ Jasper Yellowhead Museum

This little museum is the most recent addition to the sights to see in Jasper. It features exhibits on aspects of local pioneer life, such as the fur trade and the building of the railway. Most children relate very well to the exhibits here. 400 Pyramid Lake Road, (403) 852-3013. Open 10 am to 4:30 pm. Admission by donation.

## // Gondolas

□ Jasper Tramway

Rising up the Whistlers to 2,277 metres, this wheelchair-accessible tramcar takes families high into the alpine zone of pikas, marmots and fragile wildflowers, where a short trail 45-minute trail leads to the summit. Panoramic views of the Athabasca and Miette River valleys are well worth the trip. Children will love the ride and the view. Open spring-fall. Daily, mid-June to Labour Day, 8 am to 9:30 pm. Cafeteria, restaurant and lounge. Adults $9, children $4.50, under 5 free.

## // Cinema

□ Chaba Theatre — 604 Connaught Drive, (403) 852-4749.
□ Marmot Lodge — 94 Connaught Drive, (403) 852-4471.

Screens *Challenge of the Canadian Rockies* daily at 7 and 9 pm. A mountain adventure film which thrills children of all ages. Also playing daily at the Chaba Theatre, daily at 4 pm.

## // Playgrounds

□ Lake Edith and Lake Annette.
□ Beaches, playgrounds and picnic sites are located at Lake Edith and Lake Annette, just 3 kilometres from Jasper on Lodge Road. There is a paved, wheelchair-accessible, trail around Lake Annette, and a bike trail around Lake Edith.
□ Pine Avenue between Tonquin and Turret Streets.
□ Between Pyramid Lake Road and Bonhomme Street.
□ Whistlers' Campground.

## // Recreation Centres

□ Jasper Activity Centre — 303 Pyramid Avenue, (403) 852-3381; racquetball, tennis, volleyball, weightlifting.
□ Jasper Aquatic Centre — 401 Pyramid Lake Road, (403) 852-3663;

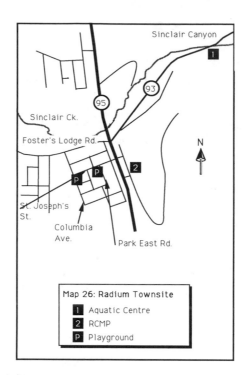

Map 26: Radium Townsite
1 Aquatic Centre
2 RCMP
P Playground

pool and waterslide. Families $10, adults $3.75, children 5-13 $2.25, children 3-5, $1.

## Radium Hot Springs

### // Swimming Pools

- Radium Hot Springs Aquacourt.
- Hot and cold pool. Summer hours 9 am to 11 pm hot pool; 10 am to 11 pm cool pool. $2 adults, $1.25 children.

### // Playgrounds

- Columbia Avenue and St. Joseph's Street.
- Park East Road, and St. Joseph's Street.
- Redstreak Campground.

## Golden

### // Museums

- Golden and District Historical Museum

This small museum presents displays of artifacts from the mountaineering, logging and mining activities in this historic area. 1302 11th Street S, (604) 344-5169.

- B.C. Wildlife Museum

Located on the Trans-Canada Highway on the hill above Golden, this recently opened wildlife museum offers a fine display of Rocky Mountain wildlife. Open 9 am to 9 pm during the summer. (604) 344-6330.

Map 27: Golden
1 B.C. Wildlife Museum
2 Historical Museum
3 Recreation Centre
4 RCMP
5 Library
? Information
H Hospital
P Playground

## // Cinema

- Yoho Theatre — 802 South 10th Avenue, Golden, (604) 344-5510.

## // Playgrounds

- 6th Street South and 6th Avenue South.
- Alexander Park on Alexander Drive.
- 10th Street South and 9th Avenue South.
- Keith King Memorial Park, end of Maple Drive.
- ball diamonds and playground.
- Municipal Campground, 9th Street South and Spruce Drive.

## // Recreation Centres

- Golden and District Centennial Arena and Golden Community Park for swimming, curling, skating, racquet sports and weightlifting. 1418 South 9th Street, (604) 344-6511.

## Field

## // Playgrounds

- Information Centre on Trans-Canada Highway.
- School playground on Stephen Avenue.

# 13 // Playing It Safe

Our family has never had a major safety problem in all our years of hiking together. We've certainly made many mistakes, but none have caused more than inconvenience and discomfort. The real story on hiking is that it is very simple if you plan ahead and take precautions.

Nevertheless, travelling into the backcountry wilderness can be a scary idea for many parents, especially those with younger children. Most of their fears are unspoken, but they are the kind of concerns that keep people in the towns or on the highway looking at the mountains from a distance. What if we get lost? What happens if a bear attacks us? What if one of the kids falls in a river or breaks his leg? What do we do so far from help?

These anxieties are natural. The mountains are monstrously large and intimidating, even when you know them well. As you leave town or your car behind on a hike, you are leaving behind a familiar world that you understand and have some control over. In the mountains, you live by the rules of nature, where people just don't seem all that significant. The old idea of dominating nature, seems to be a feeble joke, especially when you are watching out not only for your own safety, but the safety of unpredictable children in a new environment.

Let's face it, people do get lost, hurt and even killed in the mountains every year. This is a cold, hard fact. But don't give up your dreams of backcountry adventure now just because you have to protect your kids. Remember: most accidents involve people who are doing high-risk activities such as glacier-walking, mountaineering or ice-climbing. Most families don't run the same risks. Family activities in the mountains tend to range from nature hikes to several-day backpacking expeditions. While these explorations are not risk-free, most of the risks can be minimized through a combination of preparation, knowledge and humility. Do your worrying before the trip and translate it into planning. This way, you won't have to worry once you are on the trail. See **At a Glance** for information on emergency contacts.

Most safety is a matter of common sense. But it is easy to lose this in an unfamiliar environment. We've seen children go crazy when they find snow in the middle of summer and then fall and smash themselves badly on the rocks because of their carelessness. In another incident, two children ran ahead of their families and almost battered their heads against a huge mountain ram coming around the corner. Setting boundaries for children before you begin hiking has a sobering effect that doesn't need to diminish a child's sense of play and fun, unless parents get too heavy-handed. Children can be responsible for each other by using a buddy system. Parents will still have to supervise and give guidance, sometimes quietly checking up on the children to ensure safety systems are working. Small things, like checking to make sure a child packing for herself has packed her sleeping bag and not just toys, may also be necessary. It is also important that parents agree on the objectives of the hike. If mom wants to scale a peak and dad wants to snooze in the sun like a marmot, the children can be caught up in the indecision and frustration, increasing the likelihood of rash actions. By anticipating potential problems, families can hike safely and happily in the Rockies.

## // Weather

It doesn't take long before you realize the folk wisdom of the people who live in the mountains. The local residents will often be overheard saying, "If you want the weather to change, just wait five minutes." Indeed, this is almost the case. The most important thing to know about the weather in the Rockies is that it is CHANGEABLE. The postcard pictures of snow-capped mountains thrusting nobly into a pure blue sky do happen in the mountains, but they are rarities. The weather can change from sunny to stormy — and back again — in just a few hours or, sometimes, in minutes. While mountain weather is influenced by broad weather patterns, it is also extremely local. Families might find themselves in the midst of a rainstorm or snow squall at any time during a hike, yet back in town or even on the other side of a valley, the weather might be perfectly clear.

Our family has been rained on, snowed on and stormed on at one time or another. Most of the time, it hasn't been a problem because we've had everything we needed to protect ourselves. Sometimes, though, we've been lazy and left toques and gloves or other equipment in the car, refusing to believe that such a beautiful, warm day could turn nasty. Of course, whenever we omit these from our packs, we soon come in need of them. We've been lucky never to suffer serious consequences, but we've often had to give up our hike or shorten our intended stay at a destination because of poor forethought.

Running into bad weather on a hike is likely to be your only complaint about hiking in the Rockies, and even this problem is usually fleeting. Bad weather on a hike is often short-lived and is usually just an irritant that dampens the bodies as well as the spirits of you and your children. Yet, even in heavy downpours, kids can hike happily if they are dressed to splash in puddles and take extra care on slippery slopes. When the hike is over, the weather will add to the memories of your adventure as you dry out around a campfire or at the laundromat.

At its most extreme, bad weather can lead to hazardous hiking conditions, such as slippery, wet paths and flooding rivers. These dangers can be avoided with caution and common sense. A greater problem is hypothermia, a gradual lowering of the body's temperature which prevents vital organs such as the brain, heart and kidneys from functioning properly. Hypothermia can cause confusion and poor coordination, which can both result in mistakes or accidents. In extreme cases, it can cause death. For more details on hypothermia, see **Good Health.**

## // Weather Forecasting

Mountain weather is fascinating. The sky is always moving and changing. Knowing what the sky is doing and understanding its meaning can help you predict what the weather will do and help you decide whether to start or continue your hike. Weather forecasting is a great problem-solving game for children.

Major weather patterns are caused when cold, dry air meets warm, moist air. As these two types of air meet to form a weather front, the cold air pushes the moist air upwards, where it cools and condenses to form clouds. Fronts bringing bad weather can be easily recognized because of their association with clouds, precipitation and temperature changes. (Weather forecasters will also tell you that a drop in pressure also indicates a spell of bad weather. This is true, but not usually helpful when you are out in the wilderness without a barometer.) In the mountains, these weather fronts often move through passes or gaps because these areas offer the least resistance. When trying to predict the weather, it is often helpful to look between the mountains to see what is happening over the passes.

The general rules of weather prediction are:

- Bad weather is approaching if layered clouds are moving in from the south, especially if they are getting lower.
- Broken clouds from the north indicate good, dry weather.
- Stationary clouds usually mean an impending storm.
- The darker the clouds, the thicker they are and the more moisture they contain.
- Weather usually deteriorates as the day progresses. Usually, it is wise to begin hikes early in the day.
- Check the weather reports at the information centres before leaving on a hike. This will give you a general expectation of the day's weather, although it will not account for localized weather patterns.
- Remember that it can snow any time of year, at any altitude.
- Remember that the weather gets colder and wetter as you gain altitude or get closer to the Continental Divide.
- Be an optimist in your daily planning and a pessimist in your preparations. In other words, don't let the weather stop you; just take along rain gear.

## // Lightning

On most hikes, lightning simply won't be a problem because families usually don't hike up high enough to be in the primary danger zones. However, the risk is always there and bears discussion.

Lightning frequently occurs during mountain storms, particularly on summer afternoons and evenings. Lightning storms occur most often over ridges and peaks, and it is naturally here that they are the most dangerous to hikers. This danger shouldn't be exaggerated: injuries or deaths caused by lightning are quite rare and can usually be avoided.

Lightning flashes when electricity builds up in moist air which is pushed upwards in the formation of cumulonimbus clouds. This potential energy is released as the air ionizes and loses its ability to insulate the accumulated electrical pressure. When lightning strikes, it seeks the shortest route through the air to a good conductor. Mountain ridges and peaks, being so close to the clouds, normally make attractive targets for lightning. However, because electricity seeks the best conductor for its energy, humans make better conductors than rocks, trees or earth and may become targets even if other objects are closer to the lightning source. Wet objects or people make excellent conductors, as does metal.

Watch for these signs of a coming thunderstorm:

- Thunderclouds (cumulonimbus).

- A sudden drop in temperature.
- Large raindrops, snowflakes or hailstones.
- Corona: The seldom-seen corona is a bluish glow around a potential target. It is caused by ionizing air and is accompanied by the sour smell of ozone and crackling noises. For example, if a person is a potential target, her hair will stand on end and crackle as she is surrounded by a halo-like glow.

Many people survive even direct lightning strikes. The degree of danger from lightning depends on the size of the current passing through the body and the points through which it passes. The worst threat comes from a direct strike or ground current that passes through the vital organs. Large strikes will also cause burns at points of entry and exit and may also startle or paralyse a victim to such a degree that a fall or other accident results. Protecting yourself from the dangers of lightning primarily involves staying away from areas where storms might occur. Because the current diminishes as it gets farther from the strike point, it naturally follows that the farther your family is from a strike, the less danger you are in. If a storm comes up while the family is on a ridge, get off it as fast as possible to put the greatest distance between you and possible strikes. Because lightning travels so well on wet surfaces, soils and lichen patches holding water, and wet people, get off even faster if it starts to rain.

The following is a list of general safety rules during a thunderstorm:

- Stay calm and seek safety quickly. Children are easily frightened by lightning.
- Avoid strike areas.
- Get off ridges and shoulders if possible.
- Avoid wet areas.
- Find shelter among taller — but not the tallest — objects, such as mid-sized trees.
- Keep your hands off the ground. A ground current could enter through one hand and would pass through the vital organs before finding an exit point.
- If standing, keep your feet close together. This minimizes the voltage of the ground current flowing through your body. The wider the span between entry and exit points, the greater the voltage difference and the greater the flow of current.
- Sit on insulating objects such as backpacks, sleeping bags, foam mattresses.
- Sit on detached rocks.
- Avoid sitting in depressions. People do this to get as low as possible, but because the current travels along the ground like water and wants to find the shortest route, you make a better conductor than the ground and become a shortcut for the current.
- Avoid overhangs.
- If you can't get off a ridge, try to stay in the middle. Edges and ends attract lightning and are too easy to fall from.

## // Getting Lost

Few things are worse than not knowing where our children are, and for some parents, venturing into the wilderness seems to be a folly that must inevitably lead to children wandering off and falling off a waiting ledge or into a swallowing stream.

Our family has been lost several times. On the most serious occasion, we left late in the day to do what we thought was a simple nature hike lasting perhaps an hour. Because it was so straightforward, we brought no maps, no water, no food, no extra clothing, nothing. Getting carried away playing and looking at things, we overstayed our time and darkness fell. We tried to hurry back along the loop as best we could in the darkness. At one point, Ged did a bit of bushwhacking where the trail was unclear. About to take a step forward, he drew back just in time to avoid stepping into empty space. Even though we knew we were still on or near the trail, it was so black in the forest that it was dangerous to go on.

So we stayed put. We wrapped Bronwyn up in Ged's sweater and she lay between us as we huddled to keep her warm. She went to sleep counting stars and singing songs and slept all night while we shivered and shared a single pair of gloves, staring sleepless into the darkness. We knew we would make it through unless it started to rain. Fortunately, the rain held off until dawn, and at first light, we hiked quickly back to the car and turned the heater on full blast. On our way out, we passed the place where Ged had decided to take back his step and found he had almost walked himself off a twenty-foot cliff. But we got out safely — that time. And it was a lesson we haven't forgotten!

Staying found on most trails in the Rockies is actually quite simple. All of the trails in the parks are quite wide and easy to follow. They are also very well maintained, with bridges over most streams, so there is rarely any need to leave a trail to pick it up again after crossing a river. Trail crews are constantly at work building more bridges, clearing blown down trees, making the trails more passable and building new trails. You may still encounter obstacles, but these should be minor.

Signs are usually posted to identify trailheads and trail junctions so that you don't accidentally get on the wrong trail or take a wrong turn. Many of these signs also indicate distances to destinations, so you can assess how far you have gone and how much of the hike remains. Looking for signs can motivate children to continue hiking. The signs are not foolproof, however. Some have been destroyed or turned by winter storms or vandals, so it is wise to bring a map or guide along with you to guarantee that you stay on the right track.

Also remember that distances in the wilderness can be a bit disorienting. The mountains are beyond any scale of size we can comprehend, and so what seems so close might still be quite far off. Hiking several kilometres through the wilderness takes a lot longer than the same distance on paved sidewalks and roads, especially when you're carrying weight on your back or tired kids in your arms. You will often be sure that signs which say kilometres must really mean miles. Sometimes this can be discouraging, but be patient and learn to travel at the slower pace of mountain time.

The easiest way to get lost is to leave the trail. Some hardy souls think they can take a shortcut or resent following a trail that other people have travelled, and so they decide they can have a better hike by finding their own route. This rash activity is known as bushwhacking. Not only is bushwhacking

*Balancing on adzed bridges*

almost guaranteed to get you lost, scratched, frustrated and possibly injured, it is very damaging to the vegetation and soil, which gets crushed and thrashed at as you struggle up the slopes. Don't do it. Apart from getting lost, your children would find bushwhacking very difficult: the ups and downs of the raw mountainside are difficult for little legs to negotiate; the undergrowth tends to scratch unprotected faces and also makes it difficult for children to see where to take the next step. Even if you don't get lost, slow progress and accidents are inevitable, especially with children.

Staying found isn't difficult, but follow these common-sense suggestions:

- Always stay on the trail.
- Talk about the hike in advance with your children. Discuss expectations, the motivating destination and identifiable landmarks that mark the progress of the hike. Encourage team effort.
- Have a safety plan in case anyone gets lost. Review safety plans with the children and make sure everyone is working with the same plan. It's no help at all if a lost child heads back for the car and her frantic parents are racing ahead to the terminus of the trail in the opposite direction. Usually, the best plans involve all hikers trying to reach an agreed-on destination, such as a prominent landmark or the trailhead. Get the children's suggestions for meeting places. Plans that suggest

returning to the last spot your family was together usually don't work because each person remembers a different spot.

- Each hiker should carry a whistle to blow if he or she gets lost.
- Lost hikers can also leave messages with arrows of sticks or piles of stones.
- If someone gets lost, don't panic. Stay calm, assess the situation and act quickly to begin a search. Panic usually only leads to accidents and rash decisions.
- Always hike with two or more adults when hiking with young children. Never hike alone even without children. If an accident happens, someone must be able to run for help.
- Stay together. Don't let children run out of sight on the trail.
- Bell the children. Tie a bell to the children's clothing so that you can tell where they are by sound. This also functions well as a bear bell.
- Wear bright clothing. It clashes with the greens and browns of the wilderness, but it is easily visible and can be used for signalling.
- Take frequent rest and snack breaks to avoid exhaustion, which can lead to straggling children, accidents and poor decisions.
- Exercise good judgement. No destination is worth risking injuries or the trauma of getting lost.
- Make sure someone knows where you are going. On overnight hikes, you are required to register with the parks and to leave a receipt on the dashboard of your car. Wardens will note cars left beyond their allotted time and investigate the reason.
- Start hikes early in the day to avoid being caught by darkness. This isn't too much problem in the summer, when the days are so long, but precautions against hiking in the dark should always be a consideration.
- If you do get lost at night, find a sheltered area and stay there.

## // Survival

In the unlikely event that you get lost and stuck on a mountainside without tents and camping equipment, your safety and comfort depend on staying warm and dry. You are in for a long, cold night after the sun sets.

- Don't worry about who got you into this mess; put up and shut up. Blaming and complaining only makes everyone frustrated and miserable.
- Before it gets dark, find a safe, sheltered spot away from the wind.
- Keeping the children warm is more important than your own comfort. Their smaller bodies can lose heat more rapidly and so they need more protection. From a more selfish point of view, warm children will also complain less, helping all of you to make the best of a bad situation.
- Stay close together. The more of you there are, the more body heat you can share. Pile up like mice in a cage. Keeping your head and torso warm is more important than keeping your hands and feet warm.
- Collect branches and dry leaves to sit and lie on. Sitting on rocks will only draw the heat out of your bodies; sitting on moss will get you wet,

*Staying dry on the snow*

which will make the coldness worse. If absolutely necessary, break or cut branches off living trees to create an insulating layer between you and the ground.

- Small children may be able to find shelter inside hollow logs or stumps.
- Leaves, pine needles and sawdust from rotting stumps will all provide some insulation from the cold. Cover the children up just as if you were playing with sand at the beach.
- Campfires are illegal in the backcountry (except in designated firepits) because of the fire hazard and the ugly scars they leave. However, the temperature drops severely overnight in the mountains, so you must stay warm. In these circumstances, a campfire is a necessity. Collect enough dry wood to last all night. You don't want to be wandering around in the darkness. Use old tissues or dry leaves to get the fire going and then use your wood sparingly. A big blaze will use up your supply very quickly for little benefit.
- Don't cut down branches from growing trees for firewood; the wood is green and will give you nothing but smoke.
- Use smoke to let rescuers find your position only during the daytime and only under controlled conditions to minimize the risk of a forest fire.
- Rub two sticks together to start a fire if you don't have matches. This is most likely to keep you warm by the energy you burn up rather than by getting a fire going. Still, in these extreme cases, it is worth a try.
- Ration whatever food you have to keep your energies up and to maintain your body temperature. Try to drink water mostly in the daytime when it is warmer, so that you cool yourself down less from the inside out.

- Stay in one spot;
- Choose to stay in open areas such as meadows so that you can be seen from the air. Spread bright clothing on the ground and flash mirrors or metal objects to increase your chances of being seen from the air.
- Keep up morale by singing songs, playing word games and telling stories.

## // Animal Confrontations

Families travelling in the Rocky Mountains can sometimes forget that they are not visiting a zoo. These animals are not behind bars and none of them are tame in any way. They are all very wild. It is easy to forget this. Children, particularly, are naturally drawn to animals and want to feed and cuddle them as if they were small puppies or bunnies. While this may make for a great memory or photograph, it can be dangerous to children and adults. A pika can bite; many animals carry ticks and fleas; a porcupine's quills can be imbedded in skin; moose, elk and sheep are exceptionally strong and are known to charge at people; bears can kill.

Feeding animals as if they were tame pets reduces their dignity. In search of easy food, they become scavengers haunting roadsides and campgrounds. There they become nuisances that break into tents and even cars to get at food. They will destroy or carry off your supper without regret, adding insult to injury by leaving you the mess to clean up. Because the lure of easy food brings many animals to campgrounds and highways, they are often killed in traffic accidents. The fortunate ones die instantly; those that aren't so lucky are just wounded and usually drag themselves off the road into the bush to die in slow agony.

Also remember that even the best human food is junk food for animals. It can make animals sick and can eventually cause their death because of the internal and nutritional disorders created. If children ate nothing but chocolate bars and potato chips, they would soon get sick, too. Encourage your children to let the wild animals stay wild. Do not feed or approach them. Enjoy them from a respectful distance and use binoculars if you want to get a closer look at them.

## // Bears

In all of our years of backpacking, we have seen bears only on roadsides and in campgrounds, never on the trail. Our closest encounter, however, could have been devastating. When Bronwyn was just seven months old and unable to crawl, we hiked up to a high meadow. She fell asleep and so we set her down to sleep in a blanket on the grass, knowing that she couldn't go anywhere while we explored a ridge and mountain tarn. We returned to find her still sleeping. Since it was getting late, we settled her in her backpack and returned the way we had come up earlier in the afternoon. Not a hundred metres down the trail from where Bronwyn had been sleeping, we found a freshly uprooted tree, huge claw marks and large green scats. These weren't there when we had passed by on our way up to the meadow. Bronwyn had been left unprotected within sight of a grizzly digging for insects.

All of us want to see the bears in the parks. We are often so eager to make a sighting that any dark object — a stump or a porcupine — can work on our imaginations and transform itself into a bear. In fact, bear sightings on the trails are fortunately few. Like most wild animals, bears enjoy their own company best. Both the grizzly and the smaller black bear avoid human contact unless easy food is available. Bears are most commonly seen where food is most plentiful. In the early spring after awakening from hibernation, these primarily vegetarian animals seek out roots, new growth and rodents in the low, snow-free valleys, preferring hillsides where digging is easier. As the snow melts, the bears will move up the mountain slopes in search of horsetails, cow parsnip and berries.

Like skunks, bears are best at a distance. Should you happen to see one across a far meadow, you can watch it at your leisure. Bears smell better than they see. If you see a bear in the distance, make sure she is aware of your presence by getting upwind of her. This might sound like exactly the wrong advice, but if a bear is aware of you, she will likely move on. It is when a bear is startled and feels threatened by a surprise encounter that it is most dangerous. If the bear is in a meadow close to you or, worse yet, on your trail, make a calm but hasty retreat. The worst scenario is coming across a sow and her cub(s), especially if you happen to get between the two of them. Like most good mothers, the mother bear will do anything necessary to protect her baby. Curiosity or bravery have no place here. Get out fast.

In addition to following the campground rules outlined in **Walking Softly**, families can do other things to avoid bear encounters:

- Make lots of noise. This shouldn't be hard with kids around. You can get extra help by wearing bear bells, clapping, singing and shouting. Bears hate to be surprised. They will leave the area if they hear you coming.
- Children often want to treat tents like their bedrooms, eating food in them and keeping them messy. Do not allow them to eat, drink or chew gum inside the tent. This applies to snacks and treats as well as proper meals.
- Don't carry firearms as protection against bears. They are illegal and useless against 600 pounds of charging claws. Any injury they could cause to the bear would only infuriate her.
- Look out for bear scats. They vary according to the bear's diet and are usually quite large. In summer they will be greenish-brown; in the fall they will become berry-red.
- Menstruating women should avoid hiking in the backcountry because the odour can attract bears.
- Family camping usually means no attempts at making bigger families anyway, but avoiding sex in the backcountry is usually advisable because the odour might attract bears.

If you do chance to meet a bear, you have several options. The most important thing is to keep the kids quiet and for everyone not to panic. Speak in a low voice and back away from the bear without running or turning your back on her. Do not run, yell or make fast movements that might startle the bear. If your backpack has a lot of smelly food, try sacrificing it to distract the bear while you make your escape. Remove it slowly and place it on the ground as you back away.

If you cannot back away from the bear, or if it charges you, the best option is to fall to the ground, curled up in a ball with your hands over your

*Helping hands get everyone to the top*

neck. Many school-aged children will be familiar with this drop-and-cover technique from earthquake drills. If you have small children, get on top of them and try to protect them with your body. A mauling may occur, but you will likely survive.

Climbing trees is often suggested as a way to escape bears. However, this is next to impossible in reality. Getting everyone up fast enough is one problem; finding a tree that is both tall and climbable is another problem because most trees in the Rockies have only weak or broken branches at climbing heights. Remember that black bears can climb up after you and grizzlies can sometimes shake a tree down.

In the Canadian Rockies, bear problems have been drastically reduced and incidents between bears and people are few. Normally, bears will ignore people unless provoked.

# 14 // Good Health

Stay calm! It takes effort to get into serious trouble in the mountains. Most hiking-related injuries and illnesses are minor. The trails are well marked and well maintained, generally avoiding hazardous areas. Most problems that occur are caused by hikers leaving the trail, over-exerting themselves, getting caught in bad weather, hiking after dark or being careless.

However, medical conditions that are easily treatable in the city can become more dangerous in the backcountry simply because of the time delay before treatment is available. Rescue workers travelling by horse, foot or helicopter respond as quickly as possible, but the logistics of running for help and getting help to the accident site takes time. See **At a Glance** for emergency contact information. While broken legs, heart attacks and appendicitis can't always be anticipated, be careful to consider the current health and ability levels of everyone in your family before starting out on the more demanding trails. As in the city, good health in the mountains is first a matter of prevention, then a matter of cure.

A first-aid kit is mandatory equipment on any hike, no matter how short. A good first-aid kit can carry all of your basic health necessities and yet take up no more room than a large pencil case or a small toilet kit. Such a kit should include:

✓ several sizes of bandages for cuts
✓ three squares of sterile gauze
✓ one three-inch tensor bandage for sprains
✓ soap (biodegradable; small bar or liquid)
✓ butterfly dressings or adhesive tape for gaping wounds
✓ lip balm; gives lips extra protection, especially for use if hiking in snowy areas

| | |
|---|---|
| ✓ scissors | ✓ needle and thread |
| ✓ tweezers for splinters, ticks | ✓ safety pins for slings etc. |
| ✓ moleskin for blisters | ✓ insect repellent |
| ✓ sunscreen | ✓ aspirin or liquid Tempra |
| ✓ pencil for writing notes | ✓ Q-tip for cleaning wounds |

## // Blisters

Blisters are the most common health problem in the mountains. They can turn a simple hike into an agony and sweet-tempered children (and adults) into whining monsters. Caused by poorly fitting boots or socks rubbing against the skin, blisters are made worse by sweat and moisture. They occur most commonly on heels and toes.

At the first hint of a warm or sore spot on the feet, take a break from your hike and deal with the problem. Check your children's feet at least once an hour to prevent them from ignoring the warning signs. Small blisters should not be opened. Just wash and dry them well and then surround them with a piece of moleskin. Cut a hole in the moleskin and place the remaining piece around the blister to relieve the pressure from the sore spot. Placing a bandage over the blister will merely put greater rubbing pressure on the affected area.

*Improvised sunglasses*

If the blister is large, treat it the same way as a small one but remove the excess fluid from it. This can be done by sterilizing a needle in flame and then pricking the blister. Make the tiniest hole possible and leave the skin over the wound to protect the raw skin beneath. If the skin is broken already, clean it and then cover it with a sterile dressing. Surround the wound with extra tape or bandage to relieve the rubbing pressure. Don't force children to continue hiking if they have bad blisters. Put yourself in their shoes — if you can! Remember how painful blisters can be and cut the hike short if necessary.

## // Sprains

Almost everyone takes a wrong step once in a while, especially kids running along a trail or tripping over a root. Sprains vary greatly in their seriousness, but usually involve some pain and tissue swelling. Minor sprains can be ignored if the victim can put up with a bit of discomfort. More serious ones should be wrapped in a tensor bandage that is wound alternately above and below the affected joint to stiffen it. Severe sprains shouldn't be walked on and may require a premature end to the hike or even that the victim be carried out to the trailhead. As with blisters, try to think of the pain from your child's perspective when judging whether or not to continue the hike.

## // Fractures

Fractures should be immobilized as soon as possible. An arm can be tied to the torso, a leg can be held in place by tying it to a stick, a fractured jaw can be held in place by tying it in a loop of cloth that encircles the face and knots at the crown of the head. Further treatment should be administered by experienced medical staff.

## // Severe Injuries

Severe injuries resulting from a fall of a metre or more or from a strike by lightning require immediate attention. These are your treatment priorities:
1. restore breathing and/or heartbeat
2. stop blood loss
3. treat for shock
4. treat wounds

Do not move a child or adult until you are certain of the extent of her injuries. If she is unconscious, assume injuries to the head and spine and do not move her. If she is conscious, get her to attempt moving limbs by herself. If she is able to move them, she can be cautiously moved; if not, move nothing unless life-saving requires it. Time is of the essence when treating severe injuries. Usually, you do not have the knowledge or equipment to adequately deal with the emergency. One person should apply immediate first aid to address the major problems. Some one else should RUN for help. At the road, flag down the first car and drive to the nearest phone to call the warden service for emergency aid.

## // Heart Arrest

Heart attacks are usually suffered by older or unfit adults, but a severe shock, such as that caused by a lightning strike, can stop a child's heart also. Whatever the cause, you must get it going again as soon as possible. Lie the victim on his back. With your hands on top of each other and using your body weight, press on his chest until it depresses three to five centimetres. Do this fifty to sixty times a minute for at least one hour or until the heart starts beating on its own. While one person is restarting the heart, someone else should work on restoring breathing with mouth-to-mouth resuscitation.

## // Stopped Breathing

Lie the injured child on her back and remove any food, dentures or other obstructions to clear the airway. Pull her head back to extend the neck and to straighten the airway. Pinch her nostrils to prevent air from escaping and place your mouth against her mouth. Exhale into her mouth and then watch to see that her chest rises and falls. If the chest rises and falls and if her body colour is good, your resuscitation is working. If the skin turns or remains bluish, check the airways for blockages. Resume resuscitation until the patient is able to breathe freely by herself.

## // Blood Loss

Stopping the loss of blood is vital, particularly if an artery has been cut and the blood is spurting out in time with the heartbeat. Use the first available clean fabric and apply pressure to the bleeding area to stop the flow. If this doesn't work, use a tourniquet as a last resort. A tourniquet is a cloth or rope tied tightly between the wound and the torso. Remove the tourniquet as soon as the flow of blood stops. Some experts feel that a tourniquet should never be used because the limb can be damaged by the loss of blood flow; however, if the wound is bleeding so profusely that pressure will not stop the flow, the blood isn't going to the rest of the limb anyway.

Routine cuts and scrapes should be cleaned and bandaged normally. Gaping wounds should be cleaned and then pulled tight with tape or a butterfly bandage. Minimize the risk of infection by leaving dirty wounds open or lightly covered if they cannot be cleaned.

## // Shock

Shock is usually caused by blood loss or a lightning strike. It can be recognized by paleness, clammy skin, sweating, nausea and vomiting, a low blood pressure and a fast, feeble pulse. Shock is common after major injuries, but can occur even after minor injuries, especially in children. It is made worse by fear or pain. Severe cases of shock can cause the body to lose its ability to create heat, resulting in hypothermia.

Assume that a person has gone into shock after any accident, since it can develop immediately or hours after the event. Keep the accident victim flat on her back and raise her legs if possible. Use everything you have to keep her warm. In cases of severe shock, clothing won't transfer heat fast enough. In this case, skin to skin contact is the quickest way of transmitting heat. Concentrate on warming the torso and vital organs first.

Comfort and companionship are especially necessary for children in shock. Soothing words, hugs and special treats or privileges can help reduce shock, fear and the awareness of pain.

## // Hypothermia

Hypothermia is a condition in which the body loses heat more rapidly than it can be produced. Hypothermia develops gradually and is a condition in which prevention takes priority over treatment. It most commonly sneaks up on hikers when they are cold, tired and hungry. Wet clothes almost guarantee the onset of hypothermia. Children are particularly susceptible because the rigors of hiking will tire them more quickly than adults and they will expend more energy on the trail. Watch for excessive whining, listlessness and stubbornness in children as early warning signs of hypothermia.

Hypothermia's symptoms slide along a continuum. In its mildest form, victims show goose pimples and shiver. They become lethargic and pale and tend to lag behind the rest of the group. As hypothermia becomes more severe, the victim stops shivering and becomes confused and makes poor decisions. It is at this point that hypothermia becomes more dangerous, because decision-making and coping abilities are impaired and the problem might be ignored until the condition becomes irreversible. As hypothermia continues, the muscles will become rigid, reflexes will be lost and mental abilities will diminish. Eventually, the victim can slip into a coma and die.

This grim scenario rarely happens, except in extreme conditions and situations. However, most hikers suffer mild cases of hypothermia without realizing it. They quickly recover by wearing more clothes and having a hot drink. Everything is fine. Hypothermia can be prevented by wearing warm clothing in layers, eating very regularly (almost constantly), taking frequent rest stops and staying dry. Take along a change of clothing for each hiker and lots of food loaded with carbohydrates, such as sugar, honey and candy. Keep the kids from wading or splashing in the icy mountain streams.

If hypothermia does begin to set in, deal with it immediately by adding more clothing, eating and resting. Get the sufferer into a sleeping bag if necessary and if that still doesn't work, heat the torso with hot water poured into an improvised waterbottle. Skin to skin contact works fastest. In extreme situations, warm the body with anything short of burning it.

## // Heat Exhaustion

Heat exhaustion is almost the opposite of hypothermia and is rarely a serious problem in the mountains. Caused by strenuous activity in a hot environment, a victim can begin to sweat profusely, feel faint, nauseated and weak, and develop cramps or a headache. Unfit adults or over-exerted or over-dressed children most commonly suffer from heat exhaustion, but the consequences are rarely serious. To recover from heat exhaustion, drink lots of fluids and lie down for a while in a cool place.

## // Giardiasis

Also known as "Beaver Fever," giardiasis is severe diarrhoea caused by a parasitic protozoan known as *Giardia lamblia*. This microscopic parasite attaches itself to the small intestines of animal and human carriers and finds its way into mountain lakes and streams in the form of cysts when feces are dropped close to surface water. Giardiasis is contracted by drinking the contaminated water. Some experts believe that we all carry some of the protozoans around in our bodies all of the time and suffer giardiasis only when we get an acute accumulation of them.

Although an increased beaver population in the parks does correlate with an increase in "beaver fever," unsanitary hikers have been most responsible for its spread. Pets such as dogs are also common carriers of the parasite.

In addition to diarrhoea, other symptoms can begin about two weeks after contracting the parasite. These include nausea, gas and lack of appetite. Giardiasis can lead to weight loss and malnutrition. Children suffer from giardiasis more acutely than adults because of their susceptibility to malnutrition.

Although all mountain water is potentially rife with the *Giardia lamblia* protozoan, we have hiked for years without taking precautions and have never suffered from giardiasis. Now that we hike with children, however, we always carry our water or purify any water we get in the backcountry to guarantee our continuing good health. Don't let the kids cool off by guzzling water from rivers and lakes. This classic pleasure must, unfortunately, be denied on the off-chance that the water is contaminated. The protozoan can be killed by boiling all of your drinking and washing water for 20 minutes or it can be filtered out using a portable ceramic filter. The cysts are not killed by iodine tablets or chlorination. Keep your hands clean at all times and defecate 100 metres away from all streams or lakes if washroom facilities are not available. Use washroom facilities if they are available, even on dark nights when kids would rather just "go" in the bushes nearby.

If giardiasis is contracted, it is treatable with anti-protozoan medicine; however, this is one illness you will never want to repeat.

## // Sunburn

Most families are aware of the need to protect everyone from the cancer-causing radiation from the sun, especially between 11:00 and 3:00. The problem of sunburn is even more acute in the mountains. The ultraviolet radiation that causes sunburns becomes stronger at higher elevations, and people burn faster the higher up a mountain they go. Sitting by mountain lakes, glaciers and snowpools will also increase the chance of a burn because the light is reflected back at you as well as hitting you directly. Hikers also tend to be out in the open air for long periods of time, thus increasing the likelihood of a burn, even on hazy or cloudy days.

Preventing sunburn is easy. Protect everyone from the sun at all times by wearing hats, sunscreen on all exposed skin and lip balm. The higher the PABA number on the sunscreen, the more protection you will get. Also, wear long-sleeved shirts and long pants to protect you from the sun. (These will also protect you from insects, scratches and hypothermia.)

If anyone does get a sunburn, there is little to be done but endure it. It can be cooled with lotions. Drink lots of water to prevent dehydration.

## // Ticks

Wood ticks look like walking reddish-brown lentils and are relatives of the spider. Only five millimetres long, these insects are frequently found between April and June in grassy places frequented by elk, pikas and marmots. Adult ticks will be waiting for hikers on grasses and low-lying plants. If hikers brush by them, the ticks will hook onto them and then crawl upwards looking for a place to attach. Ticks will latch onto skin with their mouths and gorge themselves on blood for several days and then drop off.

Most people find the very idea of blood-engorged ticks quite revolting. The real problem with ticks, however, is that some of them carry diseases. Rocky Mountain Spotted Fever is carried by some ticks. Characterized by a high fever, headaches and muscular pain beginning three to twelve days after a person has been infected, the disease will gradually cause an infected-looking rash over the whole body. The illness is more severe in children than in adults. Now easily treatable with antibiotics, this fever used to cause delirium, brain and heart damage and even death.

The best way to prevent these diseases is to prevent ticks from attaching. During tick season (early spring and summer), wear clothes that are tight at the wrist; tuck pants into socks. Repellents are only mildly effective. Fortunately, ticks usually take several hours to decide where they want to attach themselves. Check everyone's entire body for ticks daily. Ticks especially like hairy areas, behind the ears and the nape of the neck. They will also attach where clothes fit tightly, such as the waist, or near underwear or a bra. If checking yourself or your children at your campsite, you must kill ticks by flushing them down a toilet or burning them. (They are impossible to squash and can live for several years without food or water.) If you show them mercy, they will merely find you again.

If a tick attaches to someone, pull it off with tweezers. Pull straight back and gently, without yanking. The tick must come off intact so that any existing infection in its body is not spread by crushed body parts. Immersing the tick in oil or insect repellent may cause the tick to drop off on its own. If the tick is removed but the mouth remains imbedded, remove the parts with a sterilized knife or pin. Wash the wound well and sterilize it. If you develop any signs of weakness after this incident, get to a doctor as soon as possible.

# 15 // Eating Right

Chocolate cake, cheesecake, ratatouille, stew . . . it is possible to eat mouthwatering, delicious meals while backpacking or on a dayhike. Although our own meals tend to range from bland to bland because we are lazy cooks, we have from time to time gotten our act together to serve elaborate casseroles, tasty snacks and even camembert by candlelight.

Eating in the backcountry isn't all nuts and granola, although these can be an important part of a healthy, high-energy diet. Before going on to the suggestions and recipes, consider the following limitations which will affect your meal planning.

## // Weight

You have to carry whatever you will eat. With the exception of a few trails, such as the one to Lake Agnes, there is no restaurant or teahouse at the end. There are no corner stores that you can nip out to, either. Everything you are going to eat will be on your back in your pack. However, how much weight you carry is an individual choice. If you really want to eat it, you will convince yourself to carry it. For example, I cannot stand powdered milk and carried several heavy litres of whole milk at a time into the backcountry while pregnant. We also prefer block cheese to the powdered stuff, even though the blocks are far heavier and more perishable.

To minimize the weight, carry as much food as possible in a dried format. Many tasty dried meals ranging from scrambled eggs or chili to more exotic concoctions such as veal parmigiana are available in outdoor stores. We don't take this option ourselves because these meals are expensive and the small portions always seem to leave us hungry.

The next lightest option is to take whatever you want, but substitute dry food for liquid foods whenever possible. This is what we prefer. For example, we carry powdered spaghetti sauce, soups and juices that we have to reconstitute at our campsite instead of carrying heavier but ready-to-eat canned products. If we are well prepared, we will dry our own fruit and vegetables rather than packing them in whole and heavy. They are a bit chewier, but quite flavourful. Using home-dried food also limits the garbage you have to pack out. This option usually requires extensive food preparation at your backcountry campsite.

Canned foods are conveniently packaged, preserve food well and simply require heating, but they are heavy. Canned tuna is a staple on our hikes. Occasionally we will lug a can of beans into the backcountry, but we find most canned stews, soups and pastas contain more water than food. Because we tend to be spontaneous hikers and fail to prepare for trips in advance, we carry a lot of fresh vegetables and fruits. The extra flavour and nutrition they add to our diet compensates for their weight. Carry your weight the shortest possible distance. This means planning to eat your heaviest foods first. For example, if you will have two suppers at different locations in the backcountry, eat the heavy canned beans the first night and the lighter dried fettuccini on the second night. If possible, distribute the weight among all members of the family. Kids can help out a bit and every little bit helps. Perhaps their loads can be the first to be lightened.

## // Bulk

Next to weight, bulk is our biggest packing problem, especially when we are carrying enough food for ravenous children. We try to package most of our food in plastic bags, often double wrapping them for extra security and water-tightness. (We've learned through sad experience that a hole in the sugar bag can make a wet backpack a sticky home for an ant colony!) We try to select foods that will take up minimal space for their weight. For example, we will often carry flat, foldable pita breads instead of ordinary bread or buns, rice instead of noodles, or flat noodles instead of hollow noodles weighing the same amount, because we can squash these packages into a spare corner of our packs more easily. Film cans are invaluable as bulk and weight reducers. Spices, sugar, salt, pepper, matches (even toothpaste, soaps and shampoos) can be easily transported this way. Children with daypacks can take light, bulky items, too.

## // Needs

Minimizing both weight and bulk requires an accurate assessment of your needs. Doing this requires a mix of experience and careful planning. Usually, you learn by your mistakes and by being forced to pack out unnecessary food. Planning for your needs requires walking a fine line between providing for necessities and being prepared for unaccustomed hunger or unforeseen delays in returning to the trailhead. You want to carry as little food as possible, but you are safer to carry too much food than to go hungry. Plan your meals precisely, so that you know what you will be eating at each meal and how much of each meal you and your children will each eat. Remember that exercising and being outdoors make everyone eat more than they do at home, especially children. Like bridge-building engineers, fudge your precise measurements by as much as 25% so that you are sure to take enough food. Even if you don't eat it all, it will be lighter on the way out.

Where most hikers err is in overestimating the number of snack foods or the amount of rice or noodles needed as bulk carbohydrates for the evening meal. Another problem lies in the area of packing and preparation. Because it is already packaged, hikers will often pack a half-kilogram of cheese when they will only eat half of it. Or they will throw in an entire bag of noodles instead of separating out what they need into a smaller bag. Each overweight or oversized item seems light and packable in isolation, but when they are added together they account for a lot of unnecessary bulk and weight. Film cans, plastic bags and margarine tubs are all immensely helpful for down-sizing your food supplies to fit your needs. Take the time to make your preparations. Every part of your body will thank you.

## // Perishability

The lack of refrigeration is the greatest limitation to the type of foods you can eat. On short hikes, this is likely no problem, but several days in the backcountry during the long hot summer can spoil the food as it perspires along with you up the trail. Unless we will eat it by lunchtime, we don't carry

*Chocolate pudding hits the spot*

many perishable foods: meats go rancid; bananas turn brown; cheeses sweat; butter melts; milk sours; bread moulds. Other foods are easily crushed. We've stared, open-mouthed, watching hikers pack in a half-dozen eggs for breakfast. The risks of breaking them, the danger of salmonella, and the trials of frying them just aren't worth it.

What's left? Lots. Dried foods, hard vegetables and fruits (such as onions, potatoes, zucchini, eggplant, carrots, cabbage, apples, oranges, raisins), canned meats (tuna, salmon, luncheon meat), nuts, compact breads and cakes (Christmas cake), rice, noodles, powdered mixes etc. can all be kept quite fresh without any need for refrigeration. Even softer fresh foods (grapes, tomatoes) can be kept for some time if they are carefully packed so that they don't get crushed. Cheeses can be brought along in dried form or wrapped in paper and then double-bagged to avoid leaks. You can even have the luxury of fresh meat on your first night in the backcountry if it starts the day frozen and thaws in your pack. (Avoid this on the hottest days because of the risk of food poisoning.) Bulk coil sausage is another option we rely on a lot. You can also keep perishables cool by packing them together with a can of frozen juice. And remember, if your destination is near a snowfield, or a glacier-fed lake or stream, you can put nature's refrigerator to work for you. Kids love this return to nature's methods. Cold water can keep things cool and slow the deterioration of food, but remember that it can't reverse spoilage.

## // Nutrition and Taste

We likely err by focusing on our energy levels too much instead of ensuring that we have a well-balanced diet. We like sweet things too much. Cookies, cakes and sugar-laced drinks are, I blush to confess, staples of our camping diet, rather than the healthier nuts, fruits and vegetables. Our own foibles aside, you can eat well from all four food groups with a bit of planning. Powdered milk, dried vegetables, canned meats and portable fruits are easily carried and eaten by themselves or combined in one-dish casseroles. For example, one of our staple suppers combines rice, cheese and vegetables to give us all the complementary proteins, carbohydrates and vitamins we need from a single main course. Be sure to pack foods your children like and will eat. They need the energy. Most kids don't want to eat the same lunch or supper day after day, so be sure to plan a varied menu. Try to include some of your children's favourite foods.

## // Single-Burner Stove

Unless you are roasting hotdogs on a stick (a popular and fun family meal) or sharing cooking equipment with other hikers, your culinary prowess will be limited because you can only heat one pot at a time on a single stove or, occasionally, a campfire. We've been spoiled by microwaves, multiple-burner stoves and ovens, but in the backcountry, we're back to basic, sequential cooking again. This limitation usually means that we cook casserole-style, where everything gets dumped unceremoniously into one pot. This means that recipes requiring a lot of fuss or simultaneously cooked ingredients are almost out of the question. The best we manage is to cook our meal in a pot and to warm other ingredients, such as cheese, on a lid, which doubles as a plate. Some slow-burning stoves can actually be turned into ovens capable of baking breads or cakes; however, you are most likely to be boiling your food and pouring off any excess water. Frying is also possible and increases your meal types significantly, but again, you are limited to one pot at a time. We avoid frying because of the terrific mess it makes of the pots and because the smell of fat attracts animals.

## // Cleanliness

Campground etiquette can be disgusting. Out of our normal routine, we tend to break a lot of our household rules: To save dishes, we eat out of the cooking pots, often sharing the same dish. We have even been known (in our grosser moments) to eat our meal out of a pot and then make our tea in the same pot, using our drink as wash water. Fortunately for our reputation, we've succumbed to social pressure and given up this extreme practice. Pots, dishes and eating utensils can be washed well if you have a scrubbing pad and some biodegradable soap. You can even use hot water if you heat some up on the stove. To make cleaning easier, we never fry food. We also avoid burning. Burnt food is not only a hassle to remove with your limited cleaning supplies, it tastes terrible and will be a wet, soggy mess to pack out if your kids refuse to eat it. Most stoves burn quite hot, so give your full attention to your food and stir it constantly.

It is also important to pack out all food, leftovers, scraps and packaging. Leaving a dirty campsite insults the environment you are a guest in, leaves a mess for others to clean up, attracts wildlife and possibly makes it dangerous for the next group of hikers, and can harm the wildlife that ends up eating it. Even organic remains like orange peels must be carried out. They can take several years to compost.

The following are some food and recipe suggestions. Don't let these suggestions limit you. What you eat on the trail and in the backcountry is limited only by your willingness to carry weight, your ability to keep foods fresh, your flair for cooking and your personal tastes.

*Taking a break*

## // Snack Foods

- ▢ trail mix: this varies from the standard Gorp (Good Ol' Raisins and Peanuts) to deluxe concoctions of various nuts, dates, dried apricots, coconut, seeds of all sorts etc. Experiment. Try to avoid chocolate chips, which melt.
- ▢ fruit of all types, especially apples, oranges, bananas, kiwis, hard plums. Softer fruits can be taken with care.
- ▢ vegetable sticks: carrots, celery, zucchini
- ▢ baked goods: cookies, muffins, dense brownies, cake breads such as banana bread, marzipan bread, Christmas cake
- ▢ packaged snacks such as granola bars and fruit leathers
- ▢ juice carried in place of water or from crystals
- ▢ chocolate bars, if weather is cool enough
- ▢ marshmallows
- ▢ hard cheeses and tightly packed crackers

## // Breakfast

What you choose for breakfast depends mostly on your personal style. If you are in a rush to get on the trail, a piece of fruit may be enough to get you going. Others prefer leisurely cooked breakfasts complete with a hot drink. Whatever you choose to eat, remember that you are building your energy levels for the day of hiking ahead. Foods high in carbohydrates and calories — and lots of them — will keep you going. One thing you don't need to worry about on the trail is gaining weight. Try these foods for breakfast:

- fruit
- cakes such as Christmas cake or marzipan bread (icing is neatly on the inside)
- pita with jam or peanut butter
- muffins
- cooked porridge with brown sugar and reconstituted powdered milk (not too difficult to clean if you hurry)
- cold cereals and powdered milk, especially non-crushable cereals like granola, muesli, perhaps Cheerios
- juice, tea, coffee or powdered milk

## // Lunch

Our lunches tend to be cold and are often pre-made before a hike. Like normal lunches everywhere, lunch on the trail is usually quick and simple:

- pita sandwiches: garbanzo, hummus, sausage, cheese, cream cheese, cucumber fillings
- sandwiches with perishable fillings, if eaten on day hikes or the first day of an overnight trip: egg salad, tuna, luncheon meats, tomato etc.
- bagels and cream cheese
- alfalfa sprouts pack well and add flavour to sandwiches and bagels
- vegetable pieces: mushrooms, cucumbers, carrots, celery
- nuts
- cookies
- fruits

## // Supper

Supper can be lunch repeated, but most often, we expect and prepare a more elaborate cooked meal. Perhaps this is because we have reached our destination for the day and, with the tent pitched and the sleeping bags out, we feel more settled, more established. The following meals can all be made in one pot and without frying and can help you avoid the expense of the specially dried foods available in outdoor equipment shops and heavy canned foods from supermarkets:

### Dave's Glorp

*This is our staple casserole, one we tend to eat again and again because it is easy to pack, nutritious and easily varied.*

*Boil water. Cook rice. Then add tuna, fresh or dried vegetables, salt and pepper and, finally, cheese. Serve when cheese is melted.*

*Almost everything can be substituted in this recipe. Use sausage or salmon as a tuna replacement, or omit meat altogether. Any combination of carrots, onions, snow peas, potatoes, tomatoes, green peppers, zucchinis or other squash works well. Couscous and noodles can be substituted for rice. Cheddar, mozzarella, havarti and especially blue cheese produce flavourful results. Your favourite spices or various dried cream soups, such as mushroom or chicken, can also be added.*

## Macaroni and Cheese

*This is a simpler version of Dave's Glorp. You can make it from store-bought packages or simply add noodles to boiling, salted water. When the noodles are cooked, add in chopped cheese. Melt cheese and serve.*

## Spaghetti

*Like macaroni and cheese, but add in tomato paste and a packet of sauce seasoning, available in all grocery stores. Mix the sauce right in with the noodles, to eliminate the need to shift pots on the burner. Zucchini goes well in the sauce.*

## Beef Jerky

*This is a food you must prepare ahead of time, but is suitable for snacks and supper. Slice 2-cm-thick cuts of roast or steak as thinly as possible. Marinate one hour in soy sauce. Bake at 60°C for 8 – 9 hours or for 45 minutes in the microwave. These are done when crisp.*

## Ratatouille

*Cook pared eggplant, zucchini, onions and tomatoes together in one pot. Use a bit of salted water to keep the vegetables from burning before the vegetables provide their own juices. Add pepper, oregano and cheese if desired.*

## Lentils and Rice

*Lentils are a great meat substitute. Very light and high in protein, they are a very nutritious and can be cooked in a variety of ways. For this basic dish, boil 1 cup lentils and 1 cup rice in about 3 cups of water. Flavour with 2 – 3 bouillon cubes, a bay leaf and salt to taste. The basic recipe can be flavoured with brown sugar and soy sauce, tomato paste, garlic and onions, curry powder, oregano, honey and mustard, or cheese.*

## Lentil Stew

*Combine 1 cup lentils, 1 cup rice, 250 grams of garlic sausage, small can of tomato paste, 2 cups water, bay leaf, bouillon cubes, 1 onion, 1 clove garlic, celery or celery seed, 1/4 teaspoon oregano, salt to taste. Bring to boil and simmer 25 minutes.*

## Hungarian Goulash

*Brown 4 onions, 4-6 potatoes with 1 kilogram of garlic sausage or canned meat. Season with pepper, paprika and salt. Add 1/2 litre beef bouillon (from cube). Add carrots, turnips as desired. Cook over low heat until vegetables are tender. Thicken with flour if desired.*

## Spanish Michel

*Boil 1/2 kilogram broken spaghetti until tender. Add large can tomatoes, 1 onion, 1 green pepper, and 1/2 kilogram canned meat, garlic sausage or boiled ham. Cook over low heat about 15 minutes more.*

### Melted Camembert

*Place a tin of camembert or brie in boiling water and cook for several minutes. When the tin is opened, slice the melted cheese and eat with whole almonds or apple slices. This makes a delicious and elegant snack, especially late at night.*

### Clam Chowder

*This delectable treat won't make a full meal, but adds luxury to a primitive campground. Combine one can of minced or whole clams with canned or dried potato soup and corn. Add 1 cup liquid milk (reconstituted from powder), salt and pepper.*

### Avocado Pâté

*Prepared in advance and tightly stored in a plastic bag, this smooth green ooze is a great sandwich filling or vegetable dip. It stores best in cool weather, but is very transportable. Mash 2 large avocados, 2-3 cloves of crushed garlic, juice of 1 lemon and a bit of salt. Chill. Black pepper, chili powder or sunflower seeds can be added if you wish.*

### Hummus

*Like the avocado pâté, hummus makes a great vegetarian sandwich spread. It must be prepared in advance and stored for hiking in a plastic bag. Soak 1 cup dry chick peas overnight, then simmer for 2 hours until tender. Blend peas, 1/4 cup bean liquid, 1/4 cup lemon juice, 1-2 cloves garlic, 3 tablespoons sesame butter (tahini) and 1 teaspoon salt together. Store. Add chopped parsley if you wish.*

### Bannock

*This traditional bread, baked by Natives and explorers alike, doesn't get dry or mouldy and is easily transportable. The dry ingredients can be combined at home: 3 cups flour, 1 teaspoon salt, 2 tablespoons baking powder, 1 tablespoons sugar, 2 tablespoons lard. Mix together in a plastic bag. The lard may get soft, but resists melting. At your campsite, mix the dry ingredients with 3 cups cold water. Turn your stove into an oven by nesting the pots as you would a double boiler, with water in the bottom pot. Cover the pot filled with the bannock dough to keep the heat in. Bake 35 – 45 minutes. Serve with jam or honey. You can also add raisins, nuts or cheese to bannock. The children may enjoy toasting thickened bannock dough that has been wrapped around a stick.*

## // Desserts

### Apple Crisp

*At home, mix together 1 cup flour, 1 cup brown sugar, 1 teaspoon each of salt, cinnamon and nutmeg. At your campsite, combine dry ingredients with 5 – 6 pared and sliced apples. Cook in a double boiler until apples are soft. Oatmeal may be added to the dry ingredients.*

### Cakes

*A slow-burning stove is your main requirement for this extravagance.*

*Snack time*

*Available cake mixes sometimes require only water and eggs. Dried eggs are available at many outfitting stores. Kids can be occupied making sure the cake doesn't burn.*

### Cheesecake

*Uncooked cheesecake is a fun project for kids which relies heavily on pre-made foods. Cook or buy a pie shell. Make or buy a topping. Strawberry topping, for example, can be made by combining 2 cups strawberries with sugar to taste and 1/4 cup starch. Cook this on a double boiler until thick and then store in a tightly sealed plastic bag. Buy a package of refrigerator cheesecake. At the campsite, follow the package directions to prepare cheesecake mix and place filling in the pie shell. Add topping. Double-bag the whole cheesecake and seal both bags very tightly. Place this package in a lake or river, sheltering it so that it doesn't float away. Chill. The novelty of using what nature provides will please you and your children. Enjoy.*

### Pudding

*Packaged puddings can also be prepared in much the same way as the cheesecake and appeal greatly to children. Follow package directions and combine dry ingredients with reconstituted powdered milk. Chill, either in dishes or directly in a plastic bag. The bag corner can be cut and the pudding squeezed out onto dishes. Make pudding preparation your children's contribution to the meal.*

## // General Cooking Tips

- Add variety and flavour to your food with spices brought along in film cans.
- Plan your cooking sequence in advance so that additions to the pot —

such as vegetables and cheeses that need to be cut — are ready for the pot when needed, not when the rest of the food is cold or burnt.

□ Most stoves burn very hot and so pot contents must be stirred constantly. Steel pots also get a lot hotter than aluminum ones. The steel pots seem to distribute the heat more evenly also.

□ Cook on stable surfaces to avoid tipping your pots and stove.

□ Aluminum windscreens improve cooking time and help keep your stove from blowing out.

□ Hot-burning stoves can be turned into ovens by making a covered double boiler out of your pots to even out and sustain the heat.

□ Never leave children unsupervised near the stove.

□ Cook well away from your tent and dispose of cooking and dish water away from the tent and away from surface water.

□ Cook only what you will eat to avoid packing out the wasted food.

□ Water-based cooking is the easiest to clean up after.

□ Avoid frying whenever possible.

□ Fast-drying J-cloths are ideal for cleaning.

□ Use biodegradable soap to wash up.

□ Sand can help scour pots if you have forgotten your scrubber.

□ Pack out all garbage.

# 16 // Taking Stock

Almost everything families need can be found in the park towns of Jasper and Banff. Other towns just outside the parks, such as Golden, Radium Hot Springs, Canmore and Calgary can supply the rest. In addition, several convenience stores are located near several park highways and junctions. Film, snack food and souvenirs can be found everywhere. The selected listings below should help you find your essential supplies:

## // Food and Groceries
- Banff Red Rooster — 202 Caribou Street, Banff.
- Canada Safeway — 318 Marten Street, Banff.
- Village Market — Samson Mall, Lake Louise.
- Mountain Foods — 606 Connaught Drive, Jasper.
- Nutter's Bulk Foods — 622 Patricia Street, Jasper.
- Super A Foods  — 601 Patricia Stret, Jasper.
- Robinson's IGA Foodliner — 218 Connaught Drive, Jasper.
- The Siding — 318 Stephen Street, Field.
- Golden IGA  — 624 North 9th Avenue, Golden.
- Overwaitea — 1014 South 10th Avenue, Golden.
- Radium Super Mart — Highway 93 and 95, Radium Hot Springs.

## // Gas
Gas is available at Banff, Lake Louise, Jasper, Field, Radium Hot Springs and all outlying towns. It is also available at several junctions, such as Johnston Canyon, Saskatchewan River Crossing in Banff; Sunwapta Falls, Icefield Centre and Pocohontas in Jasper; West Louise Lodge in Yoho; Vermilion Crossing in Kootenay.

## // Laundromats
- Laundry Co. Ltd. — 203 Caribou Street, Banff.
- Chalet Grocery and Coin Laundry — Tunnel Mountain Road, Banff.
- Lake Louise Laundromat — Samson Mall, Lake Louise.
- Coin Clean — 601 Patricia Street, Jasper.
- Super Suds Coin Laundry — 801 South 10th Avenue, Golden.

## // Pharmacies
- Gourlay's Pharmacy — 229 Bear Street, Banff.
- Harmony Drug — 111 Banff Avenue.
- IDA — 8th Avenue and 8th Street, Canmore.
- Cavell Value Drug Mart — 602 Patricia Street, Jasper.
- Whistlers Drugs — 100 Miette Avenue, Jasper.
- Golden Drugmart — 1106 S 10th Avenue, Golden.

## // Sporting Equipment

Many of the larger hotels sell sporting equipment and fashions. Other stores include:

- Abominable Ski and Sportswear — 229 Banff Avenue, Banff.
- Mountain Magic Equipment — 224 Bear Street, Banff.
- Mountain Trekker — 204 Caribou Street, Banff.
- Monod Sports — 129 Banff Avenue, Banff.
- Wilson Mountain Sports Ltd. — Samson Mall, Lake Louise.
- Pinnacles Sports with Fashion — 621 Patricia Street, Jasper.
- The Sports Shop — 416 Connaught Drive, Jasper.
- Mountain Equipment Co-op — 1009 4th Avenue, Calgary.
- Selkirk Sports — 504 N 9th Avenue, Golden.
- MacLeods: The Hardware Store — 914 10th Avenue, Golden.

## // Children's Wear

Children's clothing can be found in most department stores, some sportswear stores and in specialty souvenir and T-shirt shops. Other sources include:

- Hudson's Bay Company — 125 Banff Avenue, Banff.
- Kindersport — Banff Avenue Mall, Banff.
- Scallywags — Banff Springs Hotel, Banff.
            — Chateau Lake Louise, Lake Louise.

## // Toys

Gift shops galore can provide amusing diversions for little people. Among stores specializing in children's toys are:

- Banff Bears  — Banff Avenue Mall, Banff.
- Vic's Corner — Bear Street Mall, Banff.
- Hobby House — 215 Banff Avenue, Banff.
- Hudson's Bay Company — 125 Banff Avenue, Banff.

## // Books

Many gift shops also carry a selection of picture books and guidebooks on the Rockies. Stores that specialize in books include:

- Banff Book and Art Den — 110 Banff Avenue, Banff.
- Books and Gifts — 223 Bear Street, Banff.
- Woodruff and Blum — Samson Mall, Lake Louise.
- Mountain Lights — Chateau Lake Louise, Lake Louise.
            — 119 Banff Avenue, Banff.
- Reader's Choice Bookstore — 610 Connaught Drive, Jasper.
- Golden Book Store — 515B N 9th Avenue, Golden.

# 17 // Resources

## // Addresses

Canadian Parks Service
220 Fourth Ave. S.E.
Box 2989, Station M
Calgary, Alta. T2P 3H8
(403) 292-4401

Banff National Park
P.O. Box 900
Banff, Alta.
T0L 0C0
(403 762-3324

Jasper National Park
P.O. Box 10
Jasper, Alta. T0E 1E0
(403) 852-6161

Kootenay National Park
P.O. Box 220
Radium Hot Springs, B.C. V0A 1M0
(604) 347-9615

Yoho National Park
P.O. Box 99
Field, B.C. V0A 1G0
(604) 343-6324

Lake O'Hara Lodge and Reservations
Lake O'Hara Lodge Ltd., Box 1677,
Banff, Alta. T0L 0C0
(403) 762-2188
Summer: (604) 343-6418

Yoho Information Centre: (604) 343-6433

Alpine Club of Canada
Box 1026
Banff, Alta. T0L 0C0
(403) 762-4481
Bookings: (403) 678-5855

## // Books

Beers, Don. *The Magic of Lake O'Hara: A Trail Guide.* Calgary: Rocky Mountain, 1981.

This small book is the definitive work on the Lake O'Hara area. It provides a comprehensive guide to the many trails that radiate out within five kilometres of Lake O'Hara. The Lake O'Hara area has so many trails which intersect each other that this guide is almost indispensable for families wishing to make the most of their time in this wonderful mountain retreat.

Beers, Don. *The Wonder of Yoho.* Calgary: Rocky Mountain, 1989.

Like its sister, this book is a guidebook to the trails in the area. This book includes the Lake O'Hara area but doesn't restrict itself to that hiking hotspot. Hikes throughout the park are given extensive detailing and beautiful photos complement the text.

Gadd, Ben. *Handbook of the Canadian Rockies*. Jasper: Corax, 1986.

Although illustrated only in black and white, this naturalist's guide book provides a wealth of information on everything you want to know about mountain geology, insects, wildlife, birds, trees and flowers.

Langshaw, Eric. *Animals of the Canadian Rockies, Birds of the Canadian Rockies* and *Wildflowers of the Canadian Rockies*. Banff: Summerthought, 1987, 1987, 1985.

These three small guidebooks provide full colour photos and brief descriptions of a wide array of entries under each topic. Full colour pictures and the low price make these good guidebooks for the beginning or casual naturalist. There are several other books in the series for those interested in geology and herbal medicine.

Marty, Sid. *A Grand and Fabulous Notion*. Toronto: NC Press, 1984.

Written to commemorate the centenary of Canada's national parks, this book focuses on the discovery of the Banff Hot Springs and the heady, formative early days in Banff, Canada's first national park.

Marty, Sid. *Men for the Mountains*. New York: Vangard, 1978.

A wonderful anecdotal volume about working as a warden in the parks, including many tales about the men and women who explored and established the parks.

Patton, Brian and Robinson, Bart. *The Canadian Rockies Trail Guide*. Banff: Devil's Head, 1971. 4th ed. Banff: Summerthought, 1990.

This classic first came out in 1971 and has been updated several times since. Covering the four contiguous national parks as well as Waterton, this guide is the best and most used of all Canadian Rockies hiking guides.

*Peterson Field Guides* on Rocky Mountain Wildflowers, Animal Tracks, Western Birds, etc. Boston: Houghton Mifflin.

The entire Peterson series, sponsored by the National Audubon Society, provides comprehensive, detailed information for nature enthusiasts. The books include both colour photos and pen-and-ink drawings.

Pole, Graham. *Canadian Rockies SuperGuide*. Banff: Altitude, 1991.

This colourful and beautifully presented guidebook provides brief descriptions of the geological and historical highlights of the Canadian Rockies. Well-researched and thorough, the book is divided into geographical areas of interest and the small articles are highly readable. The book also boasts excellent photographs.

Spring, Vicki. *95 Hikes in the Canadian Rockies*. Vancouver: Douglas and McIntyre, 1982.

One of several fine hiking guides written by Spring, this book focuses on Banff and Kootenay, as well as Assiniboine Parks.

Urbick, Dee and Spring, Vicki. *94 Hikes in the Northern Canadian Rockies.* Vancouver: Douglas and McIntyre, 1983.

This guidebook concentrates on the trails in Yoho, Jasper and Mt. Robson Provincial Park.

Wilkerson, J.A. *Medicine for Mountaineering.* Seattle: The Mountaineers, *1985.*

This small, compact guide covers the basics of wilderness first aid and is the backpacking standard. Although aimed at people doing extreme activities, such as glacier walking and mountain climbing, this first-aid guide is comprehensive and very useful for backpackers and casual dayhikers.

# 18 // Photo Credits

# Index

# Index

# Index